Navies and Soft Power

Historical Case Studies of Naval Power
and the Nonuse of Military Force

Bruce A. Elleman
and S. C. M. Paine, Editors

NAVAL WAR COLLEGE PRESS
Newport, Rhode Island

To the unsung heroes of crisis response—federal, state, and local government employees, members of firms in the private sector and of faith-based organizations, tribal representatives, political representatives of the people, and volunteers. Each contributes to a collective capacity and capability that is unmatched in any other nation.

Naval War College

Newport, Rhode Island
Center for Naval Warfare Studies
Newport Paper Forty-Two
June 2015

President, Naval War College
Rear Adm. P. Gardner Howe III, USN

Provost
Dr. Lewis M. Duncan

Dean of Naval Warfare Studies
Thomas J. Culora

Naval War College Press

Director: Dr. Carnes Lord
Managing Editor: Pelham G. Boyer

Telephone: 401.841.2236
Fax: 401.841.1071
DSN exchange: 841
E-mail: press@usnwc.edu
Web: www.usnwc.edu/press
Twitter: http://twitter.com/NavalWarCollege

Printed in the United States of America

The Newport Papers are extended research projects that the Director, the Dean of Naval Warfare Studies, and the President of the Naval War College consider of particular interest to policy makers, scholars, and analysts.

The views expressed in the Newport Papers are those of the authors and do not necessarily reflect the opinions of the Naval War College or the Department of the Navy.

Correspondence concerning the Newport Papers may be addressed to the Director of the Naval War College Press. To request additional copies, back copies, or subscriptions to the series, please either write the President (Code 32S), Naval War College, 686 Cushing Road, Newport, RI 02841-1207, or contact the Press staff at the telephone, fax, or e-mail addresses given.

ISSN 1544-6824

ISBN 978-1-935352-33-4
e-book ISBN 978-1-935352-34-1

Contents

Foreword

This book is the last in a series of seven collections of case studies over the past twelve years that have examined the institutional roles played by navies throughout history. The series has collected an impressive group of scholars who have examined a variety of topics from the history of blockades and commerce raiding, the role of navies in coalitions, and naval mutinies in the twentieth century. This final volume, edited by Bruce A. Elleman and S. C. M. Paine, expands the series to cover the use of navies as instruments of "soft power," which includes a wide variety of missions.

The use of navies for purposes other than war is a phenomenon that goes back to antiquity and has continued ever since. For example, the great historian and keen observer of *res navales* Thucydides was well aware of the importance of ancient Greek antipiracy operations for promoting wealth and security. Perhaps one of the most interesting cases from antiquity is the humanitarian mission led by Pliny the Elder in AD 79, when, as commander of the Roman fleet at Misenum, he went to Pompeii to rescue civilians imperiled by the eruption of Mount Vesuvius, losing his life in the process.

Navies have thus always carried out a variety of operations that went beyond those necessary for the fighting and winning of wars and they continue to do so. During the last two centuries the U.S. Navy has engaged in an ever-broader array of non-war-fighting missions. For example, the Navy was famously involved protecting against piracy in the Mediterranean in the early nineteenth century and carried out equally important patrol missions, such as attempts to stop the illegal slave trade beginning in the mid-nineteenth century. After the end of the Cold War, many other nonmilitary missions came to the fore, in particular maritime humanitarian aid missions after natural or man-made disasters. One recent example of such a mission was the post-tsunami Operation UNIFIED ASSISTANCE in Southeast Asia during 2004–2005.

Beginning in 2006, the U.S. Naval War College was engaged in the process of writing the Navy's latest strategy document, called *A Cooperative Strategy for 21st Century Seapower*. This document was published in October 2007, and updated in March 2015. While the *Cooperative Strategy* has a strong focus on traditional missions, embedded in concepts such as deterrence, sea control, and power projection, it also discusses broader missions such as maritime security and humanitarian assistance / disaster relief. It is the latter two missions that form the focus of the current volume, which examines nine

case studies ranging from the nineteenth through the twenty-first century on a wide
spectrum of non-war-fighting missions.

MICHAEL F. PAVKOVIĆ
William Ledyard Rodgers Professor of
Naval History
Chair, Strategy and Policy Department
Naval War College

Preface

For well over two centuries, the U.S. Navy has engaged in an ever broader array of nonmilitary missions. Although a fundamental raison d'être of navies concerns hard power, in the twentieth century an awareness of the uses of soft power developed. For example, since ancient times protecting against piracy has been a common naval problem, while since the mid-nineteenth century equally important patrol missions, such as attempts to stop the illegal slave trade, have been conducted by the U.S. Navy. After the Cold War, many other nonmilitary missions became important, in particular maritime humanitarian-aid missions like the post-tsunami Operation UNIFIED ASSISTANCE in Southeast Asia during 2004–2005.

Beginning in 2006, the Naval War College, in Newport, Rhode Island, hosted a "blue-team/red-team" process for writing the Navy's latest strategy document, called *A Cooperative Strategy for 21st Century Seapower* (CS-21, for short). These teams addressed a wide variety of naval missions, including offshore balancing versus high-end and low-end strategies, to consider how aggressive, forward-positioned naval forces could be used both for war-fighting and for "lesser and included" missions, such as humanitarian assistance and disaster relief. According to Adm. James Foggo III, former Commander, U.S. European Command, "You can be out there forward, totally isolationist, or do what we call offshore balancing. Or you can be reactive and go where you are needed or surged. Or you can do . . . a mixture: to be combat capable but also at the same time able, in a phase zero situation, . . . to provide humanitarian assistance for disasters."[1]

In five different scenarios, named "Alpha" through "Echo," writing teams discussed the goal of humanitarian missions, anticipating that global climate change might create an increased demand for them.[2] Much of this thinking was reflected in CS-21, which was published in October 2007 and updated in March 2015. To supplement this effort, this volume presents nine historical case studies examining the use of navies in nonmilitary missions.

Notes

1. Rear Adm. James Foggo III, telephone interview, 6 February 2013.
2. Bryan McGrath, "Maritime Strategy Option Echo," spring 2007.

List of Acronyms and Abbreviations

C	**CIC**	Combat Information Center
	CRB	Commission for Relief in Belgium
	CS-21	"A Cooperative Strategy for 21st Century Seapower"
	CTF-151	Combined Task Force 151
D	**dB**	decibel
	DCE	Defense Coordinating Element
	DCO	Defense Coordinating Officer
	DoD	Department of Defense
	DSCA	defense support of civil authorities
E	**EPA**	Environmental Protection Agency
	ESA	Endangered Species Act
	EU NAVFOR	European Union Naval Force
F	**FAA**	Federal Aviation Administration
	FEMA	Federal Emergency Management Agency
	FOSC	Federal On Scene Coordinator
H	**Hz**	hertz
I	**ICS**	Incident Command System
J	**JOPES**	Joint Operation Planning and Execution System
L	**LAMPS**	Light Airborne Multipurpose System
	LFA	low-frequency sonar

M **MARAD**   Maritime Administration

MFA   midfrequency sonar

MMPA   Marine Mammal Protection Act

MOOTW   military operations other than war

MPHE   Master Plan for Habitat Enhancement

MPRSA   Marine Protection, Research, and Sanctuaries Act

N **NATO**   North Atlantic Treaty Organization

NCP   National Oil and Hazardous Substances Pollution Contingency Plan

NDRF   National Defense Reserve Fleet

NEO   noncombatant evacuation operation

NIHL   noise-induced hearing loss

NIMS   National Incident Management System

NOAA   National Oceanic and Atmospheric Administration

NRC   National Research Council

NRF   National Response Framework

O **OPA 90**   Oil Pollution Act of 1990

P **PCB**   polychlorinated biphenyl

PLA   People's Liberation Army

PLAN   People's Liberation Army Navy

PPD   Presidential Policy Directive

PSO   Peace Support Operations

PTS   permanent threshold shift

R **RAND**   Research and Development

RDT   Roving Diver Technique

	REEF	Reef Environmental Education Foundation
	RIMPAC	Rim of the Pacific [exercise series]
S	**SDOF**	San Diego Oceans Foundation
	SDP	Ship Disposal Program
	SHADE	Shared Awareness and Deconfliction
	SINKEX	sinking exercise
	SLOC	sea line of communications
	SONS	Spill of National Significance
	SPL	sound pressure level
T	**TTS**	temporary threshold shift
U	**UAE**	United Arab Emirates
	USCG	U.S. Coast Guard
	USN	U.S. Navy
W	**WHEC**	Coast Guard high-endurance cutter

Introduction
Navies Are Not Just for Fighting
BRUCE A. ELLEMAN AND S. C. M. PAINE

Navies are most commonly thought of in terms of warfare. Naval blockades, commerce raiding, and expeditionary warfare are basic missions. However, since almost their very beginning, professional navies have conducted many operations that are not strictly war related; antipiracy patrols, dating back at least to the Roman Empire, if not before, are just one example. In more modern times, patrols against the transportation of African slaves—and more recently, refugees—have become common. In addition, navies can be tasked to respond to a wide range of both man-made and natural disasters, including oil spills, hurricanes, and tsunamis.

Previous related volumes by the editors of this publication and in this series have examined the many force-based maritime operations that are considered to be the norm for professional navies.[1] This volume is different, however, in that it focuses primarily on the nonmilitary uses of naval forces—in other words, naval actions that are conducted outside of the normal actions associated with war and often (although not always) avoiding the firing of weapons or other uses of lethal force. With the end of the Cold War in 1990, the U.S. military created a special term, "military operations other than war," or MOOTW, to describe such operations; not to be outdone, the United Kingdom created "Peace Support Operations," or PSO. However, nonmilitary naval operations have existed longer than these terms and can include, but are not limited to, humanitarian-aid missions, civilian evacuation operations (often referred to as "non-combatant evacuation operations," or NEOs), and a wide variety of non-war-related patrol functions, including (during the nineteenth century) antislavery patrols and more recently (in the twenty-first century) antipiracy patrols.

In the modern era, navies can also be called on to respond to a wide range of natural or man-made threats that have little or nothing to do with questions of war or peace, including disasters at sea like the *Deepwater Horizon* fire and oil spill. They can also sponsor fundamental research on ecological or environmental problems, including

the possible impact of sonar on marine mammals. Finally, naval operations originally
created in wartime, such as the intentional sinking of ships to block important channels, have in recent years borne fruit in more peaceable endeavors, such as the sinking of decommissioned naval ships to form artificial reefs for recreational diving and
sportfishing.

While the military use of navies during times of international tension or war is obvious
and well reported by the press, these nonmilitary uses can be equally important, even
when largely ignored by the media and public at large. As with the "negative space" in
an abstract picture, so long as the global commercial system is functioning, international trade is conducted without interruption, and peacetime maritime activities—including fishing, mining in or under the seas, and recreational pursuits, such as yachting,
sportfishing, and scuba diving—can be carried out safely, there is no need to highlight
the usefulness of navies. It is often only when problems arise and catch maritime security organs unawares that media organs report on them. Nobody appears very interested
in reporting "business as usual."

In the more than twenty years since the collapse of the Soviet Union, global navies
appear to have adopted many new nonmilitary responsibilities—including patrolling
sea-lanes for pirates and assisting in oil-spill cleanups—that break the traditional mold
regarding what most people think are navies' primary duties. But as the first chapter
will show, such operations are not new. Although the U.S. government outlawed the
transatlantic slave trade in 1808, only after the 1842 Webster-Ashburton Treaty with
Britain did the U.S. Navy actively enforce this prohibition, by conducting antislavery patrols off the coast of Africa. As John Pentangelo discusses in his contribution,
the sloop of war USS *Constellation* served as flagship of the African Squadron from
1859 to 1861. During *Constellation*'s two-year cruise, this squadron of eight sail- and
steam-powered vessels captured fourteen slave ships and liberated almost four thousand
Africans from involuntary servitude. Arguably, the most important capture during
Constellation's patrol occurred on 25 September 1860, when it stopped the slave ship
Cora and discovered 705 African slaves—men, boys, women, young girls, and even
babies—whom it subsequently freed.

Naval forces can play a very important role in diplomacy without ever firing a shot. As
Henry "Jerry" Hendrix argues, by sending practically the entire U.S. Navy Atlantic Fleet
to conduct "winter exercises" in the Caribbean during 1902–1903, under the command
of the famous Adm. George Dewey, President Theodore Roosevelt was able to pressure
the German and British governments to back down from a threat to use military force
against Venezuela and to seek arbitration instead. It is notable—although "war by alge-
bra" has been much criticized, especially in land warfare—that in this case fifty-three
American ships opposed only twenty-nine British and German ships; while additional

ships could have been sent by each of these major European powers, to do so would have taken considerable time and left other parts of their respective empires undefended. Thus, an American "fleet-in-being," backed up by U.S. Marines stationed strategically on island bases throughout the Caribbean, produced a diplomatic coup not only for President Roosevelt but also for a rising American sea power.

While blockades have always been considered an important naval operation during times of war, in the twentieth century the focus of "starvation blockades" could be fine-tuned by simultaneously conducting humanitarian relief operations. As shown by Bruce A. Elleman, one of the first large-scale humanitarian-aid missions by sea occurred during World War I, with the creation of the nonprofit Commission for Relief in Belgium (CRB). This organization distributed $927,681,485.08 worth of foodstuffs and clothing to Belgium and to German-occupied areas of northern France. Before this aid could be delivered, however, its director, Herbert Hoover, had to persuade England and Germany to let ships carry it through the maritime blockade lines. From 1 November 1914 until the summer of 1919, over nine hundred CRB-leased ships successfully navigated not only the British naval blockade but also German minefields and swarms of U-boats conducting unrestricted submarine warfare. By delivering this essential food aid to helpless civilians in Belgium and northern France, the CRB helped the British focus the full impact of the starvation blockade against Germany and its allies.

An embargo is an important naval function that includes patrols but usually does not require force. During the years immediately prior to the U.S. entry into World War II, the American government tried to force Japan to pull out of China by imposing progressively more restrictive embargoes. As S. C. M. Paine discusses, following Japan's invasion of Manchuria in 1931 and the creation of Manchukuo in 1932, Washington adopted a nonrecognition policy toward Japanese territorial expansion in northern China. After the war escalated in July 1937, the United States imposed economic sanctions on Japan, including an ever more restrictive naval embargo intended to halt deliveries to Japan of war matériel and, most notably, U.S. petroleum. This chapter outlines the historical background of the imposition of sanctions and of the Japanese reaction, which proved to be not a withdrawal from China but a massive escalation on 7 December 1941, with an attack on Pearl Harbor and invasion of British and Dutch interests throughout the Pacific.

Navies can assist refugees to relocate during crises and wartime. Jan K. Herman recalls a formerly secret U.S. Navy mission that occurred during April 1975, in the final days of the war in Indochina. Although most of the South Vietnamese army had already surrendered to the approaching North Vietnamese, senior South Vietnamese naval officers refused to surrender their ships. With time running short, Richard Armitage, an agent for the Secretary of Defénse, offered U.S. Navy assistance to rescue what remained of their navy. As a result, thirty-two ships and approximately thirty thousand refugees were safely escorted by USS *Kirk* across the South China Sea to Subic Bay in the Philippines.

Decommissioned or stricken naval vessels can still make important and honorable contributions to the common good. Tom Williams shows that navy ships can continue to serve a military by being turned into naval museums or by being sunk—during wartime as blockships, in peacetime in gunnery exercises. On 25 November 2003, President George W. Bush authorized, as a provision of the Defense Department budget, U.S. Navy ships to be donated for use as artificial reefs. Although ships have been made artificial reefs for years, the first to be sunk in the new program was the aircraft carrier USS *Oriskany* (CV 34) on 17 May 2006, south of Pensacola, Florida. Sinking naval vessels to form artificial reefs can offer important economic benefits for coastal communities, by increasing maritime tourism and fishing, even while playing a positive ecological role by boosting local marine life.

The U.S. Navy's use of sonar has been blamed for numerous whale strandings and other damage to sea life. Darlene Ketten argues that the relatively small threat of sonar to the populations of whales compared with those posed by other anthropogenic dangers—fisheries, ship strikes, indigenous hunts, etc.—puts these concerns into perspective. While acknowledging the coincidence of strandings with some U.S. Navy exercises, she believes there must be an attempt to find the boundaries of the problem, as well as a retrospective analysis of the events under investigation. This requires outside support for research on multiple fronts to address the mechanisms that can trigger strandings and methodologies to avoid them. Naval participation in federal panels to address public concerns is also crucial, since the largest impediments to seeing these events clearly are widespread public misperception of the magnitude of the events per se and of their implications, and skepticism about why results sometimes appear to come slowly. To correct media errors would require better dissemination of these results plus constant explanation of the broader impacts of these results on other areas of marine science.

Navies can respond in nonmilitary ways to natural, and especially man-made, disasters. Rear Adm. Mary Landry, U.S. Coast Guard (Ret.), relates the background of the 20 April 2010 fire on the offshore oil rig *Deepwater Horizon* in the Gulf of Mexico, resulting in the rig's sinking and an oil spill. Not only did eleven of the 126 crew members perish, but from 20 April through 19 September 2010 about five million barrels of oil leaked out of the five-thousand-foot-deep well, creating the largest offshore spill in American history. In response, Coast Guard cutters and personnel became the first line of disaster response. Rear Admiral Landry, commander of the Eighth Coast Guard District, headquartered in New Orleans, Louisiana, was the top Coast Guard official coordinating, using the incident command system, what grew to be the largest fully integrated response ever mounted in the United States, including approximately forty-seven thousand people from federal, state, local, tribal, and private-sector entities.

Not just established navies but also emerging and reemerging ones can conduct nonmilitary operations. For the first time in its modern history, the People's Republic of China has deployed naval forces operationally beyond its immediate maritime periphery to protect merchant vessels from pirates in the Gulf of Aden. Andrew S. Erickson and Austin M. Strange show that beginning in December 2008, China has contributed more than ten thousand naval personnel in almost twenty successive task forces and has escorted nearly six thousand commercial vessels, approximately 70 percent of them foreign flagged, in seven hundred escort missions.[2] The People's Liberation Army Navy has carefully crafted its antipiracy operations to portray China's blue-water operations abroad in a positive way. These Gulf of Aden deployments might increase the Chinese navy's prospects for cooperation with other navies as well as impact China's future naval development.

The conclusions examine the targets, audiences, objectives, effects, and outcomes of such operations. Long before the MOOTW and PSO were invented, navies were deeply involved in the conduct of nonmilitary operations. Given that peace is the norm and war the exception, such nonmilitary missions occur much more regularly and produce significantly greater effects than most people would think.

Notes

The thoughts and opinions expressed in this essay are those of the authors and are not necessarily those of the U.S. government, the U.S. Navy Department, or the Naval War College.

1. Christopher M. Bell and Bruce A. Elleman, *Naval Mutinies of the Twentieth Century: An International Perspective* (London: Frank Cass, 2003); Bruce A. Elleman and S. C. M. Paine, eds., *Naval Blockades and Seapower: Strategies and Counter-strategies, 1805–2005* (New York: Routledge, 2006); Bruce A. Elleman and S. C. M. Paine, eds., *Naval Coalition Warfare: From the Napoleonic War to Operation Iraqi Freedom* (New York: Routledge, 2008); Bruce A. Elleman, Andrew Forbes, and David Rosenberg, eds., *Piracy and Maritime Crime:* *Historical and Modern Case Studies,* Newport Paper 35 (Newport, R.I.: Naval War College Press, 2010); Bruce A. Elleman and S. C. M. Paine, eds., *Naval Power and Expeditionary Warfare: Peripheral Campaigns and New Theatres of Naval Warfare* (New York: Routledge, 2012); Bruce A. Elleman and S. C. M. Paine, eds., *Commerce Raiding: Historical Case Studies, 1755–2009,* Newport Paper 40 (Newport, R.I.: Naval War College Press, 2013).

2. "中国海军护航编队执行第700批护航任务" [Chinese Naval Escort Task Force Carries Out 700th Escort Mission], 中国新闻网 [China News Web], 5 April 2014, www.chinanews.com/mil/2014/04-05/6034225.shtml.

CHAPTER ONE

Sailors and Slaves
USS *Constellation* and the Transatlantic Slave Trade
JOHN PENTANGELO

The United States outlawed the transatlantic slave trade in 1808 but provided for little in the way of enforcement to stop the slave ships at sea. In 1819 Congress authorized the president to use U.S. Navy ships to seize American-flagged slavers and the next year equated slave running with piracy, with death as the maximum penalty. During 1820 the corvette *Cyane* was sent to western Africa, where it "captured a number of ships suspected of intent to carry slaves."[1] Such efforts were haphazard, however, and Great Britain eventually convinced the U.S. government to establish its own permanent African Squadron. The Webster-Ashburton Treaty, signed in 1842, declared that the two nations would maintain separate naval squadrons on the West Coast of Africa to enforce their respective laws against the slave trade. A major reason in the United States behind the creation of the patrol was to avoid allowing British warships the right to search American-flagged vessels, a legal issue that had been at the heart of the War of 1812.

Although the American antislavery patrol lasted for almost two decades, up through the beginning of the Civil War in 1861, the sharp divisions on the legality of slavery between North and South meant that "it was never intended to be effective." Between 1842 and 1861 only thirty-six vessels were captured by the African Squadron, an embarrassingly low figure when compared with the hundreds of slave ships captured by the Royal Navy's antislavery patrols; in 1843 alone, the British seized forty-four slavers and "nearly double that in 1845."[2] Only for a short period during the late 1850s was the antislavery patrol truly active, and this came about mainly because slave-ship owners appeared to thumb their noses at Washington when they "openly landed slaves in Georgia in 1858."[3]

From 1859 to 1861 the sloop of war USS *Constellation,* launched in 1854, served as flagship of the U.S. Navy's African Squadron. The squadron in those years was composed of eight sail and steam-powered vessels and had orders to protect American commerce and suppress the transatlantic slave trade off Africa's western coastline. During *Constellation*'s two-year cruise the squadron captured fourteen slave ships and liberated almost four thousand Africans from lives of involuntary servitude. The crew endured the hardships of the station, worked with local Africans to suppress the trade, and experienced on the fateful night of 25 September 1860 what is arguably the most important moment in *Constellation*'s century of service to the U.S. Navy, the capture of the slave ship *Cora*.

Early History of the African Squadron

While the first American antislavery patrols off the coast of Africa date to 1820, for over twenty years they were conducted only intermittently. Few slave ships were captured, since there were insufficient warships deployed to cover over three thousand miles of African coastline. As one critic of the Navy's antislavery patrols openly acknowledged, "So great is the extent of coast from which slaves can be shipped, and so constantly do the traders change the places of embarkation, that the few vessels employed by the American government are easily deceived and avoided."[4] After Congress ratified the Webster-Ashburton Treaty, signed on 10 August 1842, this situation began to change for the better. Commo. Matthew C. Perry was the first full-time commander of the permanent African Squadron, and more ships were assigned.

In late June 1844, USS *Truxtun,* under Cdr. Henry Bruce, left the United States to join the African Squadron, off Tenerife in the Canary Islands. During its sixteen-month deployment, it captured only one small, hundred-ton slave ship, *Spitfire,* off the coast of Guinea. *Truxtun* freed 346 slaves as a result of this capture. Bruce reported that the captured ship was so cramped that "there was not room enough for a man to sit, unless inclining his head forward; their food was half a pint of rice per day, with one pint of water. No one can imagine the sufferings of slaves on their passage across, unless the conveyances in which they are taken are examined."[5] Rather than being sold at auction, *Spitfire* was refitted for use in antislavery operations.

During September 1845, USS *Yorktown,* commanded by Capt. Charles H. Bell, captured two slave ships, one of them *Pons,* a 196-ton ship transporting between 850 and nine hundred slaves. When the ship was sold the following year it brought over five thousand dollars in shares for the crew, plus another nineteen thousand dollars for the 756 slaves landed safely in Liberia. Interestingly, during 1847 this same ship was seized again by American authorities, this time for transporting 110 Irishmen, which was thirty more than the registered limit of eighty (but only about one-eighth the number of African slaves it transported in 1845).[6]

In 1847, USS *Perry,* under the command of John A. Davis and attached to the Brazil Squadron, seized the American ship *Ann D. Richardson,* on its way to Africa bearing fake papers, and two days later a second ship, *Independence.* Both ships were shown to be participating in the illegal slave trade and so were sent back to the United States as prizes. On 6 February 1849, *Perry* seized *Susan,* also off Brazil. *Perry* captured *Martha* on 6 June 1850 and *Chatsworth* on 11 September 1850, both off the coast of Africa. *Martha* was waiting to load 1,800 African slaves when *Perry* captured it. On 10 March 1854 *Perry* captured *Glamorgan,* for a total of six captures—three off Brazil and three off Africa, more than any other U.S. Navy ship on antislavery patrol.

Both the British and American squadrons faced a significant problem in their inability to search *all* suspected vessels. The American fleet could board and search only vessels flying the American flag or no flag at all. The British had many more ships on station but could not search a vessel flying an American flag. Thus slavers greatly minimized the risk of capture by flying the Stars and Stripes. They knew there was a substantial chance of being spotted by a British vessel and almost none of being stopped by an American. Much of the American slave trade was in fact carried out not by U.S. citizens but by proxies. An American-flagged slave ship might sail to Africa with an American crew, but then a foreigner would purchase the ship and use a non-American crew, "composed of Portuguese, Spaniards, or other non-U.S. citizens," all measures designed to avoid being stopped by the U.S. Navy and to protect either crew from being accused of piracy, which could be punished by hanging.[7] Unexpected as it might seem today, many slave ships hired Africans into their crews. Between 1794 and 1805, as "many as seventy-seven Africans served on board Liverpool slavers."[8]

The American squadron did not have much success in directly combating the slave trade. The group was small, often about four vessels. Four vessels were far too few to cover the mouth of the Congo River, let alone the three thousand miles of coast. The types of vessels deployed also adversely affected the squadron's capabilities. The department often sent large oceangoing frigates and sloops of war instead of the schooners and gunboats more suitable for inshore patrols and pursuit of fast merchant clippers. There were steam-powered vessels in the Navy, but they had yet to be deployed to Africa. These vessels would have been much more effective in pursuing fleeing slave ships. Finally, the Secretary of the Navy's order making the protection of American commerce the primary mission relegated the suppression of the slave trade to a secondary duty. From 1843 to 1859 the squadron captured only twenty-two vessels. During a similar time frame the British navy captured approximately six hundred. This was the climate in April 1859, when the U.S. Navy sent USS *Constellation* to the west coast of Africa with orders to become flagship of the African Squadron.

Constellation Outfits a Crew

Constellation, under the command of Capt. John S. Nicholas, weighed anchor in Boston Harbor and set sail for Africa on 19 July 1859. The all-sail, twenty-two-gun sloop of war served as the headquarters of the African Squadron's new flag officer, Commo. William Inman. *Constellation* arrived at the Portuguese island of Madeira in August to relieve USS *Cumberland*. In October it sailed south to Monrovia, Liberia, to augment its crew with African Kroomen, members of the Kroo tribe who came on board as paid crew members. According to crew member William Ambrose Leonard, vessels of the African Squadron were allowed to ship two Kroomen for every gun on board.[9] Since *Constellation* carried twenty guns, it was allowed to hire forty additional hands.[10] These Kroomen served for the entire cruise and so were actively involved in freeing other, less fortunate Africans from enslavement.

While images of the slave trade are appropriately associated predominantly with the African slaves, who endured unspeakable horrors during the Middle Passage on their way to North and South America, very little has been written about the role that some West African seafarers played in combating the trade. For decades, commanders of the African Squadron employed Kroomen as auxiliary seamen and as lightermen and long-shoremen, transporting men and supplies from ship to shore. Kroomen were recruited from shore often on a "first come, first served" basis. Renowned for their physical strength, they often worked nude or with just cloths wrapped around their waists.

The arrival of the Kroo on board *Constellation* in October 1859 made quite an impression on the American sailors. Leonard later recounted that "the ship is swarmed with them presenting their recommendations, . . . to our captain. They are a fine looking set of men. They now began to come a little faster than they were wanted and contrary to the orders of the 1st lieutenant they hung on to the ship's side, and resisted all attempts to drive them off."[11] Kroomen relied on written testimonials from previous employers to prove their worth to naval officers. They carried these recommendation papers, called "books," in wooden or tin boxes tied around their necks. Sailors who worked with them typically renamed their new shipmates after items of importance in the seamen's world. *Constellation*'s Kroomen included men renamed Fresh Water, Bottle of Beer, Tom Rattlin, Jim Bobstay, and Jack Half Dollar. These often recycled names, perhaps considered insulting by modern standards, were powerful status symbols in the Kroo villages at Freetown, Sierra Leone, and Monrovia.

As temperatures rose above 110 degrees Fahrenheit, the suffocating heat made ordinary shipboard routines almost unbearable. Leonard explained of the Kroo that "the object in having them is to man the boats so as to keep the white men from being exposed to the sun which is dreadful hot all along the Coast. They are a very hardy race of people and can stand a great deal of fatigue. They require no bedding; they sleep on deck."[12]

Another description claimed the Kroo were "an easy tempered set of men, very respectful in their manners, willing to work and withal very muscular and powerful." In addition to possessing physical prowess, the Kroo were excellent swimmers. On one occasion when a turtle happened to swim by, three of the Kroo "divested themselves of their clothing in a twinkling" and dove in after it; the turtle immediately dived deep, but "the chase did not end here, and a submarine pursuit took place which was astonishing as well as amusing to witness; one would hardly suppose that men could acquire such perfection in swimming as they practice."[13]

Resistance to Illness

In addition to their other fine qualities, squadron commanders recognized that Kroomen were more resistant than white crew members to tropical diseases. Since the beginning of the patrol it had always been disease, not belligerent slave runners, that had been the greatest threat to personnel. While the British view was that periodic visits onshore, for "seasoning," would reveal who was best suited to survive African illnesses, the U.S. Navy adopted a rule "against anyone spending a night ashore in Africa." This rule wisely sought to avoid the 20 percent mortality rate experienced by the first set of American slaves returned to Liberia.[14]

A good example of the dangers inherent in service in the African Squadron was shown during October 1844, when USS *Preble* joined Commodore Perry's African Squadron. Operating out of the Cape Verde Islands, the ships would cruise for five months at a time. Owing mainly to the chance of malaria, these missions were described as "dark and horrible cruising."[15] The actual carrier of the disease, mosquitoes, was as yet unknown; Perry's sanitary regulations included smoking the ships with "smudges," drying them out with coal stoves, and keeping them well ventilated. As for personal hygiene, the "men had to wear a flannel undershirt night and day, bathe every week, and not be on the African coast later than eight o'clock." To ready a ship for service, it "was cleansed, ventilated, and purified with fire." Without realizing it, Perry's sanitary "precautions kept to a minimum his squadron's contact with mosquitoes, the carriers of both malaria and yellow fever."[16] Nevertheless, *Preble,* before even beginning its antislavery cruise, was struck by malaria. By early December the majority of its crew, ninety-three of 144, had the disease; eventually sixteen died.

Fifteen years later, medical science had still not made the link between mosquitoes and disease. Understandably, *Constellation*'s sailors dreaded the strains of malaria and yellow fever prevalent along the coast. Disease killed hundreds in the British and American squadrons during the nineteenth century, earning Africa the sobriquet "the White Man's Grave." Officers and seamen believed the fever was contracted from breathing "bad air" close to the coastline. These diseases directly interfered with the suppression of the slave trade, inasmuch as the U.S. Navy ships were frequently ordered not to linger close to shore, which was exactly where they might have been able to observe and catch slavers loading their cargo.

During *Constellation*'s cruise, dozens of men in the squadron were infected with fever, and several died from it. In 1861, the sloop captured the brig *Triton* and discovered that its crew was sick with the fever. Captain Nicholas's clerk, Stephen B. Wilson, a member of the prize crew detached to sail *Triton* to Norfolk, died of the fever and was buried on Ascension Island. One month later wardroom steward James George died of the same illness. A sailor recalled George's ordeal the night before he expired: "All hands were kept awake by a young fellow that is sick with the coast fever; he is out of his head. His lungs must be in good condition, for he hollered like a bull."[17] Many slaves also died of the illness. For example, on 14 January 1861, USS *Saratoga*, commanded by Capt. Alfred Taylor, captured *Nightingale* with 961 slaves on board. The slaves were freed and eventually taken to Liberia, but not before 160 had died of malaria.[18]

Constellation's officers employed the Kroomen in many different ways, including scouting the shore for disease outbreaks. They also worked side by side with seamen in sail handling and lookout duty. The Kroo were also adept at navigating the difficult coastal surf zone where protected harbors were absent. As warships of the African Squadron required constant (if brief) contact with the shore for resupply and other operations conducted on land, these African mariners provided crucial support.

After embarking the Kroomen, Commodore Inman sailed south for a short cruise around the Congo River and spent the next four months around St. Paul de Loando, overseeing the completion of a new storehouse, replacing one at the distant port of Porto Praya. On 21 December 1859, while cruising off Cabinda Bay, *Constellation* captured its first prize, the brig *Delicia,* after a ten-hour chase. *Delicia,* Inman reported to Secretary of the Navy Isaac Toucey, "was completely fitted in all respects for the immediate embarkation of slaves."[19] The boarding party discovered a slave deck and large copper cauldrons intended to feed a cargo of Africans. Questioning the mate, Captain Nicholas discovered that *Delicia*'s master had been on shore purchasing a cargo of Africans when *Constellation* discovered the brig. A prize crew sailed *Delicia* to Charleston, South Carolina, for adjudication, but there having been no Americans on board and no papers, logbook, or colors, the American courts eventually declared the brig was beyond federal jurisdiction.

Satisfied with its success to date, *Constellation* sailed to Madeira for repairs and liberty in February 1860. Intensely displeased with this decision, however, Secretary of the Navy Toucey ordered Inman to return to the cruising ground immediately. Unlike many former secretaries, Toucey took the patrols seriously. He restricted the cruising ground to twenty degrees north latitude and directed that no vessel could leave it without permission from the department. Several months after *Constellation*'s return to the coast, the African Squadron had the most successful day in its eighteen-year history: on 8 August 1860, USS *Mohican* captured the slave ship *Erie,* with 897 slaves, and USS *San Jacinto* seized *Storm King,* with over six hundred Africans crammed belowdecks. The African Squadron was suddenly showing signs of life. Unbeknownst to its crew, the recently returned flagship, *Constellation,* was about to join the fray.

Constellation Captures *Cora*

On 27 June 1860 the bark *Cora* departed New York bound for the West African coast on what would prove to be an ill-fated slaving voyage. After a decade of legal merchant activity, the 431-ton Baltimore vessel was sold by E. D. Morgan & Co. to John Latham for fourteen thousand dollars. In May 1860 Latham took the bark to Pier 52 on the East River to refit its rigging and load cargo. The cargo, containing large quantities of lumber, freshwater, and provisions, raised suspicion among local authorities that the owner intended to use *Cora* as a slave ship. A U.S. district attorney detained *Cora* for examination but later cleared the bark for its voyage.

All evidence that would have confirmed *Cora* was intended for a slaving voyage was hidden deep within the ship. *Cora*'s hold contained fifty cases of muskets (likely intended to purchase slaves), more than twenty cases of drugs (to treat disease outbreaks), and forty-seven tierces—barrels holding about forty gallons or six hundred pounds—of rice (to feed the captives). Other suspicious cargo might include large copper pots for cooking food, hundreds of wooden spoons, swords, firearms, shackles, and chains.[20]

When *Cora* sailed for Africa, it carried over ten thousand feet of lumber—enough to build a slave deck. Slave ships were originally built for legal trade and needed substantial alterations to carry human cargoes. Thus a slave deck, a middle deck installed between the hold and upper deck, became the "smoking gun" for a vessel that had not yet loaded slaves.[21]

On 27 August *Cora* arrived at Punta da Lenha, a major slave-trading center thirty miles up the Congo River. Three weeks later, having made all the necessary arrangements, Latham sailed *Cora* to Manque Grande, where in the late hours of 24 September he supervised the hasty loading of African slaves from the shore to the waiting ship. Once the slaves were loaded, *Cora* sailed for Cuba to unload its cargo.

On 25 September 1860, *Constellation* parted company with *San Jacinto* and began a southerly cruise toward the Congo River. At seven bells in the second "dog watch" (7:30 PM), a lookout on the starboard cathead (where the anchor was made fast) spotted *Cora* about two miles away on the weather bow. The flagship changed course and began its pursuit. Midshipman Wilburn Hall remembered, "The *Constellation* was simply superb in tacking, and round she came, raising her sharp bow from the sea like a racer ready for the signal."[22] In an attempt to escape, *Cora* hauled up sharp on the wind, set all its canvas, and began evasive maneuvers.

Sometime after 9:00 PM, as the moon lit up the night sky, *Constellation's* starboard thirty-two-pounder long gun fired a shot across *Cora's* bow to signal it to heave to and prepare to be boarded. *Cora* ignored the shot and raced along the coast. *Constellation* closed the gap to within a half-mile and fired several more warning shots, but to no avail. In a desperate attempt to gain speed, the slaver's crew frantically began lightening the ship. They threw an empty boat, hatches, anchors, spars, and casks into the ocean. Despite all of their efforts, the flagship continued to draw closer. *Cora* cut across *Constellation's* bow in a final attempt to make it out to sea. *Constellation's* next shot cut away a part of *Cora's* rigging and forced the bark to give up.

A boarding party led by the first lieutenant, Donald M. Fairfax, boarded *Cora* and immediately discovered a slave deck with 705 Africans crammed together—men, boys, women, young girls, and babies. According to Leonard:

> This being the first slaver I ever saw with slaves in, my curiosity led me upon the slave deck. The scene which here presented itself to my eyes baffles description. It was a dreadful sight. They were all packed together like so many sheep—men, woman [sic], and children entirely naked, and suffering from hunger and thirst. They had nothing to eat or drink for over 30 hours. As soon as the poor negroes were aware that we were friends to them, they commenced a shouting and yelling like so many wild Indians. They were so overjoyed at being taken by us that I thought they would tear us to pieces.[23]

Midshipman Wilburn Hall later recalled the revolting stench of so many men, women, and children crammed together with little or no sanitation. The young officer wrote, "The slaves were nearly all on the slave-deck, shouting and screaming in terror and anxiety. I leaned over the main hatchway holding a lantern, and the writhing mass of humanity, with their cries and struggles, can only be compared in one's mind to the horrors of hell as pictured in former days."[24] As the ship's hatches were opened, the captives "came tumbling out of the hold, yelling and cringing. They ran forward and crouched on the bow. . . . They were nearly starved."[25]

Upon hearing that they had captured a slaver with hundreds of terrified Africans packed below, *Constellation's* crew let out a thunderous cheer. Each member of the crew was entitled to a bonus for every recaptured African slave landed in Liberia, as well as a portion of the proceeds gained if the slave ship were sold at auction. By law, half the proceeds of a ship sale went to the Naval Retirement Fund, but the other half was divided among the crew. Interestingly, federal courts had earlier upheld the rights of Kroo sailors to their shares of the proceeds—almost sixty-five dollars apiece for the capture of *Pons*.[26]

Returning the Slaves to Africa

Taking the slaver *Cora* was just the first step, since now the Navy was responsible for the well-being of the captured slaves. On 27 September sailors from *Constellation* finished repairing *Cora*'s rigging for the journey back to the United States. Inman ordered a prize crew of eleven sailors and three Marines, led by Master Thomas H. Eastman, to sail the bark to Norfolk, Virginia, for adjudication. The crew first sailed to Liberia and delivered the Africans into the custody of Rev. John Seys, the U.S. Agent for Recaptured Africans. Despite measures to improve living conditions and orders "to enable them to have as much pure air as possible," eleven Africans died before reaching their destination.[27]

The Republic of Liberia was the designated haven for Africans on board slave ships seized by the U.S. Navy. The American Colonization Society originally founded Monrovia in 1822, and in 1847 Liberia became an independent state; later it absorbed other, adjoining returned-slave colonies at Bassa Cove, Sinoe, and Cape Palmas. The American Colonization Society "supported it year after year with money, shipments of goods, and occasional infusions of new settlers." There was no single "home" to which rescued slaves could be returned, and many American officials feared that returning them to the Congo River basin would only result in their recapture and resale as slaves. So the U.S. government supported their relocation to Liberia. By 1844, about 250 of these "recaptives" had been landed there.[28]

Local committees assisted the traumatized Africans, called "Congoes," after their arrival. Many of the Africans were apprenticed to Americo-Liberian families. Over two hundred of the Africans liberated from *Cora* settled in Careysburg, where they performed sawmill work. For example, ten males from *Cora* were apprenticed to a sawmill near the Junk River. One of the younger ones, Reverend Seys reported, had "already learned sufficient of the business as to be able to take the place at the engine of a man who had been receiving $4 a month wages. The place is one requiring much vigilance in the application and stopping of steam at certain junctures, and so steady, so punctual and reliable is the Congo lad, that the Liberian's services are no longer required."[29]

Between August and October 1860, Liberia was overwhelmed with some 3,600 freed slaves.[30] Such success in so short a time taxed Liberia's ability to care for new arrivals. Some of the Congoes apprenticed that year ran away, and a small number committed suicide. But with no family or friends and no way to return home, most conformed to the dominant culture and adopted new lives.

Master Eastman, meanwhile, departed Monrovia and sailed *Cora* to Norfolk to deliver its first mate (Morgan Fredericks), second mate (John Wilson), and third mate (Hans Olsen) into the custody of the U.S. marshal. Owing to adverse weather, however, he instead sailed *Cora* to New York, anchoring off the Brooklyn Navy Yard on 8 December

1860. The U.S. district court in New York found the evidence damning and confiscated the bark, auctioning it for $8,900. (On 7 March 1861 it was seized once more for suspected slave running by the revenue cutter *Harriet Lane*.)

Some of *Cora's* officers did not wait for a verdict on their guilt. Less than twenty-four hours after *Cora's* arrival in New York, Morgan Fredericks broke out of his stateroom, climbed through a porthole, plunged into the East River, and made his escape. Captain John Latham, who had been brought to New York in the U.S. store ship *Relief,* was denied bail. A mysterious friend negotiated Latham's furlough from prison to buy him a suit at Brooks Brothers on Broadway. While an escorting deputy marshal was himself trying on a suit, Latham and his friend escaped in a carriage waiting outside. Mates John Wilson and Hans Olsen denied having known that they were on a slaving voyage until they reached Africa. They pleaded guilty to violating the act of 1800—a lesser crime of voluntary service on board a slaver. The court sentenced them to ten months in prison and a fine of five hundred dollars each. Four other seamen were brought into court, but their cases were dismissed.

While these court proceedings were taking place, USS *Constellation* stayed on African station, where it captured one more slave ship, the brig *Triton,* on 21 May 1861. On 11 August it set sail for the United States for reassignment. During the Civil War the ship protected commerce and conducted diplomatic functions as part of the Mediterranean Squadron. Meanwhile, the Abraham Lincoln administration, occupied by a war on American soil, finally agreed to allow the Royal Navy to search American vessels suspected to be slavers. This Anglo-American treaty was signed on 7 June 1862. The African Squadron was no more.

Conclusions

During the period that the USS *Constellation* was its flagship, the U.S. Navy's African Squadron captured fourteen slave ships and freed almost four thousand Africans from lives of servitude in the Americas. In just over two years, Commodore Inman's cruisers achieved nearly half the captures made during the squadron's entire existence (1842–61). The Navy achieved these results by increasing the number of vessels on station, introducing smaller, steam-powered vessels, relocating the supply depot from the distant port of Porto Praya to St. Paul de Loando, and restricting the boundaries of the cruising ground. More aggressive cruising and better cooperation with the Royal Navy's West Africa Squadron were also important factors. Unfortunately, however, squadron commanders were ordered to prioritize protection of American commerce over suppression of the slave trade, which hampered their success with the latter. Also, as one elderly slave smuggler affirmed in 1856, there was so much profit in smuggling slaves from Africa that even "if you should hang all the Yankee merchants engaged in it, hundreds would fill their places." According to this expert in the trade, there was only one possible solution: "Take the word of a dying man, there is no way the slave-trade can be stopped but by breaking up slave-holding."[31]

The U.S. Navy's African Squadron was "temporarily" canceled during the Civil War, when the Royal Navy was given permission to board and search American ships. To make an example in support of the Union's antislavery policies, President Abraham Lincoln ordered one American slaver captain, Nathaniel Gordon, to be hanged on 21 February 1862.[32] Because many other equally guilty slave traders were "quietly let off with light sentences," this conviction was described as "obviously a fluke."[33] Once the Confederacy was defeated, slavery in America was finally abolished. With increased efforts of the Royal Navy, plus Cuba's abolition of slavery in 1867, the transatlantic slave trade was dealt a decisive blow. Although the end of this trade was mainly the result of "breaking up slave-holding," it should not be forgotten that during the preceding two decades U.S. Navy ships like *Constellation* had played significant roles in the American effort to combat the transatlantic slave trade on the open seas.

After the war, the U.S. Navy quickly decided to reactivate the European, East India, and Brazil Squadrons, but the "African Squadron was abandoned." The Assistant Secretary of the Navy, Gustavus Fox, wrote the secretary, Gideon Welles, on 26 August 1865 that "it would be infinitely preferable to give up the African Squadron and have the same force in the West Indies under a special Commander. Such a transfer of ships would increase our influence in the seas adjacent to our coasts and which are really our waters." In December 1865, the Navy Department agreed with this suggestion, creating instead a West Indian Squadron, on the basis of the argument that "slave ships could be apprehended as effectively off the Cuban coast as off Africa."[34] In 1869, with all North American markets closed to slave ships arriving from Africa, the British government decided to abolish the Royal Navy's West Africa Squadron, "because there were no slave ships to catch."[35] Although French and Portuguese slave traders continued to participate to some degree in the transatlantic trade, "by the 1870s it had dwindled to insignificance nearly everywhere in the Atlantic."[36]

Notes

The thoughts and opinions expressed in this essay are those of the author and are not necessarily those of the U.S. government, the U.S. Navy Department, or the Naval War College.

1. C. Herbert Gilliland, *Voyage to the Thousand Cares: Master's Mate Lawrence with the African Squadron, 1844–1846* (Annapolis, Md.: Naval Institute Press, 2004), p. 3.

2. Donald L. Canney, *Africa Squadron: The U.S. Navy and the Slave Trade, 1842–1861* (Washington, D.C.: Potomac Books, 2006), p. 68.

3. Andrew Lambert, "Slavery, Free Trade and Naval Strategy, 1840–1860," in *Slavery, Diplomacy and Empire: Britain and the Suppression of the Slave Trade, 1807–1975*, ed. Keith Hamilton and Patrick Salmon (Portland, Ore.: Sussex Academic, 2009), p. 66.

4. Society of Friends, Philadelphia Yearly Meeting, *An Exposition of the African Slave Trade, from the Year 1840, to 1850, Inclusive, Prepared from Official Documents, and Published by Direction of the Representatives of the Religious Society of Friends, in Pennsylvania, New Jersey, and Delaware* (Philadelphia: J. Rakestraw, 1851; repr. Detroit, Mich.: Negro History, 1969), p. 157.

5. George Francis Dow, *Slave Ships and Slaving* (Salem, Mass.: Marine Research Society, 1927), p. 273, citing Andrew H. Foote, *Africa and the American Flag* (New York: D. Appleton, 1854).

6. Gilliland, *Voyage to the Thousand Cares*, pp. 298–99.

7. Ibid., p. 5.

8. John Pinfold, "Introduction: Captain Hugh Crow and the Slave Trade," in *The Memoirs of Captain Hugh Crow: The Life and Times of a Slave Trade Captain* (Oxford, U.K.: Bodleian Library, 2007), p. viii.

9. C. Herbert Gilliland, *USS Constellation on the Dismal Coast: Willie Leonard's Journal, 1859–1861* (Columbia: Univ. of South Carolina Press, 2013), p. 45.

10. USS *Constellation* only carried twenty guns during this cruise, having removed its two ten-inch pivot guns to provide greater stability. Its main battery consisted of sixteen eight-inch shell guns and four thirty-two-pounder long guns. It sailed for Africa with 285 officers, seamen, and Marines.

11. Gilliland, *USS Constellation on the Dismal Coast*, p. 48.

12. Ibid., p. 49.

13. Gilliland, *Voyage to the Thousand Cares*, pp. 39, 64.

14. Ibid., p. 110.

15. Ari Hoogenboom, *Gustavus Vasa Fox of the Union Navy: A Biography* (Baltimore, Md.: Johns Hopkins Univ. Press, 2008), pp. 14–15, 318 note 2.

16. Ibid.

17. Gilliland, *USS Constellation on the Dismal Coast*, p. 316.

18. Dow, *Slave Ships and Slaving*, p. 275.

19. Inman to Isaac Toucey, 21 December 1859, Squadron Letters, Record Group [RG] 45, M89, roll 110, National Archives and Records Administration, College Park, Md. [hereafter NARA].

20. "The Slave-Trade: The Bark *Cora*, of New-York, Captured on the African Coast," *New York Times*, 8 December 1860, p. 5.

21. Ibid.

22. Wilburn Hall, "Capture of the Slave Ship *Cora*," *Century* 48, no. 1 (1894), p. 116.

23. Gilliland, *USS Constellation on the Dismal Coast*, p. 148.

24. Hall, "Capture of the Slave Ship *Cora*," p. 120.

25. The account of Landsman William French published in 1924 is quoted in Glenn F. Williams, *U.S.S. Constellation: A Short History of the Last All-Sail Warship Built by the U.S. Navy* (Virginia Beach, Va.: Donning, 2000), p. 21.

26. Gilliland, *Voyage to the Thousand Cares*, pp. 298–99.

27. The first mate, Morgan Fredericks, stated that *Cora* took on 705 Africans. Loyall to Inman, 26 September 1860, Letter—Lt. Benjamin P. Loyall and 1st Lt. John R. F. Tatnall, USM, Letters, RG 45, M89, roll 111, NARA. In a letter to Toucey of 8 December 1860, Eastman reported that eleven Africans died on the way to Monrovia; John Seys reported that 694 were delivered to him on 14 October. *Constellation's* officers estimated that among the 694 freed slaves that completed the journey to Monrovia, 175 were men, 320 were boys, and 199 were women, young girls, or babies. See Karen Fisher Younger, "Liberia and the Last Slave Ships," *Civil War History* 54, no. 4 (December 2008); and Rev. John Seys, Monrovia, to Rev. W. McLain, 17 October 1860, in American Colonization Society, *African Repository* (Washington, D.C.: C. Alexander, 1861), vol. 37, pp. 1–2.

28. Canney, *Africa Squadron*, p. 71.

29. American Colonization Society, *African Repository*, vol. 37, p. 62.

30. Younger, "Liberia and the Last Slave Ships," p. 435.

31. Richard Drake, *Revelations of a Slave Smuggler: Being the Autobiography of Capt. Rich'd Drake, an African Trader for Fifty Years—from 1807 to 1857; During Which Period He Was Concerned in the Transportation of Half a*

Million Blacks from African Coasts to America (New York: Robert M. DeWitt, 1860; repr. Northbrook, Ill.: Metro Books, 1972), p. 98.

32. Lambert, "Slavery, Free Trade and Naval Strategy," p. 78.

33. Canney, *Africa Squadron,* p. 216.

34. Hoogenboom, *Gustavus Vasa Fox of the Union Navy,* p. 278.

35. Lambert, "Slavery, Free Trade and Naval Strategy," p. 78.

36. Joseph C. Miller, "The Abolition of the Slave Trade and Slavery: Historical Foundations," in *From Chains to Bonds: The Slave Trade Revisited,* ed. Doudou Diène (New York: Berghahn Books, 2001), p. 174.

CHAPTER TWO

Overwhelming Force and the Venezuelan Crisis of 1902–1903

HENRY J. HENDRIX

Few incidents of recent history have remained as clouded as the Venezuelan Crisis of 1902–3. For more than a century historians have disputed the accuracy of Theodore Roosevelt's recollections of the events of the winter of 1902. The confusion surrounding the Venezuelan Crisis stems from assertions made in Roosevelt's later correspondence. His claim that he actively coerced European blockaders to accept arbitration did not emerge publicly until October 1915, when one of his letters appeared as an appendix to a biography of former secretary of state John Hay.[1]

The biography's author, William R. Thayer, included the letter to highlight a previously undisclosed diplomatic crisis in the early days of Roosevelt's administration. Written in early 1915, the letter vividly recalls the events of late 1902 from the president's perspective: "I assembled our battle fleet, under Admiral Dewey, near Porto Rico, for 'maneuvres,' with instructions that the fleet should be kept in hand and in fighting trim, and should be ready to sail at an hour's notice . . . I saw the [German] Ambassador, and explained that in view of the presence of the German squadron on the Venezuelan coast I could not permit longer delay in answering my request for arbitration, and that I could not acquiesce in any seizure of Venezuelan territory."[2]

The records of the operational units and commanders of the naval forces involved in the "winter exercise" of 1902–3 present a clear picture of the events in the Caribbean. For eleven days, between 8 December and 18 December 1902, the future of U.S., British, German, and Venezuelan relations hung in the balance as Theodore Roosevelt discreetly pursued diplomatic negotiations between Venezuela and the two great European powers. When Germany, intent on nullifying the Monroe Doctrine and gaining a colonial possession in South America, repeatedly ignored the American president's call for arbitration, Roosevelt committed the combined U.S. Atlantic Fleet to the task of establishing the supremacy of American interests in the Western Hemisphere.

Defining Factors

In May 1901 a German warship appeared off Margarita, Venezuela, and began mapping approaches to the harbor. Although Venezuela had maintained its independence for more than seventy-five years, it continued to suffer the common ailments of many Latin American republics: a growing debt to international powers and a corrupt and weak government incapable of paying it off. Venezuela's constitutional structure maintained many of the authoritarian attributes of its colonial past, and the continuing presence and influence of institutions such as the Catholic Church, the military, and an organized landowning class acted to create and support a highly hierarchical social system that was prone to graft and corruption.[3]

Five Venezuelan presidents came and went during the 1890s, each alternately playing the role of reformer and strongman, all gaining wealth from commissions received for negotiating loans to their nation on terms very favorable to the European leaders. When Venezuela became so indebted that it could no longer afford to pay the interest on the notes, the European powers moved to collect. In 1895 this resulted in a loss of "disputed" territory to British-held Guiana, but Venezuela warded off outright colonial assimilation.[4] Concern that this surrender of territory might encourage the ambitions of other European powers eager to expand or establish colonial possessions in the area is evident in the strongly worded response and activities of the United States throughout this crisis.[5]

In 1902 the mantle of leadership rested on the shoulders of Gen. Cipriano Castro, who appears from the vantage point of history to be a caricature of the stereotypical Latin American dictator. A career army officer who had spent much of the 1890s exiled in neighboring Colombia, he launched a revolution on 23 May 1899 with the stated intent to create the strong central government he and his supporters felt was necessary to advance the cause of progress in the nation.[6] Castro's military strongman background heavily colored his foreign policy, which was a conglomeration of heavy-handed, aggressive initiatives that lacked sophistication or nuance. The American representative to Venezuela described Castro as "ignorant, obstinate and willful [sic]. He evidently thinks that he is a Power in the World . . . He has never traveled: he knows nothing of the outside world; he can not realize the force and power of virtue and justice; he believes he is the Child of Fortune, and that he alone is able to govern his country and control its destiny."[7] Castro spent much of 1901 fomenting unrest in Colombia in hopes of overthrowing its government and creating a greater Venezuelan Republic out of Bolivia, Colombia, and Venezuela.[8]

By late 1901 Venezuela's European creditors had become strident in their demands that President Castro pay more attention to his mounting foreign debts. Venezuela had not paid even the interest on its loans in several years, and Germany, Britain, and Italy were increasingly concerned. Castro diverted their requests for economic redress into the Venezuelan court system, whose bench was loaded with Castro supporters who rendered verdicts in Venezuela's favor. Additionally, Castro's navy seized foreign ships and their cargos at sea, and foreign-held homes in Venezuela were raided and looted.[9] When faced with the threat of European armed intervention to collect on debt and address the additional crimes against foreigners, Castro made it clear that he believed that the Monroe Doctrine would effectively shield his country.[10]

The Monroe Doctrine, first enunciated in 1823 by President James Monroe and his secretary of state, John Quincy Adams, forbade the expansion of European colonial efforts in the Western Hemisphere.[11] The combined effects of the Civil War and the abysmal state of the Navy left the United States without the tools to enforce this doctrine for most of the nineteenth century, however, and the responsibility for containing European expansion into the Western Hemisphere actually fell on the shoulders of Great Britain. Britain's colonial and commercial interests in Canada and the Caribbean made it a silent partner in the U.S. strategy, even when the two nations' policies were in conflict in other arenas.[12] The United States was willing to accept the dependent relationship until the final decade of the century, when the burdens of a worldwide empire on Britain, the burgeoning American Navy, and three successive crises (Brazil, 1891; Nicaragua, 1894; Venezuela, 1895) forced the two nations to reconsider the nature of their relationship.[13] With regard to Venezuela, however, Secretary of State John Hay, a noted anglophile, made it clear that the Monroe Doctrine was never intended to shield a wrongdoing state from justice. A consortium of European powers led by Germany and Great Britain prepared to test the limits of the United States' passivity.

While President William McKinley nominally supported the Europeans by urging Castro to make a good-faith effort to repay the loans, his vice president took a harder line.[14] Vice President Theodore Roosevelt reassured America's southern neighbors that while the doctrine posed no threat to them, it promised certain conflict for any "Old World Power" that sought to permanently acquire territory in the New World.[15] He took the additional step of spelling out his personal interpretation of the Monroe Doctrine directly to the German consul general, who was encouraged to convey it to Ambassador Theodor von Holleben and Kaiser Wilhelm.[16] This conversation must have weighed heavily on the mind of the German ambassador two months later when he called on Roosevelt to express his nation's sympathies to the new president of the United States following William McKinley's assassination.

In the opening days of the first Roosevelt presidency in September 1901, the European powers, with their numerous colonies scattered throughout the Caribbean and their sizable business investments in South America, exercised substantial influence over the Western Hemisphere (Table 1). Roosevelt was well aware that the leading nations of Europe did not welcome his expansive interpretation of the 1823 Monroe Doctrine. If the policy was to be effective, he needed to back it up with credible combat power and convince the imperial powers of Europe that he would use that power.

TABLE 1
Naval Order of Battle, 1901

	GREAT BRITAIN	FRANCE	GERMANY	USA	JAPAN
Battleships	28	9	15	10	6
Cruisers	120	37	26	20	31

Source: Navy Yearbook (Washington, D.C.: Government Printing Office, 1909), 655–657.

Naval Coercive Diplomacy

Shortly after entering the White House, Theodore Roosevelt accepted a report prepared for his predecessor by Rear Adm. Robley D. Evans that called into question "the real value of our naval force for fighting purposes." Evans, speaking for the General Board of the Navy—an advisory panel of a dozen or so senior officers created in 1901 to advise the secretary of the Navy on war planning, the disposition of the fleet, the establishment of bases, and so on—went on to detail the effective strength of fighting vessels available to other major naval powers in the event of war.[17] Observing the disparity in naval strength between the United States, the imperial powers of Europe, and the rising power of Japan in the Pacific, Evans noted that "the most phlegmatic observer cannot fail to be impressed with such a striking comparison, nor can he avoid appreciating the questionable position in which our country would be found, should any one of the many international problems of the present time suddenly force us into hostilities." Evans concluded by saying that the General Board urged "greater celerity in the completion of such vessels as are already authorized . . . while an equal or greater necessity for a further increase in our limited number of fighting ships should . . . be impressed upon Congress in the most emphatic manner."[18] Roosevelt reacted with characteristic gusto. "I am straining every nerve," he commented to a friend in the opening months of his presidency, "to keep on with the upbuilding of the Navy."[19] Roosevelt clearly envisioned needing that strength in his roles as his nation's chief diplomat and the commander in chief of its armed forces.

Roosevelt represented a quandary for European leaders. The populist nature of the American democracy led to a shifting foreign policy and inconsistent statements shaped largely for domestic consumption.[20] The more cosmopolitan Roosevelt crafted his pronouncements with domestic and foreign audiences equally in mind, however, and he was not given to exaggeration when it came to foreign policy.[21] Had the diplomats in the German and British embassies understood Roosevelt's character and reviewed his prior statements, there would have been no surprise when this staunch defender of the Monroe Doctrine interpreted a German communiqué issued in December 1901 not only as a challenge to the United States but as a personal affront as well. The message stated that while Germany and its partner Great Britain did not seek territorial gains, circumstances might require them to pursue "temporary occupation" of Venezuelan harbors and their accompanying customhouses.

Roosevelt took no comfort from these assurances.[22] After all, the kaiser's brother had recently seized territory "temporarily" in China and then negotiated (at gunpoint) ninety-nine-year leases on the holdings.[23] Rear Adm. Henry C. Taylor, chief of the Bureau of Navigation and the senior uniformed naval adviser to the president, wrote Roosevelt a memorandum in which he stated that in the likely event that Venezuela ignored the European blockade, the powers would respond by bombarding port facilities and invading. Germany's by now familiar strategy in these situations would be to demand an indemnity to cover the expense of the conflict. Secretary of State Hay had voiced his opinion of this formula a few years earlier while serving as ambassador to Great Britain: "There is to the German mind, something monstrous in the thought that a war should take place anywhere and they not profit by it."[24] In a classic European policy formulation, Taylor's memo concluded that President Castro "could offer nothing but territory," ensuring Germany's acquisition of a foothold on the South American continent.[25] With Venezuela overlooking the key approaches to the long-sought-after canal through the isthmus joining North and South America, the young American president correctly perceived the scenario of the likely establishment of a German naval base, or even an active German colony, as a clear and present threat to longstanding U.S. interests. This scenario alone would have compelled Roosevelt to act, but the historical record suggests that he also saw an opportunity to use the circumstances surrounding Venezuela's difficulties to elevate his nation and himself to the level of the other Great Powers and their leaders. To maximize this opportunity, he drew on the talents of men he understood and respected.

In June 1901 the General Board of the Navy, under the chairmanship of Admiral of the Navy George Dewey, had sent a report to President McKinley detailing the scope of influence the U.S. Navy could expect to exert in the Caribbean in the event of war with an unnamed Western European power. This unnamed power was assumed to be Germany, and in fact, the Naval War College had conducted a series of war games with negative results against the "Black" (German) Navy in 1901.[26] Now Dewey, the victor in the Battle of Manila Bay and, in Roosevelt's eyes, the nation's greatest living hero, reviewed his board's report with the new president. It stated that the "Navy can control the Caribbean and its shores in war, if we retain, in peace, vantage points on the shores of Cuba and create a strongly fortified naval base in Porto Rican waters. This control will reach Orinoco [near the present-day eastern border of Venezuela] and the Guianas."[27]

Subsequently, on 1 January 1902, a detachment of five Marine officers, one surgeon, and one hundred enlisted Marines began the permanent fortification of Culebra Island, a thickly wooded, six-mile-long islet sixteen miles east of Puerto Rico.[28] Culebra possessed no natural freshwater sources aside from that which came from the sky, but it did possess a magnificent harbor, known simply as "Great Harbor," that provided valuable protection for ships during the annual hurricane season.[29] One month earlier, in December 1901, portions of the island had been permanently ceded to the Department of the Navy. The conversion of designated areas to a fully equipped naval base now began in earnest, "in case of sudden war."[30] Named "Camp Roosevelt" in honor of the president, the camp featured barracks for officers and enlisted men, a storehouse for supplies, and a field hospital consisting of an operating room and dispensary. The latter was deemed too small by reviewers from the Bureau of Medicine and Surgery, who recommended that it be enlarged to the standard size, providing additional sleeping quarters for attendants and a six-bed hospital ward.[31] Tiny Culebra and its harbor became the cornerstone of American naval activities in the Caribbean.

The Navy was also carefully monitoring the mounting domestic and international instability that surrounded the Castro regime. Small U.S. Navy vessels that pulled in and out of Venezuelan ports for resupply provided surprisingly detailed intelligence reports on events unfolding there. For much of the nineteenth century, naval officers such as Commo. William Bainbridge with the Barbary pirates, Commo. Matthew Perry in Japan, and Rear Adm. John Walker in Panama had functioned with proficiency and quiet expertise as the sole diplomatic representatives of their nation in many foreign ports.[32] They also served as frontline intelligence officers, acting as the eyes and ears of the United States with regard to matters critical to national interests. On 28 February 1901 the commander of the USS *Scorpion* reported that the president of Venezuela was encouraging public discontent with the United States over minor civil infractions involving American sailors. Lt. Cdr. Nathan Sargent reported that "President Castro is unpopular and his foothold is insecure; he feels therefore that if the natural animosity to Americans can be encouraged, he can acquire popularity by his attitude and that his position will be greatly strengthened. In addition . . . he imagines he can gain the reputation of wielding a firm foreign policy without danger of being called to account for his actions by our Government." The *Scorpion*'s commanding officer suggested that the German government was using its local immigrant population to help stir up anti-American resentment: "I am also informed upon very reliable authority that the Germans are not wholly guiltless in this antagonism to everything American. They have here . . . a large colony in Venezuela, are naturally jealous of us and our trade, and have done their best to work up and accentuate this crusade against us."[33] Reports continued to arrive at the White House via the Navy Department detailing the increasing revolutionary unrest and the rising probability of European "intervention" to restore order.[34] Roosevelt knew the nature and the extent of the challenge he faced in the Caribbean, and he set about to prepare the instrument of his forthcoming diplomacy.

Winter Exercises

At the end of the nineteenth century, the U.S. Navy made a point of focusing its influence in the Caribbean. Following the Spanish-American War in 1898 the Navy commenced a series of "winter exercises," assembling various units of the fleet to carry out inspections and simulated engagements. It fell to Dewey's General Board to draft plans, assign units, and monitor the results. So it was that in May 1901 the General Board issued preliminary orders for the winter 1902–3 exercise. The conclusion of the exercise order described a simulated battle between two opposing fleets on the high seas.[35]

This proposal was refined in November 1901 by Secretary of the Navy John D. Long. According to Long's instructions, the winter exercise would begin with a series of inspections followed by combined live-firing drills (with limited expenditure of ammunition) to test the accuracy of the battleships' and cruisers' big guns and would culminate in the aforementioned simulated battle on the high seas between two large naval forces.[36] Every action ordered appears, from a professional's perspective, to be in line with standard operating procedures. As tensions between the European powers and Venezuela began to rise, however, a not too subtle "hidden hand" gradually altered the winter "exercise" to full preparation for war.

In early 1902 Ambassador von Holleben warned Kaiser Wilhelm II that Theodore Roosevelt would respond strongly to any hint of a permanent German military presence in South America. Wilhelm dismissed his ambassador's concern, saying, "We will do whatever is necessary . . . even if it displeases the Yankees."[37] The kaiser viewed the expansion of U.S. influence with alarm, fearing that it came at the expense of Germany's imperialist plans. In 1898, following George Dewey's defeat of the Spanish fleet in Manila Bay, a squadron of German ships sailed into the harbor amid rumors that it was intent on acquiring all or part of the former Spanish possession not claimed by the previously "nonimperial" United States.[38] The United States' subsequent departure from its historical imperial reluctance and acquisition of the entire archipelago, threatening to back up its stand with force if necessary, embarrassed the German commander, and by extension the kaiser.[39] Wilhelm was not one to suffer embarrassment without retaliation. At one point he even considered invading Long Island and using it as a bargaining chip to force the U.S. government to turn over certain overseas possessions.[40] Ultimately,

Wilhelm backed away from that precipice and shifted his focus to other nations in the Western Hemisphere.

By the time Theodore Roosevelt assumed the presidency, Wilhelm had concluded that the Monroe Doctrine was a real threat to the expansion of German influence and territory in South America. In a government position paper he questioned the doctrine's legality. "The Monroe Doctrine has not become an international law, to which the European Nations are tied," he insisted, and he pointedly began referring to the "United States of North America" in his speeches and correspondence.[41] Contemporary observers discerned in Wilhelm's statements a strategy to "unite Europe, including England, in hostility to the Monroe doctrine."[42] Wilhelm II knew that he had to destroy the legitimacy of the United States' claims of preponderant interest in the Western Hemisphere to achieve the goals of German colonial expansion. To do that, he would have to take on Theodore Roosevelt.

Upon assuming the presidency, Roosevelt, for continuity, had asked McKinley's cabinet to remain in place. Within six months, however, the new president, who as assistant secretary had chafed under John Long's lethargy, accepted the old man's resignation, graciously describing him as a man who was "single-minded in his devotion to the public interest."[43] Roosevelt took the traditional route of looking to the state of Massachusetts for a replacement and quickly appointed four-term congressman William H. Moody, "whose vigor, sturdiness, and temperament . . . resembled his own," as the new secretary of the Navy.[44] Moody's four years of service on the House Insular Affairs Committee had educated him on the magnitude of the challenges of carrying out a successful imperial foreign policy.[45] With Moody's help, Roosevelt quickly modified the character of the forthcoming naval exercise.

In June, Roosevelt took the highly irregular step of asking Admiral Dewey himself to assume command of the combined Atlantic Fleet for the winter exercise. Dewey, the Navy's only "four-star" admiral, seldom went to sea, and never for extended periods. He preferred to remain in Washington, where he could monitor the Navy from his office from nine until noon and then enjoy a nice afternoon nap at home before setting out for an afternoon carriage ride followed by dinner and early retirement to bed.[46] Revealing that the broader international audience was the intended target of his decision, Roosevelt wrote to Dewey: "Your standing . . . abroad, is such that the effect of your presence will be very beneficial."[47] Roosevelt demonstrated the importance he attached to Dewey's mission when, despite being bedridden with a leg injury that would ultimately result in a painful bone-scraping procedure, he invited Dewey to his sickroom to share his private thoughts on the matter. The president made it clear that his reason for assigning Dewey was twofold: He wanted Dewey commanding the fleet to "put pride in the people and [to] arrest the attention of . . . the Kaiser." The full extent of Roosevelt's instructions during this meeting are not known, but a diary entry by Dewey's wife later that evening intimates their sensitive nature: "The Prest. [*sic*] told G. in strict confidence—what had better not be written now."[48]

In August, Roosevelt attempted to telegraph the seriousness of his intentions to the international community. Writing to his good friend, British parliamentarian (and noted European socialite) Arthur Lee, Roosevelt stated that Dewey was training the fleet for war.[49] Lee, noted for his numerous contacts in European capitals, could be counted on to make sure that this diplomatic tidbit reached the right ears. Deeply sensitive to the significance of symbolism in diplomacy, T.R. completed his summer diplomatic foray by offering Dewey the use of the presidential yacht, the USS *Mayflower,* as his flagship.[50] Any attack on this ship, an outward symbol of the American presidency, could be seen only as a personal attack on Theodore Roosevelt himself.

Secretary of the Navy Moody had already taken steps to support Dewey in his mission to the Caribbean. Prior to the president's offer of the *Mayflower,* the swift packet vessel USS *Dolphin* had been placed at Dewey's command, along with an expert staff that included Rear Adm. Henry C. Taylor as chief of staff and the newly promoted Cdr. Nathan Sargent as Dewey's personal aide.[51] Again, from an operational perspective, Taylor's assignment as chief of staff is worthy of note.

Henry Clay Taylor was regarded as one of the most gifted men of his generation. He had served at the Naval War College in Newport, Rhode Island, acquiring a reputation as an intellectual, an administrator, and an innovator. When the position of chief of the Bureau of Navigation was vacated, Roosevelt reached far down and promoted Taylor over the heads of many of his superiors into the senior Navy position in Washington.[52] At that time there was no Chief of Naval Operations. Instead, the U.S. Navy was run by eight admirals who headed up "bureaus" (navigation, shipbuilding, ordnance, etc.). While they were all equal in rank, it was accepted that the head of the Bureau of Navigation was the "first among equals." The assignment of Taylor to be Dewey's chief of staff was thus highly unusual and could have occurred only by the direction of the commander in chief. The choice of Commander Sargent, recently the commander of the USS *Scorpion* and the source of so much intelligence concerning the political unrest in Venezuela, further underlines the importance assigned to this mission.

Moody took the additional step of ordering U.S. Navy assets in July to survey the Venezuelan coast for possible German landing zones and to submit suggestions for their defense. Later, in an internal memorandum, he informed his bureau chiefs that the president was "deeply interested" in the forthcoming maneuvers. Moody directed all involved to provide "hearty and vigorous cooperation" to ensure "that this mobilization of the fleet be successfully accomplished." He concluded by reminding the recipients "that this movement is a test of our ability to meet war demands" and assured his bureau chiefs that he would "sanction all reasonable expense within the law and regulations, in order that the vessels engaged . . . may be prepared."[53] This level of personal attention at the secretarial level leaps out at the historical and professional observer. In October the secretary issued the final instructions for the winter exercise, now just two months away. In a telling and dramatic departure from the simulated battle between two fleets on the high seas contained in previous versions of the exercise, Moody ordered a battle scenario focused on the interception of an approaching naval force intent on securing an undefended foreign harbor and mining its main ship channel.[54]

U.S. Marines Build a Base

Naval power is not completely sea based, and Roosevelt's preparations did not end with Dewey and his fleet. Throughout the late summer and early fall, as the final changes were being made to the "winter exercise," the workings of the other arm of the naval service, the U.S. Marine Corps, also showed evidence of Roosevelt's hidden hand. In September 1903, on the order of the Commandant of the Corps, a battalion of Marines was consti-tuted for possible deployment to Panama.[55] The battalion comprised 16 officers and 421 enlisted men under the command of Col. Percival C. Pope, an exceedingly experienced commander of troops whose service stretched back to the Civil War.[56] The men were embarked on board the USS *Prairie,* which remained tied up at the naval base in Norfolk, Virginia, awaiting further orders. On 23 October an additional order increased the size of the force by one company under the command of Capt. Smedley D. Butler, bringing the force to 19 officers and 522 enlisted men.[57] The size and structure of this force represented a sizable percentage of the expeditionary combative power of the Marine Corps.

On 5 November this force was ordered to participate in the winter exercise, and the *Prairie* departed Norfolk for Culebra Island.[58] The Marines reached the island on 20 November, disembarked, and began constructing three defensive artillery positions, mutually supporting their fields of fire. They built roads strong enough to allow the trans-portation of heavy guns and ammunition between the emplacements and strung tele-phone lines between the various encampments. Rear Adm. Francis J. Higginson and Rear Adm. Joseph B. Coghlan, the respective commanders of the North Atlantic and Caribbe-an squadrons, inspected the positions and pronounced them satisfactory.[59] The Marines' actions constituted a major effort to establish a defensible base for fleet operations.

Kaiser Wilhelm II remained oblivious to the mounting American resistance to his plan for expansion in South America. Throughout the summer and early fall he worked to convince the British to act with Germany to coerce Venezuela into paying off its debts.[60] Two months later, in a characteristic boast, Wilhelm played up the capabilities of his navy to visiting American Army general (and known Roosevelt confidant) Leonard

Wood.[61] By early November the forces of Germany and Great Britain were in position to take action against Venezuela.[62] Rear Admiral Taylor advised Roosevelt that war between the United States and the European powers was the likely outcome if the situation developing off Venezuela turned violent.[63]

On the evening of 24 November 1902 Roosevelt hosted a private dinner for a small group at the White House to honor Baron Speck von Sternburg, a German diplomat and old friend. Both men had served in Washington during the early 1890s, Roosevelt on the Civil Service Commission and von Sternburg in the German embassy. Roosevelt hoped to use the intimacy of personal diplomacy to convey his intentions directly to the kaiser's senior staff. Also at the dinner table that evening was Admiral of the Navy George Dewey.[64]

Admiral Dewey always maintained the poise and appearance of a cultured man, but inside him raged a fierce spirit with but one focus: Germany. While he publicly restrained his comments, Washington's social elite were well aware that Dewey held the Germans in particular distaste as a result of the German navy's actions preceding and following the Battle of Manila Bay.[65] Mildred Dewey, again in the privacy of her diary, stated her unvarnished opinion of the U.S.-German relationship, "The truth is, we hate each other."[66]

Roosevelt's purpose in inviting Admiral Dewy to the White House for dinner could not have escaped a professional diplomat of von Sternburg's caliber. But events in European capitals conspired to ensure that the carefully constructed guest list and dinner conversation would not have the time or opportunity to achieve Roosevelt's aim. Events were already in motion.

Germany and Great Britain had begun to consider joint action against Venezuela in the early days of 1902.[67] Great Britain wanted to seize Venezuela's gunboats as "a convenient form of coercion" and as a means of avoiding the perception of infringing on Roosevelt's Monroe Doctrine.[68] The kaiser, however, remained convinced that Roosevelt was bluffing and instructed his ambassador to Britain to communicate his intention to blockade the South American republic. Count Paul von Metternich's arguments carried the day, and on 25 November 1902 Germany and Great Britain formally announced their intention to implement a "pacific" blockade of Venezuela.[69]

Britain's participation in the Venezuelan Crisis appears inconsistent with its evolving national interests in the Western Hemisphere. After a century of acrimony and distrust between their two respective nations, the governments of Theodore Roosevelt and Arthur Balfour seemed to be successfully knitting together the destinies of the two great English-speaking nations. Given the importance it attached to its current relationship with America, Balfour's government took the precaution of forewarning Secretary of State Hay of Britain's decision to blockade Venezuela. Hay, who was either out of touch with Roosevelt's thinking or deliberately playing his role in a grand Rooseveltian diplomatic drama, responded that while he regretted "that European Powers should use force against Central and South American countries," his country "could not object to their taking steps to obtain redress for injuries suffered by their subjects, provided no acquisition of territory was contemplated."[70] Perhaps because of the tepid nature of Hay's assurance, Britain's new ambassador to the United States, Michael Herbert, felt compelled to express his own personal reservations. "I wish we were going to punish Venezuela without the aid of Germany," he wrote to his foreign minister, Lord Henry Lansdowne, "for I am not sure that joint action will be very palatable here."[71]

On 1 December Roosevelt traveled the few blocks south from the White House to the Washington Navy Yard to see Dewey off. The exact words exchanged between the two men are not known, but the substance of the conversation is clear: while Dewey did sail with the intention of overseeing the annual winter exercise, there was the very real potential for him to play an even greater role in the developing crisis off the coast of Venezuela. As her husband sailed south out of communication, Mildred Dewey recorded in her diary, "I dread there may be war over Veequela [sic] . . . how can Georg [sic] get thru three wars unscathed."[72]

Execution

On 7 December 1902 Germany and Great Britain instituted their "peaceful blockade" of Venezuela.[73] It did not begin well. A Venezuelan mob in Porto Cabello seized the British-flagged merchantman *Topaze* at anchor there, and German ships shelled two nearby Venezuelan military installations in response. Elsewhere, students marched in the streets displaying banners that called on the United States to uphold *la doctrina* Monroe on their behalf.[74] President Castro escalated tensions and gave his opponents a legal recipe for a declaration of war when he ordered the imprisonment of all male British and German citizens and the seizure of their property.[75] On 9 December British and German naval forces proceeded to capture the ships of the Venezuelan navy then in port.[76] The Germans, in their enthusiasm, sank one of their prizes and seriously damaged another.[77] Castro, by now convinced of the seriousness of the European threat, appealed to the American minister in Venezuela, Herbert Bowen, to intercede on Venezuela's behalf and extend an offer of arbitration.[78] Britain, increasingly aware of the concern the situation had aroused in the United States, assented, but Germany attempted to sidestep arbitration.[79]

The concept of arbitration as an element of international law emerged from The Hague Peace Conference convened by Czar Nicholas II in the spring and summer of 1899. While the conference did not achieve its ultimate, idealistic aim of achieving world peace, it did result in the establishment of a Permanent Court of Arbitration where nations could seek redress for their mutual grievances without having to resort to armed conflict. Germany, not keen to see the martial advantage arising in its shipyards and the forges of the Krupp arms factories nullified by weak nations who sought equal treatment through legal venues, opposed the arbitration initiatives.[80] Now, as word of the Venezuelan offer arrived in Germany, the kaiser's earlier concerns seemed justified. Arbitration at this point in the blockade would not allow for the series of events necessary for Germany to gain the toehold of Venezuelan territory it needed to begin its slow expansion into South America and assert strategic prominence overlooking the approaches to the long-planned canal across the isthmus. The kaiser rejected arbitration.

According to Theodore Roosevelt's later accounts, as the *Mayflower* dropped anchor off Culebra Island on 8 December, he was in the White House welcoming a group of German businessmen escorted by Ambassador Theodor von Holleben. During this meeting, the president later recalled, he drew von Holleben aside and spoke sharply to him, issuing an ultimatum demanding that Germany either accept arbitration within ten days or face armed conflict with the United States.[81] The shocked ambassador responded that he could not forward such a demand, phrased as it was, to the kaiser. Apparently, von Holleben left the room convinced that Roosevelt was bluffing. He would not have been so certain had he been aware of the actions of Admiral Dewey during the period 9–18 December 1902.

Naval professionals will quickly discern within the stark events that occurred over the next week and a half the differences between a well-executed "winter exercise" and the actions of a veteran combatant commander preparing his forces for war. Background analysis also reveals the blunt hand of America's relatively new chief diplomatist and commander in chief. Unlike previous exercises, which focused on individual naval squadrons, the 1902–3 maneuvers gathered every available battleship, cruiser, and torpedo boat in the Atlantic.[82]

By combining the North Atlantic, South Atlantic, European, and Caribbean squadrons, Dewey was able to marshal fifty-three ships to counter the twenty-nine ships available to Britain and Germany in the Caribbean.[83] Although this number may seem excessive, it was necessary, in Roosevelt's mind, to demonstrate an ability on the part of the United States to concentrate an overwhelming force in its claimed "zone of influence." Both Great Britain and Germany possessed larger navies than the United States, but they would have had to strip units from other critical areas of their empires (leaving trade routes vulnerable to disruption) in order to exceed the combined American fleet. Assembling such a force would take weeks—weeks in which Roosevelt would be free to exercise his diplomacy.

While Dewey cruised down from Washington, D.C., aboard the *Mayflower* his task force was already exercising in the Caribbean. The individual components of the Atlantic Fleet had begun to assemble off Culebra in mid-November (Table 2). On 1 November the Caribbean Squadron under the command of Rear Adm. Joseph Coghlan had made the short transit to Culebra from its base at San Juan, Puerto Rico. Coghlan's division comprised the type of cruisers and auxiliary cruisers that had borne the brunt of the action during the Spanish-American War four years earlier. The North Atlantic Squadron, largely formed of battleships and under the command of Rear Adm. Francis Higginson, arrived on 21 November 1902 from Hampton Roads, Virginia. The remaining two squadrons—the South Atlantic Squadron under the command of Rear Adm. George W. Sumner and the European Squadron under the command of Rear Adm. A. S. Crownin-shield—which each comprised a single battleship escorted by three or four armored or protected cruisers, rendezvoused in the Gulf of Paria to form the simulated approaching opposing force in the winter exercise's main battle problem.

TABLE 2

U.S. Atlantic Fleet Components prior to 1902 Winter Exercise

NORTH ATLANTIC SQUADRON	CARIBBEAN SQUADRON	SOUTH ATLANTIC SQUADRON	EUROPEAN SQUADRON
Rear Adm. Francis J. Higginson	Rear Adm. Joseph B. Coghlan	Rear Adm. George W. Sumner	Rear Adm. Arent S. Crowninshield
USS *Kearsarge* (BB), flagship	USS *Olympia* (CL), flagship	USS *Iowa* (BB), flagship	USS *Illinois* (BB), flagship
USS *Alabama* (BB)	USS *Montgomery* (CL)	USS *Atlanta* (CL)	USS *Chicago* (CL)
USS *Massachusetts* (BB)	USS *Detroit* (CL)	USS *San Francisco* (CL)	USS *Albany* (CL)
USS *Indiana* (BB)	USS *Panther* (CX)		USS *Nashville* (GB)
USS *Cincinnati* (CL)	USS *Marietta* (GB)		
USS *Machias* (GB)			
USS *Scorpion* (GBL)			
USS *Gloucester* (GBL)			
USS *Aileen* (GBL)			
TORPEDO FLOTILLA			
Lt. Cdr. Lloyd Chandler			
USS *Decatur* (TB), command ship			
USS *Bagley* (TB)			
USS *Barney* (TB)			
USS *Biddle* (TB)			
USS *Shubrick* (TB)			
USS *Thornton* (TB)			
USS *Stockton* (TB)			

Abbreviations: BB, battleship; CL, unarmored cruiser; CX, auxiliary cruiser; GB, gunboat; GBL, unarmored gunboat; TB, torpedo boat.

Source: Annual Report of the Navy Department, 1903 (Washington, D.C.: Government Printing Office, 1903), 466–473.

The objective of the exercise was for the opposing White force under the command of Rear Admiral Sumner to "secure a base" in any one of the five harbors in the vicinity of Puerto Rico and Culebra by 6:00 PM on 10 December 1902. The Blue (American) force under the command of Rear Admiral Higginson had to intercept this fleet, either at sea or soon after its arrival in a port, with a superior force. The result of this exercise provides insight into the great challenges of warfare on the vast reaches of the oceans. Sumner's force transited first far to the east and then to the north of the islands before making a final swift passage down through the Mona Passage. Sumner successfully completed his task—occupying and defensively mining a harbor without resistance—on 9 December.[84]

Admiral Dewey had dropped anchor at Culebra's Great Harbor the previous day. His first step on arriving in the Caribbean was to secure fuel and ammunition for his ships as well as current intelligence on his surroundings. During his sail down from Washington Dewey had requested information on the positions of all logistics support ships in the Atlantic, and on arrival he ordered all ships to submit a list of the supplies required for them to meet "all contingencies." In the meantime, Secretary Moody had wired his naval attachés in London, Paris, and Berlin requesting the desertion rates of the respective European navies in a rough attempt to ascertain their readiness for war.[85]

Dewey continued to issue orders at odds with the planned inspection, gunnery exercise, and simulated battle. He instructed a majority of the fleet to maintain position outside Great Harbor, and all U.S. ships to "maintain sufficient steam pressure to get underway" at a moment's notice.[86] Maintaining this high readiness posture was exhausting for the men involved and used up large quantities of coal. Further, it was very difficult to perform a full material inspection of a ship with the crew manning all stations and the fires in the steam engineering plant ignited and hot. Most engine inspections were completed when the fires of the propulsion system were out and the steam plant was cold, allowing the internal workings of the boiler and the gearing systems to be opened and available for visual inspection. Dewey, it seems, was not emphasizing a rigorous material review.

Perhaps the most glaring example of Dewey's novel approach to the exercise was his order on 10 December to his medical staff to establish a sixty-bed hospital ward in Puerto Rico.[87] The Marines, as previously mentioned, had built a "standard" six-bed hospital ward the year before, and the ships in Dewey's fleet maintained their own sickbays and carried doctors or pharmacist's mates to tend to the day-to-day ills and complaints of the crew. Squadrons typically carried a surgeon who would shuttle back and forth between the ships to handle the most serious cases. But Dewey took the initiative of moving his surgeons and their equipment off the major capital ships and borrowing medical staff from the growing naval base ashore to establish a land-based hospital capable of handling an inordinate number of sick or wounded. Whether that action is viewed from the vantage point of a naval professional or an archival historian, it is clear that Dewey was making every effort to ensure that all preparatory steps for combat operations had been taken.

A message from Chief of Staff Taylor to the commanding officer of the naval base adds another clue to Dewey's intent. It is customary, when a group of navy ships pulls into port, for a shore detail to be formed to assist the local command in the logistical support of the ships. This practice maintains order among the sailors allowed ashore (the dreaded "shore patrol") and also provides for the upkeep of the piers and the waterfront. The local commanding officer sent a request to Dewey's flagship for just this sort of detail when the *Mayflower* arrived, but on 11 December Rear Admiral Taylor replied, "I regret to inform you it will be impracticable to give you any force of men or boats from the fleet at present. The intention of Admiral Dewey is to keep the fleet outside [the harbor] in a state of preparations to move at short notice."[88] This and Dewey's other instructions were not typical of a fleet commander preparing his ships for a set schedule of inspections, gun firings, and simulated battle. In fact, on his second day in the harbor, Dewey, a noted stickler for schedules and organization, scuttled a carefully prepared schedule and announced his intention to begin material inspections of the major combatants immediately.[89] He quickly moved through the material inspection phase, pushing on into instruction for all ships in the new system of marksmanship developed by Lt. Cdr. William S. Sims.[90]

Back in Washington—according to Edmund Morris' timeline, on the afternoon of Sunday, 14 December—Roosevelt held his second meeting with Ambassador von Holleben. After discussing the weather and exchanging other pleasantries, Roosevelt asked if von Holleben had a reply for him regarding his previous ultimatum. The ambassador replied that since he had assumed that Roosevelt was not serious, he had not sent the message to the kaiser. Roosevelt later remembered telling von Holleben that "instead of allowing the three days that remained for an answer I would order Dewey to sail [south to Venezuela] in forty-eight hours."[91] T.R. also began a series of hurried consultations with members of the House of Representatives and the Senate that were reported in the *New York Times* and *Washington Evening Star* for all to see.[92] Dewey, for his part, alluded to the focus of his attention when he wrote obliquely to his son the same day, "Things look rather equally Venezuela way, but we are not in it at the present."[93]

The German ambassador understood with stark clarity his predicament. Following his 14 December meeting with Roosevelt, he hurried north to New York City to meet with Karl Bunz, the longtime German consul general there and a friend of Theodore Roosevelt. Years later, a friend of Bunz recounted that von Holleben came to ask if Roosevelt's threat should be taken seriously. Bunz replied that to the best of his knowledge, Roosevelt did not bluff.[94]

That same day, Secretary Moody wired Dewey, via a secure underwater Navy cable, to maintain a swift vessel at the ready in San Juan in order to ensure continuous communications with the fleet. He sent a similar message to the naval station at San Juan to stand by to forward instructions immediately to Dewey at sea.[95] Dewey and the combined fleet had by this time progressed into a sequence of coordinated maneuvers, beginning with divisions of four ships, then combining into squadrons, and ultimately coming together as a fleet (Table 3). The new torpedo-boat flotilla practiced stealthy night attacks against simulated opponent battleships.

Dewey confided to his journal that "some of the evolutions were rather raggedly performed, owing to new ships having joined . . . [I] think angles and turning circles not yet having been determined."[96] The after action report noted that the "cruiser divisions

TABLE 3
Combined U.S. Atlantic Fleet, 10 December 1902

	Commander Admiral of the Navy George Dewey USS *Mayflower,* flagship	
First Squadron Rear Adm. Francis J. Higginson	**Second Squadron** Rear Adm. George W. Sumner	**Base Command** Rear Adm. Joseph B. Coghlan USS *Vixen* (PY), flagship
First Division USS *Kearsarge* (BB), flagship USS *Iowa* (BB) USS *Massachusetts* (BB) USS *Alabama* (BB) USS *Scorpion* (GBL), tender	**Third Division** USS *Chicago* (CL), flagship USS *Albany* (CL) USS *Cincinnati* (CL) USS *Newark* (CL) USS *Eagle,* tender	**Substitute Vessels** USS *Nashville* (GB) USS *Machias* (GB) USS *Marietta* (GB) USS *Bancroft* (GB) USS *Wasp,* tender
Second Division Rear Adm. A. S. Crowninshield USS *Illinois* (BB), flagship USS *Texas* (BB) USS *Indiana* (BB) USS *Olympia* (CL) USS *Hist,* tender	**Fourth Division** Capt. Asa Walker USS *San Francisco* (CL), command ship USS *Atlanta* (CL) USS *Montgomery* (CL) USS *Detroit* (CL)	**Torpedo Flotilla** Lt. Cdr. Lloyd Chandler USS *Decatur* (TB), command ship USS *Bagley* (TB) USS *Barney* (TB) USS *Biddle* (TB) USS *Thornton* (TB) USS *Wilkes* (TB) USS *Stockton* (TB) USS *Nina,* tender
Transports USS *Prairie* (CX) USS *Panther* (CX)	**Tugs** USS *Fortune* USS *Leyden* USS *Osceola* USS *Potomac* USS *Uncas*	
Water Supply USS *Arethusa*		**Supply and Repair** USS *Culgoa*
Colliers USS *Hannibal,* USS *Leonidas,* USS *Sterling,* USS *Lebanon,* USS *Brutus,* USS *Marcellus,* USS *Ajax*		

Abbreviations: BB, battleship; CL, unarmored cruiser; GB, armored gunboat; GBL, unarmored gunboat; CX, auxiliary cruiser; TB, torpedo boat.

Source: Journal of the Commander in Chief, Dewey Collection, Library of Congress, Washington, D.C., box 44, 15.

were handled in connection with line of battle[ships] without confusion and without the necessity of frequent signals or signaling at great distances."

Capt. Albert Gleaves, the commanding officer of Dewey's flagship, the *Mayflower,* disagreed with that assessment. Gleaves recorded in his memoirs an attempt to steam in formation from Culebra to Saint Thomas that left an indelible image of a fleet "without form and void—so to speak." Gleaves felt that the ad hoc procurement practices of the Navy Department had resulted in such a multitude of ship designs and capabilities that the U.S. Navy was practically unable to operate in formations beyond small groups of similarly designed ships. Following the winter exercise, an attempt was made to align the fleet in accordance with the ships' capabilities.[97]

In another departure from the norms of the day, Admiral Dewey directed that the reinforced Marine battalion under the command of Colonel Pope at Culebra dispatch landing parties to the eastern and western shores of Vieques, to the bay of Ensenada Honda, and to the northern shore of Puerto Rico. Those Marines left on Culebra not tasked with logistical duties were sent into that island's jungles.[98] These reconnoitering parties, each comprising an officer and twenty-five enlisted men and supplied with a week's worth of provisions, practiced armed reconnaissance, searching out possible enemy landing sites and establishing defensive positions to repel the aggressor force. While the after action report makes no mention of Venezuela, Dewey's involvement and the magnitude and realism of the Marines' activities indicate that this, too, was no mere exercise. Dewey's final report obliquely summarized the Marines' jungle training: "These various exercises proved of conspicuous value to the officers and men engaged in them and gave us much valuable experience for later use."[99]

In reply to Moody's 14 December letter, Dewey acknowledged the order to maintain a courier boat to relay messages and, in a barely disguised request for additional information, pointedly asked, "Program of exercises called for dispersal of fleet Friday night for Christmas holidays. Shall this be carried out?"[100] Earlier that day Dewey had received an intelligence report from the commanding officer of the USS *Marietta,* operating off La Guayra, Venezuela, detailing the actions taken by the British and German war vessels *Charybdis* and *Vineta* against Venezuelan military installations and port facilities.[101] Based on this information, and clearly expecting a war order, Rear Admiral Taylor sent a message to the communications center in San Juan: "Recent intelligence from Washington indicates the possibility of urgent dispatches arriving anytime . . . it is probable that such cables may be written in cipher and every precaution should be taken to expedite their delivery . . . it is advisable to avoid comment upon questions and topics in any way."[102]

Shortly after transmitting this cable, Dewey recalled all of his force's ambulatory sick from Puerto Rican hospitals in an effort to fully man his ships, and ordered all of his ships currently in or near the port to be fully loaded with stores.[103] No other indicator of the expectation of combat can be so clear as the decision to pull a sick man from his bed in order to man his battle station.

December seventeenth dawned ominously as William Moody cryptically instructed Dewey not to disperse the fleet. Such instructions along with Dewey's activities indicate that both Dewey and Moody expected the worst. Supplies of coal and ammunition had been loaded, and the force had been exercised vigorously at sea. Word from Washington indicated no change in the Europeans' position, and it was apparent that the situation was deteriorating. The U.S. Senate passed a resolution endorsing Roosevelt's public warnings to the European nations with regard to maintaining the territorial integrity of Venezuela.[104] As night fell, Dewey assembled all of his senior commanders onboard the *Mayflower* "for consultations relative to the Venezuelan question."[105]

In the United States, public reaction to events in Venezuela was decidedly anti-European, an attitude that was promptly noted in European capitals. Prime Minister Balfour learned from his ambassador in the United States, Sir Michael Herbert, "The impression prevails in Washington that Germany is using us, and our friends here regret, from the point of view of American good feeling towards us, that we are acting with her."[106] Three days earlier Herbert had cabled an encrypted message stating that the U.S. government was passing along Venezuela's renewed desire to seek a "settlement of the present difficulty by arbitration."[107] On 16 December Parliament convened to debate the situation in Venezuela and the strains it was placing on Britain's relationship with America.[108] Balfour appeared in Parliament the following day to announce, "We have no intention, and have never had any intention, of landing troops in Venezuela or of occupying territory, even though that occupation might only be of a temporary nature."[109]

The next day the American ambassador, Henry White, presented a message from Roosevelt to Balfour's government strongly urging Britain and Germany to accept arbitration. Although Balfour was irritated by the impertinence of the suggestion, he felt it necessary to maintain the goodwill of the United States and quickly accepted it. Other officials of the government stepped forward to acknowledge and recognize the Monroe Doctrine. The prime minister also took it upon himself to contact some leading American citizens to ask them to relay to Roosevelt his desire for continued good relations with the United States. The burgeoning special relationship between the two English-speaking nations remained a high priority.[110]

In Berlin, the reaction to the United States' "suggestion" of arbitration was slightly different. Much to Lord Lansdowne's consternation, Germany's ambassador to Great

Britain, Count Paul von Metternich, continued to insist that the kaiser would not stoop to arbitration.[111] The kaiser, it seems, was continuing to call what he thought was Roosevelt's bluff. Back in the United States, Ambassador von Holleben's military attachés traveled north to advise him on the strategic implications of the positioning of the American fleet.[112] Finally overcoming his "mortal terror" of the kaiser, von Holleben transmitted two telegrams to Berlin. Their contents are unknown, but their effect was immediate.[113] On the evening of 17 December Berlin signaled its acceptance of the American arbitration proposal. The kaiser had, as one observer wrote, "tested the Monroe Doctrine and discovered that it held."[114]

Soon after the crisis ended, Theodor von Holleben was recalled in disgrace by the German emperor. The Washington establishment buzzed at both the suddenness and the silence of his departure. An explanation that the ambassador's health was impaired was so at odds with his appearance and actions that speculation only increased. Some suggested that he had failed in his mission for the kaiser because he cultivated too friendly a relationship with Roosevelt rather than seek out ties with the financial community in New York so important to Germany's industrial expansion. Decades would pass before the real nature of his diplomatic demise was understood.

Following the Venezuelan Crisis, the Monroe Doctrine, which the European powers had always looked on with skepticism, gained widespread tacit recognition and respect.[115] Wilhelm had blinked, ending Germany's chance to create colonies in the Western Hemisphere. On 18 December, free of worries, Secretary Moody wired his commander at sea, "Carry out your proposed holiday itinerary. Merry Christmas."[116]

On 4 January 1903, as the *Mayflower* made its way back up the eastern coast of the United States, Admiral Dewey summarized the success of his mission in a letter to George Dewey Jr. The exercise, he wrote, "has been very interesting and I think beneficial to the Navy & Country. I have no doubt the Venezuela question would have given considerable trouble had it not been for this splendid fleet on the spot."[117] Years later, Roosevelt would sum up the role of George Dewey and his fleet succinctly during a speech given in Oyster Bay. "Dewey," the former president remembered, "was the greatest possible provocateur of peace."[118]

Conclusions

Edmund Morris eloquently described the vacant diplomatic record surrounding the Venezuelan Crisis as a "white shape of some vanished enormity, a reverse silhouette cut out of the gray text of history."[119] The naval record of the events associated with the crisis, both in the broader scope of Roosevelt's overarching naval policy and in the specific actions of Admiral of the Navy George Dewey in his role as the commander in chief of the combined Atlantic Fleet, supports Theodore Roosevelt's later version of events as expressed in his 1915 letter to William R. Thayer: ". . . less than twenty four hours before the time I had appointed for calling the order to Dewey, the Ambassador notified me that His Imperial Majesty the German Emperor had directed him to request me to undertake arbitration myself."[120]

From the outset of his administration it was Theodore Roosevelt's desire to "upbuild" the U.S. Navy, supporting the service's uniformed leadership in their desire for increased production of capital vessels. When faced with a credible threat to U.S. interests in the Caribbean and South America, he authorized the construction of a large naval base on Culebra, an island strategically located in the path of European approaches to the Caribbean. He altered the nature of a routine winter exercise—both its scenario and its composition—flooding the Caribbean basin with the near entirety of the Atlantic Fleet to ensure an overwhelming concentration of power during the critical months of the crisis. Further, Roosevelt personally made changes in personnel in key political and military positions.

Hence, both naval and historical records seem to provide more than enough evidence to support the proposition that the American fleet arrived in the Caribbean with the intent of coercing the European nations into accepting mediation. In order for this form of diplomacy to be successful, the naval forces involved had to be fully prepared to conduct combat operations. In the end, it was this high degree of preparation that helped to convince the Europeans of Roosevelt's seriousness and bring them to the bargaining table.

Theodore Roosevelt went to extraordinary lengths to inform European powers of his interpretation of the Monroe Doctrine, both formally through conversations with the German consul general and ambassador, and informally through back-channel personal conversations with his many contacts on the European continent. He telegraphed his intention to deploy a credible combat force by several means, not the least of which was naming Dewey the commander of the task force. Roosevelt set a time limit of ten days for the resolution of the crisis, and when his ultimatum was ignored, he heightened the sense of urgency by accelerating the timetable. Ultimately, it was his presence and force of will that convinced Ambassador von Holleben of the seriousness of the situation and led the ambassador to overcome the kaiser's personal resistance to arbitration. Roosevelt's discretion, employed throughout the process, enabled his strategy to succeed. Had the president gone public with his demands at any time, the kaiser, facing war or public humiliation, might well have chosen war. Yet the discreet nature of Roosevelt's demands allowed Wilhelm the opportunity to back down in private and preserved for the immediate present the future relations between the two nations.

The previous century of tacit cooperation with Great Britain suggested that the British would neither actively oppose Roosevelt's new interpretation of the doctrine nor stand in the way of his new activist foreign policy. Nevertheless, the events in Venezuela along with the events of the last decade of the nineteenth century suggest that conflict with the United States was not outside the realm of possibility.

Documents recently declassified under the "one-hundred-year rule" at the British National Archives suggest that Roosevelt's actions with regard to Venezuela may have had another, albeit unintended, result. As the winter exercise approached and tensions increased between the United States and the European powers, the British Colonial Office drafted a secret memorandum that was forwarded to the Colonial Defense Committee, the War Office, and ultimately the Admiralty for comment. The memorandum raised questions about the defensibility of British possessions in the western Atlantic in the event of a conflict with the United States. In a response entitled "Strategic Conditions in the Event of War with the United States," the Admiralty expressed doubt that "it would be possible to dispatch a sufficient naval force to maintain sea supremacy" in the western Atlantic and Caribbean "if at the time of the outbreak of war uncertain or hostile relations existed between this country and a European power." The document goes on to state that the United States would be in a position to "stop our supplies from Canada" and to secure all food imports from the United States itself, effectively cutting off two-thirds of Great Britain's food supply. The inescapable conclusion was that current realities emphasized "the necessity of preserving good relations with the United States."[121] Within two years Lansdowne and Balfour would secure an unofficial security arrangement with the United States, the beginning of what has come to be known as "the Special Relationship."[122]

Thus it was that Theodore Roosevelt established for all the world to see the two pillars on which he would construct his foreign policy: the Monroe Doctrine and the U.S. Navy. His actions during the Venezuelan Crisis established precedents for American involvement in the world throughout the twentieth century.

Notes

This excerpt from *Theodore Roosevelt's Naval Diplomacy: The U.S. Navy and the Birth of the American Century*, by Henry J. Hendrix (© 2009 by United States Naval Institute), is reprinted with permission by the Naval Institute Press.

The thoughts and opinions expressed in this essay are those of the author and are not necessarily those of the U.S. government, the U.S. Navy Department, or the Naval War College.

1. Roosevelt to Whitelaw Reid, 27 June 1906; Roosevelt to Henry White, 14 August 1906, in Theodore Roosevelt and Elting Elmore Morison, *The Letters of Theodore Roosevelt* (Cambridge: Harvard University Press, 1951) [henceforth *TLTR*], 5: 318–320, 357–359.

2. William R. Thayer, *Life and Letters of John Hay* (Boston: Houghton Mifflin, 1915), 284–285.

3. Donald L. Herman, "Democratic and Authoritarian Traditions," in *Democracy in Latin America: Colombia and Venezuela* (New York: Praeger, 1988), 5.

4. Judith Ewell, *Venezuela: A Century of Change* (Stanford: Stanford University Press, 1984), 23–28.

5. Ruhl J. Bartlett, ed., *The Record of American Diplomacy* (New York: Alfred A. Knopf, 1964), 341–354.

6. Brian S. McBeth, *Gunboats, Corruption, and Claims: Foreign Investment in Venezuela, 1899–1908* (Westport, Conn.: Greenwood Press, 2001), 15–21.

7. Herbert W. Bowen, *Recollections Diplomatic and Undiplomatic* (New York: Grafton Press, 1926), 252.

8. Ibid., 248–251.

9. McBeth, *Gunboats, Corruption, and Claims,* 82–83.

10. Sheldon B. Liss, *Diplomacy and Dependency: Venezuela, the United States, and the Americas* (Salisbury, N.C.: Documentary Publications, 1978), 27–30.

11. James D. Richardson, ed., *Compilation of the Messages and Papers of the Presidents* (New York: Bureau of National Literature and the Arts, 1920), 14: 6522–6523.

12. Walter LaFeber, *The Cambridge History of American Foreign Relations* (Cambridge, U.K.: Cambridge University Press, 1993), 60–61.

13. Ibid., 121–125.

14. Edward Wagenknecht, *The Seven Worlds of Theodore Roosevelt* (New York: Longman, Green, 1958), 119.

15. Howard K. Beale, *Theodore Roosevelt and the Rise of America to World Power* (Baltimore: Johns Hopkins University Press, 1956), 395–431.

16. Roosevelt to Cecil Spring Rice, 6 July 1901, *TLTR,* 3: 107–109.

17. Ronald Spector, *Admiral of the New Empire* (Baton Rouge: Louisiana State University Press, 1974), 126–127.

18. Report of the General Board, 27 March 1902, Dewey Collection, Library of Congress [henceforth DCLOC], box 43, folder 7,

Records of the General Board of the Navy, Washington, D.C.

19. Roosevelt to Ambassador Joseph H. Choate, 3 February 1902, *TLTR,* 3: 225.

20. Richard H. Collin, *Theodore Roosevelt, Culture, Diplomacy, and Expansion: A New View of American Imperialism* (Baton Rouge: Louisiana State University Press, 1985), 156.

21. Frederick W. Marks, *Velvet on Iron* (Lincoln: University of Nebraska Press, 1979), 37–70.

22. Howard C. Hill, *Roosevelt and the Caribbean* (Chicago: University of Chicago Press, 1927), 141–146.

23. William Hard, "How Roosevelt Kept the Peace," *Metropolitan Magazine* (May 1916): 5, Theodore Roosevelt Collection, Harvard University [henceforth TRC].

24. Holger H. Herwig, *Politics of Frustration: The United States in German Naval Planning, 1889–1941* (Boston: Little, Brown, 1976), 94.

25. Henry Taylor to Roosevelt, late November 1902, Theodore Roosevelt Collection, Library of Congress [henceforth TRLOC], box 57, Military Correspondence of the President.

26. Ronald Spector, "Roosevelt, the Navy, and the Venezuela Controversy: 1902–1903," *American Neptune* 32, no. 4 (1972): 259–260.

27. General Board Memorandum, 25 June 1901, DCLOC, box 43, folder 7, Records of the General Board of the Navy.

28. *Annual Reports of the Navy Department, 1902* (Washington, D.C.: Government Printing Office, 1902), 976.

29. "Puerto Rico, Study of Theater Operations," Geographical Files, Puerto Rico Folder, USMC Historical Center, Washington Navy Yard.

30. Beale, *Theodore Roosevelt and the Rise of America,* 356–357.

31. *Annual Reports to the Secretary of the Navy, 1902,* 977.

32. Colby M. Chester, "Diplomacy on the Quarter Deck," *American Journal of International Law* 8, no. 3 (1914): 443–476.

33. Lt. Cdr. Nathan Sargent to Secretary of the Navy William Moody, 28 February 1901, Records of the Department of the Navy, National Archives [henceforth NARA], Record Group 45 [henceforth RG], box 671, VI, Venezuela Situation.

34. Cdr. T.C. McLean, Commanding Officer, USS *Cincinnati,* to Secretary of the Navy Moody, 26 July 1902; Cdr. John Nickles, Commanding Officer, USS *Topeka,* to Secretary of the Navy Moody, 23 July 1902, both in NARA, RG 45, box 671, VI, Venezuela Situation.

35. Memorandum of the General Board, 28 May 1901, DCLOC, box 43, folder 7, Records of the General Board of the Navy.

36. Memorandum of the General Board, 2 November 1901, DCLOC, box 43, folder 7, Records of the General Board of the Navy.

37. Herwig, *Politics of Frustration,* 69.

38. Thomas A. Bailey, "Dewey and the Germans at Manila Bay," *American Historical Review* 45, no. I (1939): 63–70.

39. Terrell D. Gottschall, *By Order of the Kaiser* (Annapolis: Naval Institute Press, 2003), 206–211.

40. Herwig, *Politics of Frustration,* 47.

41. Holger H. Herwig, *Germany's Vision of Empire in Venezuela* (Princeton: Princeton University Press, 1986), 196.

42. "The German Emperor and the Monroe Doctrine," *Harper's Weekly,* 31 January 1903, TRC.

43. See "Progress in the World," *American Review of Reviews* (April 1902), TRC.

44. Isaac F. Marcosson, "Attorney-General Moody and His Work," *World's Work* (November 1906): 81–91.

45. Paul T. Heffron, "Secretary Moody and Naval Administration Reform: 1902–1904," *American Neptune* 29 (January 1969): 33.

46. Spector, *Admiral of the New Empire,* 139.

47. Roosevelt to Adm. George Dewey, 14 June 1902, DCLOC, box 13, General Correspondence.

48. Mildred Dewey Diary, DCLOC, box 73, General Correspondence, 71.

49. Marks, *Velvet on Iron,* 50.

50. Roosevelt to William H. Moody, 20 September 1902, DCLOC, box 13, General Correspondence.

51. Memorandum dated 24 April 1902, DCLOC, box 13, General Correspondence.

52. Heffron, "Secretary Moody and Naval Administration Reform," 33.

53. William H. Moody memorandum, 24 July 1902, DCLOC, box 13, General Correspondence.

54. Translations of Messages Sent in Cipher, October 1888–January 1910, vol. 4, p. 289, NARA, RG 45, Naval Records Collection, Office of the Secretary of the Navy, General Records.

55. Order dated 23 September 1902 signed by Acting Commandant, Col. Reid, NARA, RG 127, U.S. Marines Overseas Brigades, Battalions, Regiments, Panama, box 4.

56. Record of Percival Clarence Pope, USMC, Biographical Facts, Percival C. Pope Folder, USMC Historical Center, Washington Navy Yard.

57. *Annual Reports of the Navy Department, 1903,* 1232.

58. Col. P. C. Pope to Commandant, 15 October 1902, NARA, RG 127, U.S. Marines Overseas Brigades, Battalions, Regiments, Panama, box 4.

59. *Annual Reports of the Navy Department, 1903,* 1233.

60. Allan Nevins, *Henry White: Thirty Years of American Diplomacy* (New York: Harper and Brothers, 1930), 209.

61. Leonard Wood Diary, 10 September 1902, Leonard Wood Papers, Library of Congress, Washington, D.C.

62. Alfred P. Dennis, *Adventures in American Diplomacy, 1896–1906* (New York: E. P. Dutton, 1928), 287.

63. Edmund Morris, "A Few Pregnant Days," *Theodore Roosevelt Association Journal* 15, no. 1 (1987): 10.

64. Ibid.

65. Bailey, "Dewey and the Germans at Manila Bay," 62–63.

66. George Dewey, *Autobiography of George Dewey* (Annapolis: Naval Institute Press, 1987), 220–231; Mildred Dewey Diary, DCLOC, box 73, General Correspondence, 93.

67. Iestyn Adams, *Brothers across the Ocean: British Foreign Policy and the Origins of the Anglo-American "Special Relationship" 1900–1905* (London: Tauris Academic Studies, 2005), 39; memorandum for communication to the German ambassador, 22 October 1902, British National Archives, Foreign Office [henceforth BNA, FO] 115/1241, "From Foreign Office."

68. Marquess of Lansdowne to Sir F. Lascelles, 22 October 1902, BNA, FO 115/1241.

69. W. L. Penfield, "Anglo-German Intervention in Venezuela," *North American Review* 177 (July 1903): 96.

70. Warren G. Kneer, *Great Britain and the Caribbean* (East Lansing: Michigan State University Press, 1975), 22.

71. Ibid., 26.

72. Mildred Dewey Diary, 86. Dewey had previously served in the American Civil War and the Spanish-American War without receiving a wound.

73. McBeth, *Gunboats, Corruption, and Claims,* 88.

74. Liss, *Diplomacy and Dependency,* 38.

75. McBeth, *Gunboats, Corruption, and Claims,* 88.

76. Richard H. Collin, *Theodore Roosevelt's Caribbean* (Baton Rouge: Louisiana State University Press, 1990), 95.

77. Herwig, *Politics of Frustration,* 79.

78. Ewell, *Venezuela,* 40.

79. *Papers Relating to the Foreign Relations of the United States, 1903* (Washington, D.C.: Government Printing Office, 1904), 420–422.

80. Margaret Robinson, *Arbitration and the Hague Peace Conferences* (Philadelphia: University of Pennsylvania, 1936), 24, 70.

81. Beale, *Theodore Roosevelt and the Rise of America,* 419.

82. "May 23, 1916, George Dewey letter to Henry A. Wise," *New York Herald Tribune,* 27 September 1925, 9.

83. Edmund Morris, "'A Matter of Extreme Urgency': Theodore Roosevelt, Wilhelm II, and the Venezuela Crisis of 1902," *Naval War College Review* 55, no. 2 (2002): 79.

84. *Annual Reports of the Navy Department, 1903,* 647.

85. Secretary Moody to Naval Attachés, 4 December 1904, NARA, RG 45, General Records, Translations of Messages Sent in Cipher, October 1888–January 1910, vol. 4.

86. *Mayflower* Letter Book, DCLOC, box 44, 39.

87. Ibid., 41.

88. Ibid., 55.

89. Ibid., 139.

90. Elting E. Morison, *Admiral Sims and the Modern American Navy* (Boston: Houghton Mifflin, 1942), 132.

91. Hill, *Roosevelt and the Caribbean,* 133.

92. Ronald Reter, "The Real versus Rhetorical Theodore Roosevelt in Foreign Policy Making," Ph.D. diss., University of Georgia, 1973, 42–44.

93. Adm. George Dewey to George Dewey Jr., 14 December 1902 (63-291-LB), Dewey Papers, Personal Letters, Naval Archives, Naval Heritage & History Command [henceforth DPNHHC], Washington Navy Yard.

94. Morris, "A Few Pregnant Days," 3.

95. Moody to Dewey; Moody to Commandant, Naval Station, San Juan, Puerto Rico, 15 December 1902, NARA, RG 45, General Records, Translations of Messages Sent in Cipher, October 1888–January 1910, vol. 4.

96. Journal of the Commander in Chief, DCLOC, box 44, 39.

97. Albert Gleaves, *The Admiral* (Pasadena, Calif.: Hope Publishing, 1985).

98. *Annual Report of the Navy Department, 1903,* 1249.

99. Ibid., 647–648.

100. Journal of the Commander in Chief, DCLOC, box 44, 43; Dewey to Moody, 16 December 1902, NARA microfiche M625, roll 261, Area File of Naval Collection, 1775–1910, Area 8, December 1902–January 1903.

101. Commanding Officer, USS *Marietta,* to Secretary Moody, copy to Admiral Dewey, 16 December 1902, NARA, RG 45, box 671, Venezuela Situation, 4.

102. *Mayflower* Letter Book, DCLOC, box 44, 146–147.

103. Ibid., 148.

104. Reter, "The Real versus Rhetorical Theodore Roosevelt," 45.

105. *Mayflower* Letter Book, DCLOC, box 44, 44.

106. British Ambassador to British Foreign Minister, 16 December 1902, BNA, FO 115/1244.

107. Sir Michael Herbert to Lansdowne, Cipher Telegram, 13 December 1902, BNA, FO 115/1244.

108. Kneer, *Great Britain and the Caribbean,* 35.

109. Ibid., 38.

110. Adams, *Brothers across the Ocean,* 50–51.

111. Collin, *Theodore Roosevelt's Caribbean,* 106–107.

112. Morris, "A Few Pregnant Days," 11.

113. Morris, "'A Matter of Extreme Urgency,'" 82–84.

114. Burton J. Hendrick, "Historic Crises in American Diplomacy," *World's Work* (June 1916): 186.

115. Henry Mann, "The Monroe Doctrine," *Harmsworth Self-Educator* (July 1907): 1556.

116. Gleaves, *The Admiral,* 106.

117. Admiral Dewey to George Dewey Jr., 4 January 1903 (63-291-MH), DPNHHC.

118. Dudley W. Knox, *A History of the United States Navy* (New York: G. P. Putnam's Sons, 1936), 375.

119. Morris, "A Few Pregnant Days," 3.

120. Thayer, *Life and Letters of John Hay,* 284–295.

121. "Caribbean Sea and Western Atlantic: Strategic Conditions in Event of War with the United States," BNA, Admiralty Group (ADM) 1/8875, 21 January 1903.

122. William N. Tilchin, *Theodore Roosevelt and the British Empire: A Study in Presidential Statecraft* (New York: St. Martin's Press, 1997), 102–105.

CHAPTER THREE

Starvation Blockade and Herbert Hoover's Commission for Relief in Belgium, 1914–1919

BRUCE A. ELLEMAN

It may seem counterintuitive, but starvation blockades can be made more focused and therefore more effective by conducting humanitarian relief operations at the same time. In any examination of the roles of navies and soft power, humanitarian relief missions immediately come to mind, but not necessarily in connection with naval blockades. One of the most recent, and largest, humanitarian relief missions by sea was the post-tsunami Operation UNIFIED ASSISTANCE in Southeast Asia during 2004–2005.[1] Several years later, Operation TOMODACHI assisted Japan after its devastating tsunami crisis. In addition to helping those in need, global navies often use soft-power missions to compete with each other for public acclaim. This is perhaps best shown by China's recent "Peace Ark" cruises, in particular to Africa and the Middle East.

One of the first massive humanitarian aid missions by sea occurred during World War I, under the auspices of the nonprofit Commission for Relief in Belgium (CRB). From 1 November 1914 through the summer of 1919 this American-created and organized effort distributed $927,681,485.08 worth of foodstuffs and clothing to Belgium, as well as to the German-occupied areas of northern France. Organized as it was by Herbert C. Hoover along business lines rather than as a pure charity, the CRB incurred administrative costs during this five-year period of only $3,908,892.74, or just 0.43 percent of its charitable disbursement, a record that modern aid organizations would have difficulty matching.[2]

Safely transporting aid across the Atlantic was the linchpin of this humanitarian operation. All food, clothing, and other gifts were delivered by civilian cargo ships to Rotterdam, in the Netherlands, for transshipment to Belgium and northern France. The most controversial part of the operation was obtaining permission from England and Germany to let the aid ships through their respective maritime blockades. Hoover spent countless hours negotiating safe passage, and he often criticized Germany's ambiguous policies toward the aid ships: "There is no way by which they [the German government] can strike the vitals more than this diabolical attitude towards our shipping question."[3] The CRB's ships delivered aid not only through the British naval blockade but also through German minefields and swarms of U-boats conducting unrestricted submarine warfare. In the process, the CRB knowingly helped the British to focus their starvation blockade exclusively against the German people rather than against helpless neutrals.

Creation of the Commission for Relief in Belgium

When Germany attacked France through Belgian territory during August 1914, it violated the neutrality of a nonbelligerent country. After the war on this front became deadlocked in trench warfare just to the north of Paris, approximately ten million Belgian and French civilians found themselves trapped behind enemy lines. Prior to the war, Belgium had imported much of its food from its immediate neighbors to the south—now cut off by trenches—or from the Netherlands. Without access to these markets, starvation loomed. During the fall of 1914 the U.S. and Spanish governments sponsored a humanitarian relief operation designed to transport food to these inno-cent civilians caught in the midst of war. This effort was organized as the Commission for Relief in Belgium, and its volunteer director was a young mining engineer named Herbert C. Hoover.

The creation and workings of the Commission for Relief in Belgium are well document-ed.[4] During 1916, Lewis Richards wrote a lengthy internal report describing the CRB, "Some Things an American Delegate Should Know."[5] Soon after the war began, "Local Relief Committees were formed in every State in the Union and in almost every country in the World, with the result that from all parts of the globe came an unceasing flow, not only in foodstuffs but of money and clothing as well, in an 'elan' of charity, such as the World had never seen."[6] The CRB shipped in "wheat, sugar, maizes, lard, coffee, bacon, rice, margarines, beans and soup."[7] Kindhearted people around the world were eager to donate; "gift cargoes arriv[ed] with every evidence of having been packed in a way which suggests more of the heart of the donor than of practical knowledge of shipping."[8]

What made this humanitarian operation different from other previous efforts was the distribution of aid according to "business principles." According to Richards: "This is the reason that we sell some of our gifts and thus the well-to-do Belgian in buying our gifts and other food stuff is directly helping to care for his neighbour less fortunate than himself."[9] This was in sharp contrast to "professional" charities, which perhaps gave food away for free but often had much higher handling and administrative costs, including fat salaries to their directors. By contrast, many of the employees of the CRB, including Hoover, were wealthy businessmen who donated their time.

Since there was no international exchange of currency during the war, the CRB quickly ran into trouble figuring out how to use proceeds to purchase more food. In early November 1914, for example, Hoover had yet to divine a "method by which a country devoid of credit documents can translate some form of obligation into the purchase of goods." Even if "we can find a method," Hoover thought, it was unlikely that more than half of the CRB's payments could be made.[10] One idea that was eventually implemented was that Belgians living overseas who wanted to send money back home to their families could purchase food aid in the United States. A credit for this purchase was put on the books in U.S. dollars, and then an appropriate amount of Belgian money was remitted to the family members using local currency collected when selling food. By May 1917, the CRB had delivered the equivalent of some five million dollars to family members in Belgium through its Commercial Exchange Department.[11] The CRB also paid for many in-country services on behalf of the Belgian government, once again in direct proportion to the food aid being purchased overseas. Such "barter" systems proved highly effective.

For purposes of the distribution of aid, Belgium was divided into the nine provinces of Antwerp, Brabant, East Flanders, Hainault, Liege, Limburg, Luxemburg, Namur, and West Flanders; plus the city of Brussels (located in Brabant), which was treated as an equal member.[12] Later, northern France was also covered by the CRB, in six districts: Charleville, Lille, Longwy, St. Quentin, Valenciennes, and Vervins.[13] Once the aid was delivered it was consigned to the Belgian organization, which in turn handed it over to regional committees. Approximately six thousand communes in Belgium were responsible for the final distribution of the food aid. As Hoover put it, "We have attempted to handle this problem of [feeding] millions of people by intense decentralisation."[14] At this point the CRB agents' "control ceases . . . except as to the moral obligation governing the equitable distribution to the civil population."[15]

In distributing food aid, a major concern was avoiding waste. Of the estimated 2,750,000 indigent poor in Belgium, some 1,200,000 were considered to be fully destitute; these received all food and clothing for free. The less poor were required to pay 20 percent of the price, while another million or so paid 50 percent.[16] Wealthy Belgians who could afford to buy food on the free market were required to pay full price. These percentages appeared on ration cards issued by each commune. All proceeds from these sales were then used to buy and import more food. The accounting firm of Deloitte, Plender, Griffiths, & Company agreed to donate its services to make sure that no money was wasted. Hoover early on emphasized the importance of relying on outside auditors so as "to make the whole business a complete national monument of efficiency and commercial accuracy."[17]

Hoover's top priority was to ensure that no Belgian or French civilians suffered from hunger. The CRB provided wheat, rice, maize, bacon, lard, peas, and beans, and later yeast for making bread from the imported grain. Although it received requests for many other manufactured products, the CRB felt that to agree to import such items into the war zone might "bring us into conflict with normal trade." As a result, the CRB stuck to basic commodities that were in short supply in Belgium, so as to remove "us from all feeling of competition with the ordinary course of trade."[18] All aid was "distributed equitably to the Belgian civil population *only*."[19]

Other U.S. charities sought to dominate the transfer of aid to Belgium. By November 1914, however, Hoover was able to announce that the CRB had nine million dollars in funds "absolutely under our control" and that "we do not propose to be dictated to by any little hole in the corner organization in New York like DeForest's committee which might secure five or six hundred dollars."[20] The head of the CRB New York office, Lindon Bates, reassured Hoover that the CRB was the "shining mark," receiving about 80 percent of "the nationwide philanthropy of the country."[21] As for the competing groups, "We are going to get a harness on these people by sheer merit."[22]

The CRB's key leverage was over the means of transportation. On average, it took two months to purchase food in the United States, get it to a port, load it, and deliver it to Rotterdam, where it crossed militarized borders into Belgium and northern France.[23] During late 1914 it was estimated by Hoover that transportation costs would average 20 percent of the food cost; in other words, for every dollar spent on transportation a total of five dollars' worth of food could be purchased and delivered.[24] During mid-November 1914, Hoover told one of his competitors, "Through patriotic assistance of large English and continental shipping firms [we] are able [to] secure shipping on much better terms than you can secure in open market."[25]

One of Hoover's top goals was to maximize efficiency. He even told Bates in the CRB's New York office in early 1915 that "if this job is going to [be] done efficiently," the CRB must become "the complete and over-riding organisation for all relief work in Belgium."[26] As the next section will discuss, the creation of the transportation network to deliver food aid to Belgium was the most important link in the aid chain. Safe delivery of aid by sea proved to be one of the most difficult and constant challenges that Hoover faced during the five years of operation of the CRB.

Delivering Humanitarian Aid by Sea

All aid to Belgium and northern France was shipped by sea; the main office in London was responsible for purchases in Great Britain and the United States and for arranging transportation to Rotterdam. This put enormous responsibility on Hoover's shoulders, as the CRB chairman. During the fall of 1914, Hoover even complained to his wife that the "whole responsibility [for] purchase dispatch and delivery [of] some ten thousand tons of food stuffs per week rests on me."[27] The key to Hoover's success was control over maritime transportation. When the CRB was challenged by other aid societies, Bates was, he reassured Hoover, "confident our ability to take care of Inland and Ocean freights makes us impregnable."[28] Likewise, Hoover reassured W. H. Page, the American ambassador in London, that "as far as I can see we [CRB] are the only channel through which such relief can be introduced into Belgium."[29]

Hoover's efforts were fully supported by the U.S. government. On 7 November 1914, Secretary of State Robert Lansing wrote to James Gerard, the U.S. ambassador to Berlin, "Belgian Commission requests that you secure from German Government unmolested passage for neutral food ships from United States to Holland [intended] for Belgium."[30] By February 1915, the German government confirmed "the freedom of ships on the high seas and in port."[31] Even after the German submarine blockade was set to begin on 18 February, the German foreign minister, Gottlieb von Jagow, promised Hoover "to have orders issued of the most scrupulous care of [the CRB's] steamers."[32]

But the British too had to cooperate if this aid program was to work. On 8 November 1914 Hoover asked the Foreign Office contraband department official, Lord Eustace Percy, for a grant of "immunity from all British naval authorities" for CRB cargo ships heading for Belgium.[33] Against much British opposition—including from Winston Churchill and Lord Kitchener, who argued that any aid would ultimately help Germany—Foreign Secretary Edward Grey and David Lloyd George, then Chancellor of the Exchequer, supported the humanitarian operation mainly for the "great propaganda value for Britain in U.S." When Hoover was pressed for funds, the British government even agreed to back the activities of the CRB financially.[34]

While in public Hoover had to persuade opponents in Britain to support the CRB, in secret he told his closest advisers that much of the public condemnation in England was for show, so as "to maintain by all means the conviction in the German mind that the English and the Allies generally were extremely discontented with our feeding of the Belgians." Hoover was convinced that otherwise "if the German people thought for one moment that the English were anxious that the Belgians should be fed, they would at once stop food . . . as a weapon to force the hand of the Allies."[35]

As Hoover recounted in a later letter to Percy, the CRB provided a useful service for Whitehall. In particular, it was an "implement by which Allied Governments are able to secure an exception to their blockade policy, and which makes the blockade a feasible thing in the eyes of the world in general." If the CRB were not providing food to innocent civilians in Belgium and northern France, public pressure might soon turn and the

Allies "would be compelled to relax the blockade."[36] In private, therefore, Percy assured Hoover that as the U.S. ambassador in London told him of the departure of each vessel carrying CRB aid he would send a "telegraph to the [Royal Navy] fleet to allow the vessel to pass without any delay."[37]

In exchange for British promises "to place no obstacles in the moving of ships" leased by the CRB, the German government needed to agree not to requisition any food in Belgium; if food were taken from the Belgians while they were receiving aid from the CRB, Hoover could be accused of indirectly supporting Germany. During early February 1915 Hoover visited Berlin to meet with Chancellor Theobald von Bethmann-Hollweg and representatives of the Reichsbank. Hoover called the German treatment of Belgium "an undoubted blot on their whole national character" and suggested that it was "only the lack of imagination that did not lead them to see that an entire change of attitude towards Belgium would produce for them the friendship of the world." He argued that a "generous attitude toward Belgium" would help "secure the favourable opinion of the United States [at that point neutral] towards the Germans." After lengthy discussions, the German government grudgingly agreed. Although Hoover deserves much credit for this success, one cannot help but suspect that Ambassador Gerard's argument was the more convincing—that is, that the CRB's goal was to keep the Belgians from starving and "that in keeping them from starvation the greatest possible military service was being done to the Germans."[38]

To avoid delays caused by British ship inspections, aid cargoes were "consigned" to the CRB—otherwise "we must expect [the cargo ships] will be held up on voyage possibly for days."[39] To sidestep lengthy inspections, it was particularly important that the charity ships contain "whole cargoes of food for Belgian relief."[40] For example, a relief ship was held up by the British at Falmouth for two days when a "small bundle [of] tents"—considered to be a contraband item—was discovered on board.[41] Inspections were later moved to Halifax, Nova Scotia, but by August 1917 there was a shortage of fifty-nine thousand tons in the pipeline. Lord Robert Cecil agreed to eliminate the Halifax inspections.[42] With the entry of the United States into the war in 1917, the two allies could cooperate more closely. Beginning in August 1917, inspections of the cargoes could be carried out during the loading process in U.S. harbors. This reform saved an estimated thirty thousand tons in cargo capacity by cutting the total number of transit days per month from seventy-six to only sixty.[43]

Once the cargo ships arrived in Rotterdam, their aid cargoes were transshipped to lighters with flags bearing the initials "C.R.B." The lighters had to be approved by the German authorities, and all lightermen held German-issued passports.[44] While the lighters were essential for delivering aid from the Netherlands to Belgium, the lightermen had to be watched carefully to make sure they did not try to take undue advantage of their unhindered access across otherwise militarized borders. It was up to the local CRB agent to check that all seals remained unbroken, check the lighters for false bottoms, look into the bilges, and examine "other places where, unfortunately, the dishonest lighterman is likely to hide commodities in an endeavor to increase his income."[45]

To keep costs low it was determined that "as far as possible, the transportation shall take place by water."[46] But it was often necessary to transport food aid by railway or truck, usually during the final stages. German authorities provided these carriage services for free, since the CRB was providing a much-needed humanitarian service—the feeding of approximately ten million people—for which otherwise Germany would be expected to pay. In one early misunderstanding, a local stationmaster charged for a CRB shipment, but he was later ordered by the German authorities "to pay [the CRB] back at once the money collected for freight," because "the German Government [was] refusing to accept any money from [the] American Commission."[47]

Due to these procedures, shipping problems were "practically negligible"; the "administrative cost is approximately one-half of one per cent—a phenomenal achievement."[48] If the CRB's administration of the transportation of food aid and clothing to Belgium was almost flawless, however, increasingly strict German regulations affecting cargo vessels delivering aid to Rotterdam would soon cause great concern for Hoover.

German Regulations on Maritime Shipping

While the British government insisted on inspecting all CRB ships in English-controlled ports to make sure they did not carry contraband, for its part the German government issued official passes allowing the aid vessels through military lines on their way to Rotterdam. Over time, German regulations on shipping became more and more complicated, especially with the adoption of unrestricted submarine warfare. This caused enormous problems for Hoover, located in London, and the CRB agents living and working in Rotterdam, throughout Belgium, and in northern France.

London was the administrative and financial hub of the humanitarian operation, but the port city of Rotterdam acted as the main distribution hub: "Our purchase[s] arrive in Rotterdam on vessels under the protection of distinctive markings, such as side-cloths containing the words: 'RELIEF COMMISSION,' flags, etc."[49] Over time, the protections for the aid ships became more elaborate, and each vessel had two flags, two pennants, and two side cloths, or large banners.[50] On 3 March 1915, Dr. Henry Van Dyke, the American minister at The Hague, reported that the German government had declared that all ships bringing aid to Belgium were to bear "flag and markings clearly visible and lighted at night to pass through English channel unmolested." German submarines had been warned not to sink these ships, but because there was no way to turn off the many mines in the English Channel, the Germans emphasized the "impossibility of giving safe conduct."[51]

On 6 March 1915, the German minister in The Hague outlined new requirements. An official CRB pass was to list the name of the ship, its master, port of registry, and an official ship number. Second, the ship had to have "on board exclusively goods of the American Commission for Relief in Belgium intended for the suffering civil popula-tion in Belgium." Third, the German pass was valid only from an American port to Rotterdam and back home again, at which point it had to be returned to the German consul general or ambassador. Fourth, the master of the ship was to "abstain during the outward and return voyage from any and all actions that may involve assistance to Germany's enemies." Fifth, the Imperial German Navy had the right to search the ship at any time. Sixth, and finally, in "case of non-compliance with the above conditions the ship loses all right to preferential treatment."[52]

Prior to departure, each ship's captain had to sign a declaration that, first, his cargo included only food and clothing intended for Belgium; second, that he would not assist Germany's opponents; third, that after the voyage he would turn over these protec-tions to the German consul; and fourth, that his vessel could be searched by German authorities. If contraband were discovered on board the ship, he acknowledged, it would forfeit all rights to preferential treatment.[53] It was particularly important to the Germans that all CRB flags and banners be collected after arrival. As one internal CRB memo observed, "You can understand how the business of this commission might be upset should a captain hold back from delivering one of our flags and hoist it to escape from attack after he has finished his work for the Commission and [is] bound on another voy-age. Our object is to prevent any possible misuse of the Commission flag."[54]

Despite the flags and banners identifying them as carrying aid to Belgium, about a dozen CRB ships were sunk in the first years of the program, mainly by sea mines. Beginning in 1915, additional flags were draped diagonally across the upper decks of aid ships so that German pilots could more easily identify them.[55] To ensure maximum visibility, all CRB flags were twelve by fifteen feet in size, with lettering of twelve by eighteen inches; the banners were five feet by a hundred; the pennants were five feet wide, tapering down to two and a half feet, with twelve-by-twenty-inch letters.[56]

This system, while highly practical, was not foolproof. One cargo ship, *Harpalyce,* was apparently sunk by a torpedo from a German submarine on 10 April 1915. Of the forty-four crew members, seventeen perished, including the master.[57] Thirty-three of the crew members were Chinese sailors based in London; their names were not even reported, "as the crew list went down with the vessel." Although there was no proof that the ship had been torpedoed, the surviving crew members surmised that a mine would have struck the "fore-part of the vessel" rather than "against the ship's side." Furthermore, the third officer claimed to have seen a submarine, as did the captain and chief officer of the nearby cargo ship *Elisabeth*.[58]

This supposed torpedo sinking threatened the entire CRB transportation operation. The commission was partly to blame, since the German government had advised all aid ships to take a northerly route, by "way of the Shetland Islands"; the CRB later argued, "Against this we protested that it was fully and absolutely unfeasible," mainly because of the British requirement that all ships stop at an English port to be searched.[59] Hoover complained that "there is nothing in international liability, military necessity or, on its lowest plane, in military advantage, in sinking one of those ships, it is simply murder gone mad."[60] Hoover further stated that the "'relief' character must have been evident to the murderers of these innocent men engaged in a humanitarian task. . . . It is absolutely in its complete barbarism without parallel in the last century."[61]

In addition to protesting directly to the German government, Hoover turned to the U.S. government for support, asking that it "demand in common humanity, consideration for us and the people who serve us." When describing to Ambassador Page how the German attack imperiled the lives of ten million people who depended on the arrival of the food aid, Hoover declared, "I count myself as not being given to hysterics over the abnormal events of modern warfare but if this action can be reconciled with any military necessity, or, to put it on its lowest plane, . . . any military advantage, . . . we can but abandon any hope that civilisation has yet accomplished anything but enlarged ruthlessness in destruction of human life."[62]

The German torpedo attack immediately affected the other aid ships and their crews. For example, soon after this incident the mainly Chinese crew of *Lincluden* refused to sail, and the owners had to hire a brand-new crew in Rotterdam.[63] The captain of *Dowgate* evidently argued that "the pass which he secured gave him no protection if he was to be torpedoed without warning," so "he could not see any reason not to resist a submarine." Since one commitment all masters of aid ships had to make was "not to aid the enemies of Germany," *Dowgate*'s captain "preferred to go without a pass, and be perfectly free in his actions."[64]

In mid-April 1915, Hoover learned that *Dowgate*, engaged to deliver food aid to Belgium, had been refused "safe conduct" by the German authorities on its homeward journey, which imperiled arrangements for shipping for all future deliveries, and not only that—"those [ships] already fixed will[,] if they are wise[,] decline to go." Hoover condemned the torpedo attacks, stating the Germans had "no excuse under laws God or man," and immediately ordered John White, Lindon W. Bates's assistant, to go to Berlin to "take up" this issue with authorities "if this whole organization [is] not to break down."[65] Another effect of this torpedo incident, equally if not more important, was its potential impact on marine insurance. If the commission's cargo ships were refused insurance, the aid operation would probably cease to function.

The Crucial Role of Marine Insurance

Marine insurance was a very important consideration, since without it no shipping company would agree to transport the CRB shipments across enemy lines. On 21 December 1914, Hoover explained to Walter Runciman, of the Board of Trade in Whitehall, that any British-owned CRB aid ship would be given "the benefit of the Government War Risk Insurance Scheme" and that the commission had "received from the Admiralty general consent for the steamers proceeding, and they have advised that they will give special consent for each ship if required."[66] On 1 February 1915, an internal CRB memo somewhat optimistically remarked about banners on aid ships, "It occurred to us that it might also be helping our underwriters since the steamer would be less liable to be subject to attack by a German war vessel."[67]

After the sinking of *Harpalyce,* Hoover asked the German government to repay the commission a hundred thousand pounds for the lost ship, which "would be little enough to pay the extra cost of insurance which we are going to be [obliged] to [assume] over this action."[68] As Hoover explained to Brand Whitlock, the American ambassador to Belgium during World War I, the insurance issue was really the Achilles' heel of the whole operation: "If the Germans are endeavouring to break down this Commission they are going about it in the proper manner."[69] Germany's adoption in 1917 of unrestricted submarine warfare resulted in the sinking of forty thousand tons of CRB ships and the delay of 165,000 tons of food aid.[70] By June 1917 Hoover was forced to admit, "If there is any jeopardy to the Belgian people, it is due entirely to transport."[71]

However, Germany's reluctance to give safe passage to outbound ships, at least, had some validity. On 17 March 1915 the German minister at The Hague made clear that his government would not give safe passage to any ship leaving Rotterdam unless "the vessel is proceeding directly to the United States without touching at any English ports." This was to avoid the ships' taking up "other cargoes after completing their work for the commission."[72] But vessels leaving Rotterdam often needed to take on coal in Britain to reach their next destinations, whether the United States or some other country. The German requirement that they return directly to their countries of origin, therefore, was unrealistic.

On 16 April 1915, Hoover, greatly concerned, told John White that the German "refusal to grant return passes is an admission by the Germans themselves that they have torpedoed that boat."[73] White agreed that this new German requirement to return directly to the United States was detrimental to the whole aid program: "It is impossible that such an understanding of the agreement should have existed." To this point only British-flag vessels had been used to transport aid to Belgium. Because of the dangers involved, "up to the present time the commission has not been able to charter a single neutral vessel." White concluded, "This new technical interpretation of the passport would seem to have been put forward merely as a cloak to cover the torpedoing of the steamer [*Harpalyce*]."[74]

Hoover feared that British War Risk Insurance would be lost if German submarines were sinking CRB aid ships. Up until the *Harpalyce* incident, the British government had insured the CRB ships, since virtually all were British registered. But now this arrangement was in jeopardy. At one point Hoover estimated that it might cost the aid program an additional three million pounds sterling if the CRB were forced to insure all the ships itself.[75] The commission's monthly insurance premiums might increase from forty to seventy thousand pounds. Two days after the sinking, on 12 April, Hoover warned Whitlock that if the ship had indeed been torpedoed, the "English government will, certainly withdraw the Government Insurance on ships." Hoover found the timing of the sinking particularly bad: "We were just getting our programs of deliveries into shape," and so "it fills us with intense anxiety for the future."[76]

On 1 May, Hoover explained to Ambassador Gerard in Berlin that formerly all insurance coverage had been based on "the joint undertaking of the Germans and the British not to interfere with our shipping." As a result of the *Harpalyce* incident, the insurance association "[had] now put up the rates to a fabulous figure." Unless something could be done to guarantee future deliveries, "this is likely to throw the loss of the ship [*Harpalyce*] on to the Commission or an expense of, say some £90,000 odd, aside from the increase in insurance rates which would make a very large sum monthly."[77]

Throughout the spring German attacks on the relief ships continued. For example, on 14 March 1915, even before the *Harpalyce* had been sunk, SS *Sutton Hall* had reported a torpedo fired at it, though its relief flags and banners were clearly displayed.[78] Later, *City of Dortmund* and *Elfland* were also attacked: "German officers have now on four separate occasions deliberately attacked vessels bound on this philanthropic errand under guarantees given [by] the German Government itself." The CRB felt compelled to warn the German government that "the British ships will have to be withdrawn from the Commission's service if the attacks upon them continue."[79]

During May, when more information on the *Harpalyce* incident had become available, Hoover told Page that "it would appear, without doubt, that the Germans admit [in their description of events] that the *Harpalyce* was sunk by a submarine."[80] In July, however, Hoover was not very optimistic that he could convince the German government to admit guilt formally: "In general things are going rather badly, both in Belgium and here in London, and I am afraid that much friction as to detailed administrative things, which are to be imposed on us from both sides, will break down the whole machinery."[81] In a private letter, Hoover acknowledged that because the relief effort was unofficial, "We are an orphan and have to do the best we can without any right guardians."[82]

Negotiations with the German government continued throughout the summer, with Hoover seeking reparations to reimburse the shipping companies for lost vessels. But in July German officials were able to produce a photograph of *Harpalyce* unloading in Rotterdam with the CRB banner along its side rolled up, most likely to avoid being damaged. This photograph was alleged to prove that "the ship has not always been equipped with the side markings as agreed upon."[83] Hoover was not convinced, but he could not prove that the flag had been unfurled prior to the ship's departure from Rotterdam. On 9 August Hoover admitted, "I do not believe we can pursue this matter any further advantageously."[84] All further CRB claims for reimbursement were ignored by Berlin.

Under the constant threat of refusal by the war risks associations to insure "future vessels proceeding to Rotterdam," Hoover felt "compelled," he told Ambassador Gerard, to continue his investigations of the torpedo incidents.[85] Hoover was under no illusion that he would win; this was merely an effort to stave off any final action by the insurance associations, "on the ground we are still negotiating" with the Germans. If no solution could be reached, there might be a "boycott of all cargoes through Rotterdam."[86] Hoover's problems in finding adequate cargo ships to carry aid to Belgium became even worse when the British naval blockade of Germany intensified.

The Impact of the "Starvation Blockade" on the CRB

As the war entered its third year, the British "starvation blockade" began to be felt in Germany, even more so in its occupied territories. The CRB's shipments of food aid fell below expectations. In an undated report of late 1915 or early 1916, Hoover stated that the food reaching Belgium and northern France was "entirely below that generally advanced by dietary specialists" as barely "sufficient" to sustain life. The biggest problem was not money but access: "The dominant factor—even were more monetary supplies available—is the volume of shipping which can be obtained from over the seas." Due to the lower than expected shipping volume, "it has hitherto been impossible to deliver the whole programme [of aid], due to unexpected shortages in shipment, shipping, loss of ships, and various uncontrollable causes."[87]

Meanwhile, forced requisitioning of food was being carried out by German authorities in Belgium. Rice and corn were evidently being shipped back to Germany. Reports received by the British government claimed that some sixteen thousand tons of relief aid had been sent from Belgium on to Germany. This report made Hoover "so angry that I almost choke."[88] If substantiated, this misallocation of food aid might have threatened the entire humanitarian operation. Hoover, in London, told W. B. Poland in Brussels that if these rumors proved to be true, "with the state of mind in this country [Britain] at the present moment, if these facts were made public you can take it that the Relief Commission would be suppressed by popular clamour." Hoover called it the "greatest crisis" the commission had yet faced, "almost the last blow."[89]

Upon investigation, however, it turned out that of 17,499 tons of food taken by the Germans from Belgium, only 911 tons—including rice, waste corn flour, and beans—might have come, entirely or in part, from food aid delivered by the relief effort.[90] Even if all 911 tons had come from CRB aid, this was a small proportion—only about 5 percent—of the total.

To complicate matters further, it became harder to find cargo ships willing to transport the food aid to Rotterdam. On 31 December 1915 Hoover reported that "the shipping situation is becoming almost desperate."[91] One possible solution was to use a number of interned German steamers that had been detained by the Allies and were in neutral ports. These ships would sail under Dutch flags with Dutch crews.[92] While the French Foreign Department supported this plan, the French Department of Commerce opposed it, "claiming that the German submarines would capture one of their own ships and convert it into a privateer."[93] Hoover was forced to report to the CRB executive committee that the French government "absolutely refused to assent to the German shipping contract."[94] The French were particularly critical of the prospect that the German shipping company would make money off the scheme, even though it was only about two hundred and fifty pounds per ship per month, which was far below normal cargo rates.[95]

At one point Hoover, made desperate by refusals to grant the CRB additional cargo ships, warned the French that he would be put "in a [too] difficult position to go to the charitable world and ask them to subscribe money to make up a deficiency which is deliberately created for a military purpose."[96] In early 1916 Hoover announced that no more food could be delivered to northern France, a threat that "produced a perfect storm in Paris." Hoover traveled to Paris in an attempt to "direct the hurricane."[97] He warned President Raymond Poincaré that "we were in jeopardy of total failure owing to the lack of shipping."[98] On his return from Paris Hoover was pleased to be able to report that the French government had agreed to the use of the German vessels.[99] However, by now Hoover's arrangement with the German company had expired, and he was unable to renew it.

Desperate for ships, Hoover convinced the Belgian government to pass a requisition law under which, when it went into effect on 8 February 1916, the CRB was able to obtain leases on nineteen Belgian cargo vessels.[100] By mid-April, this number increased to twenty-one, plus four other Belgian-owned ships flying the British flag. However, as Hoover warned R. L. Craigie of the British Foreign Office, this was still inadequate. Over a four-month period only thirty-three CRB shiploads had arrived in Rotterdam, rather than the forty-five to fifty that were necessary to keep the aid pipeline flowing at the required levels.[101]

Hoover found all these setbacks and government obstructions very frustrating. What had initially been thought of as a temporary aid program would eventually continue for four and a half years. Several times Hoover had offered to terminate the CRB or to turn it over completely to the Belgians, but each time the British government had insisted that he remain in charge. Being "neutral," it pointed out, Hoover and his American assistants had "no official position limiting their liability."[102]

What upset Hoover more than anything else were repeated press accusations, as mentioned above, that the CRB's aid helped the Germans. For example, the English newspaper *Western Morning News* ran a series of articles accusing the CRB of a long list of infractions. These included feeding Belgians working for the Germans, on the one hand, and providing Germany with crucial strategic goods, on the other. One British journalist, J. Byers Maxwell, specialized in anti-CRB articles. In one Maxwell claimed that the "Germans are able to utilize the labour of the Belgians, who are being fed from the charitable contributions of England and other countries, and thereby the enemy directly benefits from such payment." Not only did this use of humanitarian aid show the Germans' "cleverness in breaking the British blockade," but by feeding the Belgians "we are helping the Huns to keep the population quiescent."[103] Another, similar article from the same British newspaper claimed that lard and fats being given to the Belgians as food were being turned into nitroglycerine.[104] On 13 March 1916, Hoover acknowledged to Whitlock that "these continued pin-pricks over the question of our fidelity to the guarantees are becoming simply heart-breaking."[105]

Over two decades later, on 25 August 1940, Hoover would tell an interviewer that the "British sent agents to watch the operations of the C.R.B., and they could find no instances of food being used by the Germans."[106] Meanwhile, however, Hoover and the CRB spent much time trying to disprove all accusations, no matter how groundless, because, ridiculous as some of these stories sounded, the British government was forced to react by fine-tuning the Royal Navy's naval blockade against Germany. Aid lists were constantly inspected and revised to ensure that nothing could inadvertently help Germany. For example, when the Germans requisitioned all "raw and manufactured wool" in Belgium, the CRB was ordered to halt all shipments of donated clothing.[107] Beginning in January 1916 all animal fodder was cut, it having been reported that eighty thousand German cows were being pastured in Belgium.[108] To avoid accusations that CRB-provided fats were being misused, Hoover was told to deliver only "hard soap" that could not be melted down to make explosives.[109] In reaction to news reports detailing additional German demands on Belgium, Percy was forced to tell Hoover, "In face of German [requisition] policy, we are feeling obliged to force the reservation of local stocks in Belgium for the exclusive use of the population by cutting off the prospect of any increase[d] importations."[110]

By 12 February 1917, matters had reached the point that the German government insisted that all Americans working on behalf of the CRB leave Belgium. The shipping problem became worse than ever after the United States entered the war. During July 1917, the Directeur des Services du Ravitaillement wrote to complain, "For political reasons, French or English steamers cannot go to Rotterdam; the American Government ask us not to charter American ships for any purpose and all neutral shipowners refuse at present to sail to Rotterdam on account of the risk to be sunk."[111] Desperate for ships, Hoover turned to the Scandinavian countries; a number of Norwegian and later Swedish and Finnish ships were leased.[112] By October 1918 over two hundred thousand tons of Swedish "dead weight" shipping was under contract.[113] Later still, Argentinian ships were leased. The CRB even tried to purchase its own ships from various German shipping companies, including from the Hamburg-American Line and North German Lloyd, to help alleviate its "almost desperate tonnage situation."[114]

The one positive development from the U.S. entry into the European war was that President Woodrow Wilson appointed Hoover to a newly created position of food administrator. In January 1918 Hoover wrote to a colleague in Belgium to explain his new job: "You will be astonished to realize that I am now putting the American people on a practical rationing of many of the commodities most urgently needed in Europe, with a view to saving from our consumption a sufficiency to carry the Belgian Relief and to provide their essential foods." The main CRB office was located right "next door to mine" and so was "a matter of constant solicitude." In particular, Hoover could now make certain guarantees: "As my department practically controls the dispatch of foodstuffs from the United States, you may be assured that the Belgian Relief will have full priority in shipments."[115]

Eventually, after more than four years of war, the last days of the CRB seemed to approach. By spring 1918, many of Hoover's plans to purchase cargo ships had failed, and he had been forced to appeal to Lloyd George for greater access to British shipping.[116] The CRB now faced enormous difficulties getting even minimal food aid delivered to Rotterdam. It is not altogether clear whether, had the war not ended when it did on 11 November 1918, the CRB's shipping program could have been sustained at the levels needed to get through the winter of 1918–19.

Final Delivery Statistics

On 21 October 1918, as the Great War was finally winding down and Allied victory loomed on the horizon, Herbert C. Hoover presented to President Woodrow Wilson a summary of the CRB's activities to date. Public charity had reached $32 million, in addition to which the British government had donated $120 million, the American government $200 million, and the French government $220 million, for a grand total of $572 million.[117] By the time the CRB wrapped up its operations in early 1919, this number had increased to $806,209,313.45, of which $52 million, or over 6 percent of "the total funds secured by the Commission," had been the result of charitable contributions.[118]

During the four and a half years of the CRB's existence, almost 120 million bushels of breadstuffs were delivered, almost 550 million pounds of pork products, 73 million pounds of other meat, 715 million pounds of rice, 283 million pounds of beans and peas, and 113 million pounds of dairy products, to name just a few commodities. In addition, over twenty million garments were distributed to the needy.

But despite this monumental effort, Hoover acknowledged, the local populations had been put on a "drastic regime" in which "there has been under-nourishment," though fortunately "no starvation."[119] This compared favorably to Serbia, which Hoover estimated suffered 25 percent civilian losses during the war due to starvation, and especially to Poland, which he estimated at a whopping 50 percent.[120] Two months later Hoover asserted flatly that when the experience of these two countries were compared with the "no loss" by "starvation" among the ten million inhabitants of Belgium and northern France, "the difference was simply the Relief Commission."[121]

Such a massive relief effort had first and foremost required access to international commercial shipping. Hoover reported to Wilson that the CRB had at any given time depended on seventy transatlantic steamers to transport food aid to Rotterdam and another five hundred canal boats and tugs to deliver food and clothing to Belgium and northern France. When the goods arrived, they had been housed in some two hundred central warehouses before being sent on to individual communes for final distribution.[122] Between November 1914 and April 1919 the CRB had chartered 903 separate ship passages to transport close to four and a half million tons of aid—an average of seventeen ships delivering 83,000 tons per month.[123] The final numbers were even larger, with 993 oceangoing and 1,320 cross-channel ships delivering a total of 5,174,431 metric tons.[124]

Because of the commission's almost total reliance on international shipping, the CRB was once described by a critic as a "piratical state organized for benevolence." That is, "like a pirate state, the CRB flew its own flag, negotiated its own treaties, secured special passports, fixed prices, issued currency, and exercised a great deal of fiscal independence." However, whatever the negatives, "its bold acts of benevolence were accomplished with an efficiency and integrity that later became a model for modern foreign aid."[125]

Hoover was understandably proud of the efficiency of this administration, particularly that his "overhead" costs were "less than three-eighths of one per cent."[126] He had sought men with business experience rather than "the usual charity cranks," telling a colleague that "one must have common-sensed, solid, business people, used to dealing with large affairs and doing so on an adequate, business and financial basis."[127] Hoover was particularly offended by self-serving philanthropists. Concerning the "New York bunch," he said, "There is no place in the world where there is such unlimited snobbery as New York and because we happen to be common or garden[-variety] people they do not seem to think we deserve even the treatment that is ordinarily meted out to servants."[128] Hoover especially spurned what he called "professional charity workers."[129]

Virtually everyone associated with the CRB gave Hoover most of the credit for its creation and flawless administration. Lord Curzon once referred to the CRB as an "absolute miracle of scientific organization," and even an erstwhile critic called the humanitarian operation the "biggest task ever grappled by an individual. A Joseph came to Belgium. He undertook to feed a whole country."[130]

Conclusions

Humanitarian aid layered on top of a naval blockade had the effect of making Britain's strategy more focused. If the CRB had not existed, Britain's starvation blockade of the continent would have hit friend and foe alike. Hoover understood quite well that his humanitarian efforts made the blockade more effective: "At the close of the war," he later reminisced, "the Belgians were in fine physical condition, while the German people were starving."[131] The simultaneous adoption and mutual alignment of a humanitarian relief operation and a strict naval blockade can greatly intensify the strategic impact of the latter against an enemy.

The delivery of humanitarian assistance was not a simple task. Although both London and Berlin guaranteed the aid ships' safety, of the fifty-three ships damaged during their voyages, fifteen were torpedoed, and twelve struck mines and sank. These numbers broke down to just slightly over 1.5 percent torpedoed and 1.3 percent mined, an overall loss of just under 3 percent of the number of ship passages.[132] Hoover freely admitted that the CRB humanitarian effort was not a complete success and that "much food has been lost by submarines and some native food taken by the Germans." But, in short, "We have done all that finance, shipping and administration could accomplish."[133]

Francis Cogswell Wickes, who served with the CRB for almost three years, in giving Hoover full credit for the CRB's success, emphasized his entrepreneurial spirit: "It was this spirit which alone made the work possible. And this spirit was the spirit of boundless personal loyalty felt by each and every member towards the one dominating and heroic figure, towards the great chief, Herbert C. Hoover. He had conceived the *Commission,* he had created it, he had carried it on through its countless crises. It was he who inspired it. The Commission for Relief in Belgium, was Hoover, and Hoover alone."[134]

Notes

The thoughts and opinions expressed in this essay are those of the author and are not necessarily those of the U.S. government, the U.S. Navy Department, or the Naval War College.

1. For more on this operation, see Bruce A. Elleman, *Waves of Hope: The U.S. Navy's Response to the Tsunami in Northern Indonesia,* Newport Paper 28 (Newport, R.I.: Naval War College Press, 2007).

2. Hoover to Richey, date unclear but probably 28 January 1920, Commission for Relief in Belgium [hereafter CRB], box 7, file 42, Hoover Institution Archives, Stanford University, Stanford, California [hereafter HIA].

3. Hoover to Brand Whitlock, 16 April 1915, CRB, box 3, file 4, HIA.

4. The archives of the Hoover Institution, Stanford University, have 591 manuscript boxes, forty-nine oversize boxes, and seventeen card files detailing all aspects of this operation.

5. Lewis Richards, "Some Things an American Delegate Should Know" (1916), CRB, box 1, file 1, HIA.

6. Ibid., p. 3.

7. Ibid., p. 17.

8. Ibid., p. 18.

9. Ibid., p. 4.

10. Hoover to the various CRB Honorable Chairmen, 3 November 1914, CRB, box 4, file 3, HIA.

11. Hoover's Statement, 14 May 1917, CRB, box 27, file 3, HIA.

12. Richards, "Some Things an American Delegate Should Know," pp. 5–6.

13. Ibid., pp. 20–21.

14. Hoover to the subcommittee of War Trade Advisory Committee on Supplies for Belgian Relief, 23 December 1915, CRB, box 4, file 1, HIA.

15. Richards, "Some Things an American Delegate Should Know," p. 14.

16. Hoover to the subcommittee, 23 December 1915.

17. Hoover to Bates, 19 January 1915, CRB, box 4, file 2, HIA.

18. Hoover to the Minister of Foreign Affairs, The Hague, 26 June 1915, CRB, box 4, file 8, HIA.

19. Richards, "Some Things an American Delegate Should Know," p. 5 [emphasis original].

20. Hoover to Bates, 13 November 1914, CRB, box 5, file 3, HIA.

21. Bates to Hoover, 24 December 1914, CRB, box 4, file 2, HIA.

22. Bates to Hoover, 7 January 1915, CRB, box 5, file 3, HIA.

23. Memo, 4 February 1915, CRB, box 21, file 2, HIA.

24. Hoover to the ambassadors, 3 November 1914, CRB, box 3, file 5, HIA.

25. Hoover to Robert DeForest, 13 November 1914, CRB, box 5, file 3, HIA.

26. Hoover to Bates, 19 January 1915.

27. Hoover to Mrs. Hoover, 22 October 1914, CRB, box 1, file 2, HIA.

28. Bates to Hoover, 18 December 1914, CRB, box 4, file 2, HIA.

29. Hoover to Page, 22 October 1914, CRB, box 7, file 4, HIA.

30. Lansing to Gerard, 7 November 1914, CRB, box 19, file 3, HIA.

31. Memo, 4 February 1915.

32. Jagow to Hoover, 7 February 1915, CRB, box 21, file 1, HIA.

33. Hoover to Percy, 8 November 1914, CRB, box 4, file 8, HIA.

34. Payson J. Treat Papers, box 45, "Hoover, Herbert C., Interviews," HIA.

35. Hoover to Bates, 8 February 1915, CRB, box 21, file 3, HIA. This ruse was so effective that some British firms refused to work with the CRB, and Hoover later wrote Percy for a letter that he could show these companies proving that the British government was backing him; Hoover to Percy, 7 August 1915, CRB, box 22, file 5, HIA. In addition, the British Admiralty from time to time "hectored and harassed" Hoover, accusing him of aiding the enemy; see George H. Nash, *The Life of Herbert Hoover: The Humanitarian, 1914–1917* (New York: W. W. Norton, 1988), p. 176.

36. Hoover to Percy, 16 February 1916, CRB, box 24, file 2, HIA.

37. Percy to Hoover, 18 November 1914, CRB, box 4, file 8, HIA.

38. Hoover's Notes and Transcripts: Trip to Berlin, 7–9 February 1915, CRB, box 7, file 42, HIA.

39. Hoover to New York office, 19 December 1914, CRB, box 4, file 8, HIA.

40. W. J. Bryan to Lindon W. Bates, 1 January 1915, CRB, box 4, file 8, HIA.

41. Hoover to New York, 28 January 1915, CRB, box 4, file 8, HIA.

42. Page to Hoover, 12 August 1917, CRB, box 7, file 6, HIA.

43. Hoover to Auchincloss, 14 August 1917, CRB, box 6, file 9, HIA.

44. Richards, "Some Things an American Delegate Should Know," p. 11.

45. Ibid., pp. 13–14.

46. Brussels memo, 14 April 1915, CRB, box 4, file 9, HIA.

47. Lucey to Hoover, 16 November 1914, CRB, box 4, file 3, HIA.

48. Richards, "Some Things an American Delegate Should Know," p. 17. To keep administrative costs down, complaints about potential losses along the transportation routes due to petty theft were only made if the total was over half of 1 percent in shipments over a thousand kilograms, or a quarter of 1 percent

losses in cargoes between five hundred and a thousand kilos; ibid., pp. 18–19.

49. Ibid., p. 10.

50. Memo, 6 April 1915, CRB, box 3, file 4, HIA.

51. Van Dyke to Hoover, 3 March 1915, CRB, box 3, file 4, HIA.

52. German minister, The Hague, 6 March 1915, CRB, box 3, file 4, HIA.

53. Declaration, 24 December 1915, CRB, box 3, file 4, HIA.

54. London to Rotterdam, 15 February 1915, CRB, box 4, file 8, HIA.

55. Behncke, Chief of Staff, Admiralty, note, 25 March 1915, CRB, box 3, file 4, HIA.

56. Memo, 16 April 1915, CRB, box 3, file 4, HIA.

57. Memo, 11 April 1915, CRB, box 3, file 4, HIA.

58. W. J. George, Second Officer, and John S. Turnbill, Second Engineer, testimony, n.d. but probably during April 1915, CRB, box 3, file 4, HIA.

59. Hoover to Jkr [Jonkheer] de Marees van Swinderen, 16 April 1915, CRB, box 3, file 4, HIA.

60. Hoover to Page, 18 April 1915, CRB, box 22, file 1, HIA.

61. Hoover to Page, 16 April 1915, CRB, box 3, file 4, HIA.

62. Ibid.

63. Telegram from Rotterdam, 12 April 1915, CRB, box 3, file 4, HIA.

64. C. A. Young, Rotterdam Manager, to Hoover, 12 April 1915, CRB, box 3, file 4, HIA.

65. Hoover to White, 16 April 1915, CRB, box 22, file 1, HIA.

66. Hoover to Runciman, 21 December 1914, CRB, box 20, file 2, HIA.

67. Internal memo, 1 February 1915, CRB, box 4, file 8, HIA.

68. Hoover to James Gerard, U.S. ambassador to Berlin, 28 August 1915, CRB, box 3, file 4, HIA.

69. Hoover to Whitlock, 16 April 1915.

70. Hoover to Woodrow Wilson, 23 October 1917, CRB, box 27, file 8, HIA.

71. Hoover to Baron E. de Cartier, Minister Plenipotentiary, Belgium Legation, 3 June 1917, CRB, box 27, file 4, HIA.

72. White to Hoover, 17 April 1915, CRB, box 3, file 4, HIA.

73. Hoover to White, 16 April 1915.

74. White to Hoover, 17 April 1915.

75. Hoover to John White, 16 April 1915, CRB, box 3, file 4, HIA. Even though the term "month" appears in the document, Hoover might have been thinking "year," since this estimate is about ten times too high for a monthly insurance cost.

76. Hoover to Whitlock, 12 April 1915, CRB, box 3, file 4, HIA.

77. Hoover to Gerard, 1 May 1915, CRB, box 3, file 4, HIA.

78. Memo, 15 March 1915, CRB, box 3, file 4, HIA.

79. Langley to Page, 24 May 1915, CRB, box 3, file 4, HIA.

80. Hoover to Page, 7 May 1915, CRB, box 3, file 4, HIA.

81. Hoover to Van Dyke, 5 July 1915, CRB, box 4, file 8, HIA.

82. Hoover to Page, 17 May 1915, CRB, box 3, file 4, HIA.

83. Jagow to Hoover, 22 July 1915, CRB, box 7, file 34, HIA.

84. Hoover to Young, 9 August 1915, CRB, box 22, file 5, HIA.

85. C. Hipsgood, Board of Trade, Whitehall, 11 June 1915, CRB, box 3, file 4, HIA.

86. Hoover to Gerard, 28 August 1915.

87. Hoover, memo, n.d. but probably late 1915 or early 1916, CRB, box 7, file 42, HIA.

88. Hoover, memo, 24 January 1916, CRB, box 2, file 1, HIA.

89. Hoover to W. B. Poland, 24 January 1916, CRB, box 2, file 1, HIA.

90. List of German forced exports from Belgium, 8 February 1916, CRB, box 2, file 1, HIA.

91. Hoover to CRB Executive Committee, 31 December 1915, CRB, box 23, file 5, HIA.

92. Hoover to Page, 1 September 1916, CRB, box 23, file 1, HIA.

93. Hoover's meetings in Paris, 10 February 1916, CRB, box 7, file 42, HIA.

94. Hoover to CRB Executive Committee, 12 October 1915, CRB, box 23, file 2, HIA.

95. Hoover to Chevrillon, 8 September 1915, CRB, box 23, file 1, HIA.

96. Hoover to Chevrillon, 12 October 1915, CRB, box 23, file 2, HIA.

97. Memorandum on Shipping, 8 February 1916, CRB, box 24, file 2, HIA.

98. Hoover's meeting with President Poincaré, 14 February 1916, CRB, box 7, file 42, HIA.

99. Hoover to Hymans, 17 March 1916, CRB, box 24, file 3, HIA.

100. Memorandum on Shipping, 8 February 1916.

101. Hoover to Craigie, 11 April 1916, CRB, box 24, file 4, HIA.

102. Grey to Page, 13 March 1916, CRB, box 24, file 3, HIA.

103. J. Byers Maxwell, "Relief in Belgium: Are We Helping the Enemy?," *Western Morning News,* n.d., CRB, box 4, file 1, HIA.

104. *Western Morning News,* 28 October [1916?], CRB, box 4, file 1, HIA.

105. Hoover to Whitlock, 13 March 1916, CRB, box 2, file 1, HIA.

106. Payson J. Treat Papers.

107. Hoover to Rotterdam, 15 March 1916, CRB, box 24, file 3, HIA.

108. Percy to Hoover, 25 January 1916, CRB, box 4, file 1, HIA. Shortages of animal fodder caused much distress in Belgium and northern France. One exotic-animal park in northern France wrote repeatedly asking for a special ration of fodder. It was refused, and a later report noted that the park had been forced to feed its sole orangutan to its panthers, as "an emergency measure"; Hoover to Craigie, 25 April 1916, CRB, box 24, file 4, HIA.

109. Percy to Hoover, 23 February 1916, CRB, box 4, file 1, HIA.

110. Percy to Hoover, 5 January 1916, CRB, box 23, file 6, HIA.

111. Level to Edgard Rickard, 6 July 1917, CRB, box 7, file 11, HIA.

112. Memo, 11 September 1917, CRB, box 7, file 42, HIA.

113. Hoover to Francqui, 3 October 1918, CRB, box 6, file 41, HIA.

114. Memo, 2 October 1917, CRB, box 7, file 8, HIA. One problem that Hoover encountered, however, was that he did not want the ownership of any cargo ships to be in the CRB's name, since the vessels "should be in such

shape as to easily liquidate at the end of its work"; Hoover, memo to the U.S. Shipping Board, 8 November 1917, CRB, box 7, file 24, HIA.

115. Hoover to Francqui, 23 January 1918, CRB, box 28, file 1, HIA.

116. Hoover to Lloyd George, 16 May 1918, CRB, box 7, file 42, HIA.

117. Through the spring of 1917 a total of $266,000,000—about 90 percent of the CRB's total funding—came from the British and French governments. George H. Nash, *The Life of Herbert Hoover: Master of Emergencies, 1917–1918* (New York: W. W. Norton, 1996), p. 445, citing Tracy B. Kittridge, unpublished history of the Commission for Relief in Belgium, chap. 19, Tracy B. Kittridge Papers, HIA.

118. George I. Gay, *Statistical Review of Relief Operations* (Stanford, Calif.: Stanford Univ. Press, 1925), pp. 41, 67.

119. Hoover to Wilson, 21 October 1918, CRB, box 7, file 3, HIA.

120. Ibid. Hoover later dropped his estimate for Poland to 25 percent as well; see Hoover to Rickard, 18 December 1918, CRB, box 29, file 3, HIA. While Hoover's estimates of starvation deaths in Serbia and Poland were high, in fact as many as a fifth of all Serbs and perhaps a sixth of Poles starved to death during World War I.

121. Hoover to Rickard, 18 December 1918.

122. Hoover to Wilson, 21 October 1918.

123. Transportation Summary, n.d., CRB, box 442, file 14, HIA.

124. Gay, *Statistical Review of Relief Operations,* p. 41.

125. Elena S. Danielson, "The Commission for Relief in Belgium," in *The United States in the First World War: An Encyclopedia,* ed. Anne Cipriano Benzon (New York: Garland, 1995), pp. 154–59; repr. CRB collection finding aid, HIA.

126. Hoover to Wilson, 21 October 1918.

127. Hoover to Beatty, 12 January 1916, CRB, box 23, file 6, HIA.

128. Hoover to Bates, 13 November 1914.

129. Hoover insisted that an outside audit be conducted for all charities that wanted to work with the CRB. The real reason was to scare off charities that were not conducting their operations ethically, since if they "refused to allow their books be audited by the Commission's accountants [this] would be sufficient to damn any professional charity worker for the balance of his history." Hoover to Bates, 19 January 1915.

130. Maxwell, "Relief in Belgium."

131. Payson J. Treat Papers.

132. Report on Ship Damages, n.d., CRB, box 442, file 13, HIA; Gay, *Statistical Review of Relief Operations,* lists only fifty-two ships that "met with accidents of various characters" (p. 42).

133. Hoover to Wilson, 21 October 1918.

134. Francis Cogswell Wickes, June 1917, CRB, box 7, file 45, HIA.

CHAPTER FOUR

The Allied Embargo of Japan, 1939–1941
From Rollback to Deterrence to Boomerang
S. C. M. PAINE

In the 1930s, the United States faced numerous grave national security challenges as the world appeared to be going to ruin, with global economic depression and brewing wars in Europe and Asia. To cope with Japan's expanding war in China, Washington needed to devise a low-cost and politically feasible strategy acceptable to both isolationists and financially pressed American voters. Over a decade, U.S. strategy toward Japan evolved from nonrecognition of its invasion of Manchuria through political neutrality and trade embargo to a combination of trade cessation and forward basing of the U.S. Fleet. All of these strategies attempted to exert sufficient diplomatic and economic pressure to force Japan to halt its aggression.

The Japanese government, however, did not respond to the evolving American strategy as anticipated, even though it lacked access to the wide range of natural resources necessary to fight the war it chose. U.S. deterrence ultimately backfired, because the sunk costs of Japan's own failed strategy were already so high that to back down would have emasculated the Imperial Japanese Army. Instead, the Japanese government chose a military strategy that had a remote hope of success—albeit a high chance of going down in flames—over an even higher likelihood of regime change at home if it reversed itself after incurring such huge human and financial costs in China.

This chapter examines the various stages of the U.S. deterrence strategy over a ten-year period. Each stage adopted incrementally more restrictive trade limitations that it was hoped would be sufficient to pressure Japan to back down and yet insufficient to prompt Japan to escalate instead; the U.S. Navy, in particular, hoped to delay—or better yet, avoid—war with Japan so that the U.S. military could concentrate on defeating the fascists in Europe. Rather than preserving a tenuous peace with Japan, however, the American strategy boomeranged, precipitating Japan's attack on Pearl Harbor. As Americans discovered, some nations make mistakes of such magnitude that they are immune to deterrence and insist on taking the paths to ruin for themselves and others.

The Problem: Strategy on a Shoestring versus Regional Domination

As the international order collapsed in the 1930s, the Imperial Japanese Army made policy by fait accompli. It occupied Manchuria and later Central China to protect Japan's significant investments there, restore order in a neighboring failing state, create an autarkic zone of sufficient size to compensate for Western protectionism, and prevent the spread of communist influence from the Soviet Union.[1] These goals were all big-ticket items for Japanese policy makers. Asia, however, was not at this point a big-ticket item for the United States, whose economy remained a mess, whose primary allies faced invasion by Germany, and whose trade with China remained minor. Japan was em-barked on a program of expansion of its empire—first into Manchuria (1931–33), then into North China (1934–36), and finally throughout Central and South China (1937–45). With the massive escalation of the Second Sino-Japanese War in 1937, the U.S. gov-ernment sought a low-cost strategy that would avoid American economic or military overextension and yet deter further Japanese expansion and eventually pressure Tokyo to roll back its conquests and restore the Nationalist government of Chiang Kai-shek to full sovereignty over China.

U.S. pressure increased incrementally, starting with nonrecognition. On 7 January 1932, the United States responded to Japan's occupation of Manchuria by refusing to acknowledge these conquests—the so-called Stimson Doctrine, named for American Secretary of State Henry L. Stimson—but Japanese conquests continued unabated and soon encompassed North China.[2] On 6 December 1931, the State Department Division of Far Eastern Affairs had initially examined the possibility of a boycott of Japan as re-taliation.[3] Article 16, paragraph 1, of the League of Nations Covenant required "the sev-erance of all trade or financial relations" by all league members should any resort to war in violation of the covenant, a crime Japan had clearly committed. It also required "the prevention of all financial, commercial or personal intercourse between the nationals of the covenant-breaking State and the nationals of any other State, whether a Member of the League or not."[4] The hitch was the United States was not a member; no member other than China was interested in implementing article 16. Neither was the United States. Yet without full U.S. participation, any trade sanctions would be meaningless, given American domination of Japan's foreign trade.

At the time, the State Department and the War Department disagreed on the advis-ability of imposing economic sanctions. When Secretary of State Stimson supported the idea, President Herbert Hoover "replied that that meant war and must be considered as such." But when the Chief of Naval Operations, Adm. William V. Pratt, predicted that such a war would last from five to seven years, Hoover declared he "would have nothing to do with sanctions."[5]

With World War I still looming large in American thinking, Congress passed a succession of neutrality acts, starting on 31 August 1935. These acts forbade trade with either side in a war, lest the United States again become embroiled in costly hostilities leading to disappointing results. President Hoover's successor, Franklin D. Roosevelt, chose not to apply the law to China and Japan, on the technicality that neither had officially declared war against the other. Congress simply renewed the act, on 29 February 1936, making it permanent on 1 May 1937.[6]

Once Japan's radical military escalation that began on 7 July 1937 brought hostilities into China's coastal areas central to American investment and commercial interests, the Chief of Naval Operations, now Adm. William D. Leahy, recommended that the U.S. and British fleets maintain a distant blockade, off California and Singapore, respectively, to cut Japan's imports of oil, scrap iron, cotton, and copper and thereby undermine its military operations. The State Department disagreed.[7] Instead, on 14 September, President Roosevelt announced that U.S. merchantmen could no longer transport war matériel to either China or Japan.[8] On 5 October, his famous quarantine speech signaled the American judgment that Germany and Japan were pariah states, lying outside the international order.

Tension quickly escalated on 12 December 1937, when Japanese forces attacked and sank the gunboat USS *Panay* on the Yangzi River near Nanjing. During the ensuing two-week diplomatic crisis, President Roosevelt ordered the drafting of secret plans to blockade Japan from the Aleutian Islands to Hong Kong and tried to secure British cooperation. He intended to implement the blockade upon the next provocation. Britain held that doing so would lead to war; the United States disagreed and began building a fleet capable of conducting such a blockade.[9] In March 1938, the Joint Army-Navy Board completed the last prewar version of Plan ORANGE, which envisioned rising American-Japanese tension leading to a surprise Japanese attack and then the U.S. economic and military defeat of Japan.[10] In other words, from the 1930s American military planners anticipated responding to a Japanese attack with a combined military and economic strategy.

To conduct the military part of this strategy, the United States would need a strong navy. Back in 1934 the United States had taken the first steps to create naval forces capable of insulating the country from the brewing troubles in North Africa, Europe, and Asia: the Vinson-Trammell Act authorized, but did not fund, a buildup of the U.S. Navy to the limits set at the London Naval Conference of 1930. In 1938 a second Vinson naval act finally funded the construction plans authorized under the original act for the first expansion of the fleet since World War I. In the four intervening years, however, the ceilings established in London in 1930 lapsed.[11] With the outbreak of World War II in Europe on 3 September 1939, the United States loosened the Neutrality Act's trade restrictions in favor of Britain and France and soon afterward included China.

In the same years the United States had ramped up aid to the Nationalist government to keep it in the fight against Japan—and presumably to keep Japan tied down and less able to cause problems elsewhere. On 15 December 1938, the U.S. Export-Import Bank had issued twenty-five million dollars in credits to a Chinese-owned, U.S.-based trading corporation.[12] From 8 February 1939 until 21 March 1942 it provided the Nationalist government a succession of six loans totaling $620 million.[13] Undoubtedly these loans helped keep China fighting, but they failed to roll back Japanese conquests, let alone deter new ones.

On 28 June 1940, within a week after the fall of France on 22 June, Congress passed a third Vinson naval act, funding naval expansion 11 percent beyond the lapsed London limits. A fourth Vinson bill, passed as the Two-Ocean Navy Act on 19 July, authorized a 70 percent naval expansion to build a navy of two fleets, one for the Atlantic and the other for the Pacific—a navy with four times the tonnage and four times the airpower of Japan's.[14] These prospects, however, did not deter Japanese leaders but instead led them to perceive a fast-closing window of opportunity during which they must act.

Between 1932 and 1938 the U.S. government tried to increase pressure on Japan to roll back its invasion of China. Yet nonrecognition, neutrality, and aid to the beleaguered victims all failed to dampen Japan's aggression. On the contrary, the problem of Japanese expansion quickly became worse, not better, and there were no signs of change in the adverse trend lines. Therefore, in mid-1938 the United States began implementing a new strategy of, on the one hand, escalating trade restrictions on the matériel necessary for Japan to continue hostilities and, on the other, forward basing the U.S. Fleet at Hawaii starting in 1940.

Escalating Embargoes

The new American strategy was to use a combination of a "fleet-in-being" and widening embargoes to deter and eventually roll back Japanese expansion while preventing Japan from stockpiling the resources necessary to fight the United States or, even more likely, the Dutch or British for their colonial possessions in Asia. Embargo seemed a highly promising strategy, given Japan's overwhelming dependence on imports of raw material. The Chinese clearly thought so: the Chinese Council for Economic Research fed the United States statistics on the Japanese reliance on American imports to wage war in China.[15] The Chinese government believed "that the United States, through Japan's dependence on American exports, could have stopped the invasion of China in its tracks at any moment" since the 1937 escalation with embargoes of, especially, petroleum products, copper, steel and iron semi-manufactures, and machine tools.[16]

In 1931 the United States had been Japan's most important trading partner, with a volume of trade that was a multiple of Japan's second- and third-most-important markets, China and British India. Prior to hostilities, the United States had bought 40 percent of Japanese exports and had provided 34.4 percent of Japan's imports, including 49.1 percent of its iron imports, 53.6 percent of its machine tool imports, and 75.2 percent of its oil.[17] According to a 13 October 1940 American newspaper report,

> of 32 commodities held indispensable to the prosecution of war, Japan possesses only two with exportable surpluses. These are graphite and sulphur. It is domestically self-sufficient in three— coal, pyrites and foodstuffs. Its supplies of 16 are inadequate to meet domestic demands. They are iron ore, aluminum, chromium, copper, manganese, zinc, asbestos, fluorspar, mica, phosphates, iron and steel scrap, finished and semi-finished iron and steel, machine tools, aircraft, automotive equipment and hides. It is completely or almost completely dependent on foreign sources for 11—antimony, lead, mercury, nickel, tin, tungsten, magnesiate, nitrates, petroleum, potash and rubber.[18]

Japan, then, was fatally dependent on two key resources, oil and iron. Without them, its military forces could neither move nor shoot. Moreover, its war in China had made it more, not less, reliant on imports. Whereas it had imported 67 percent of its oil in 1935, this figure grew to 74 percent in 1937 and to 90 percent in 1939.[19] It also imported more than 90 percent of its iron and 75 percent of its lead, zinc, dyes, and chemicals.[20]

This dependence had enormous military implications. A refusal to sell is easy to implement, and the denied resources ultimately proved impossible for Japan to replace. The U.S. government tightened its trade embargo against Japan over a period of three years. On 11 June 1938, in response to the many Chinese civilian deaths from the Japanese bombing of Guangzhou (Canton), Secretary of State Cordell Hull imposed a "moral embargo" on U.S. exports of aircraft and equipment to "countries the armed forces of which were engaged in the bombing of civilian populations by air."[21] On 1 July 1938, the United States required export licenses for aircraft and for the resources needed to fly, arm, and produce them.[22] According to the Munitions Control Board, American arms exports to Japan had previously soared, from $1.9 million in 1937 to $9.2 million in 1938, when 97 percent was spent on aircraft and aircraft parts and motors.[23]

Soon the United States gave Japan a heads-up for troubles to come: on 26 July 1939, Secretary of State Hull officially notified the Japanese ambassador to the United States, Horinouchi Kensuke, that the United States was invoking article 17 of the 21 February 1911 Treaty of Commerce and Navigation between the United States and Japan to terminate it, effective six months hence.[24] The Japanese derided the decision as "hasty and abrupt."[25] The United States justified its actions on the grounds that Japan had hamstrung American businesses in occupied China with "quantitative limitations, monopolistic instrumentalities, exchange control, and related measures affecting the importation and exportation of goods and remittance of funds," as well as by placing restrictions "upon the navigation of China's waterways and upon travel and residence and trade in various parts of China." Therefore, "It follows that so long as agencies and instrumentalities of the Japanese Government continue in fact to render inoperative the practice of equality of treatment for American commercial interests throughout large areas of China, there exists a serious obstacle to the conclusion by the United States of a new commercial treaty or agreement with Japan."[26] Renunciation of the treaty did not improve business conditions in China, but it did set up the United States to begin embargoing products in earnest once the treaty expired in late January 1940.

Japan, for its part, gave the United States notice of its intentions as well: in early April 1940 it claimed special economic interests in the Dutch East Indies. In response, Secretary of State Hull declared an American resolve to maintain the regional status quo.[27] In 1939 Japan had imported just 2.3 million barrels of oil from the Dutch East Indies out of that region's total exports that year of 24.4 million barrels.[28] Clearly, Japan now wanted the lion's share.

On 2 April 1940, the U.S. Fleet—minus the new but still small Atlantic Squadron— sortied from its base at San Diego for annual exercises off Hawaii. The original schedule drafted in 1939 had anticipated its departure from Hawaii on 9 May. On 7 May the stay was extended for two weeks, and on 15 May it was made indefinite. The force was to act as a fleet-in-being to deter Japan from a possible southward resource grab in the Philippines or the Dutch East Indies.[29] The timing of these naval reinforcements was intended to support the increasingly tight U.S. embargoes on Japan.

By June 1940, the U.S. government had instructed American customs authorities not to permit certain equipment exports to Japan or the Soviet Union. The Japanese were unhappy about that, since they knew of no laws requiring such restrictions.[30] On 4 June, Secretary of State Hull explained to the U.S. ambassador to Japan, Joseph C. Grew, that anticipating the imminent passage of a bill restricting the export of war matériel and dual-use commodities and manufactures, President Roosevelt had authorized the Navy Department to requisition "certain tools and supplies" and customs officials to stop their export.[31] Japanese diplomats urged the United States not to restrict trade to Japan.[32]

The pending legislation to which Hull referred marked a change in the justification for U.S. trade restrictions from the prevention of aerial bombing of civilians to the imperative to stockpile resources to meet defense requirements. On 2 July Congress passed the Act to Expedite the Strengthening of National Defense (known as the Export Control Act), authorizing the president to prohibit the export of war matériel and strategic resources in order to stockpile them at home. President Roosevelt invoked the act that very day, prohibiting a long list of items and threatening that "all violations of such provisions will be rigorously prosecuted."[33] On 26 July 1940, on the first anniversary of the American abrogation of its commercial treaty with Japan, Roosevelt invoked the new act to cut the export to Japan of aviation gasoline and various categories of iron and steel scrap.[34]

Between the introduction of the Export Control Act on 2 July 1940 and 28 May 1941, the United States repeatedly broadened the list of items embargoed (see the table). Because Japanese military activities were so prejudicial to American business interests in China, there was little private-sector pushback against these restrictions on their sales and credits to Japan.[35] In hindsight, the Japanese government would have done itself a great service had it placated neutral American businessmen, with the hope that they would stand up for continued trade rather than embargo. But, like its military strategy, which made virtually all the major Western powers its enemies, Japan's economic strategy alienated most foreign businessmen as well.

With German armies sweeping through Europe and the alarming prospects for the fall of Britain, on 14 September 1940 the United States introduced the first peacetime conscription in its history. This was clearly a step toward war. On 27 September, in response to Germany's early victories against France, Japan joined the Axis powers. This decision unwittingly transformed Japan, in American eyes at least, from a regional bully in a secondary part of the world into a pariah state in cahoots with America's most deadly enemies in Europe. Almost immediately, U.S. trade restrictions against Japan tightened even further.

U.S. Trade Restrictions

DATE	RESTRICTIONS	EMBARGOED ITEMS	SOURCE
1 Jul 38	No export licenses to countries aerially bombing civilians.	aircraft, aircraft parts, munitions	FRUS, Japan: 1931–1941, vol. 2, pp. 201–202.
26 Jul 39	U.S. renunciation of 1911 Treaty of Commerce and Navigation. Effective in six months.		FRUS, Japan: 1931–1941, vol. 2, p. 189.
15 Dec 39	Same.	aluminum, molybdenum	FRUS, Japan: 1931–1941, vol. 2, pp. 202–203.
20 Dec 39	Same.	technology transfers for high-quality aviation gasoline production	FRUS, Japan: 1931–1941, vol. 2, pp. 203–204.
26 Jan 40	Treaty renunciation in effect.		"Treaty of Commerce and Navigation between the United States and Japan," art. 17, p. 105.

U.S. Trade Restrictions, continued

DATE	RESTRICTIONS	EMBARGOED ITEMS	SOURCE
2 Jul 40	Export Control Act. United States to stockpile strategic resources. Defense-related items subject to case-by-case export licensing.	aluminum, antimony, asbestos, chromium, cotton linters, flax, graphite, hides, industrial diamond, magnesium, manganese, manila fiber, mercury, mica, molybdenum optical glass, platinum-group metals, quartz crystals, quinine, rubber, silk, tin, toluol, tungsten, vanadium, wool; ammonia and ammonium compounds, chlorine, dimethylaniline, diphenylamine, nitrates, nitric acid, nitrocellulose, soda lime, sodium acetate, strontium chemicals, sulfuric acid; aircraft parts, armor plate, nonshatterable glass,.optical elements for armaments; metalworking machinery for melting or casting, pressing into forms, cutting or grinding, or welding	FRUS, *Japan: 1931–1941*, vol. 2, pp. 211–12.
26 Jul 40	Same.	aviation lubricating oil, aviation motor fuel, iron and scrap steel, tetraethyl lead	FRUS, *Japan: 1931–1941*, vol. 2, pp. 217–18.
12 Sep 40	Same.	technology transfers relevant for the production of aircraft and aviation motor fuel; equipment or technology transfers relevant for the production of tetraethyl lead	FRUS, *Japan: 1931–1941*, vol. 2, pp. 220–21.
26 Sep 40	Unrestricted exports only to Britain and Western Hemisphere. Previous licenses to others revoked.	iron and steel scrap	FRUS, *Japan: 1931–1941*, vol. 2, pp. 222–23.
27 Nov 40	Defense-related items subject to case-by-case export licensing.	machine tools	FRUS, 1940, *Far East*, vol. 4, p. 617.
10 Dec 40	Exports outside Britain and Western Hemisphere restricted to prewar levels.	iron and steel scrap	FRUS, *Japan: 1931–1941*, vol. 2, p. 232; FRUS, 1940, *Far East*, vol. 4, p. 620.
20 Dec 40	Defense-related items subject to case-by-case export licensing.	abrasives, aviation lubricating oil equipment and technology, balancing machines, bromine, cobalt, ethylene, ethylene dibromide, gauges, hydraulic pumps, measuring machines, methylamine, plastic molding machines, strontium metals and ores, testing machines, tools incorporating industrial diamonds	FRUS, *Japan: 1931–1941*, vol. 2, p. 36; FRUS, 1940, *Far East*, vol. 4, p. 620.
10 Jan 41	Same.	brass, bronze, copper, nickel, potash, zinc	FRUS, *Japan: 1931–1941*, vol. 2, p. 238.
29 Jan 41	Additional reporting requirements for licensed exports to destinations other than the British Empire.	paperwork must include affidavits indicating the total exports of the licensed item to the relevant country since 1 January 1937	FRUS, *Japan: 1931–1941*, vol. 2, p. 241.
2 Feb 41	Defense-related items subject to case-by-case export licensing.	calf and kip skins, radium, uranium, well and refining machinery; expanded list of specific items included in the embargo of iron and steel exports	FRUS, *Japan: 1931–1941*, vol. 2, pp. 242–28.

U.S. Trade Restrictions, continued

DATE	RESTRICTIONS	EMBARGOED ITEMS	SOURCE
25 Feb 41	Same.	aircraft pilot trainers, atropine, belladonna, belting leather, beryllium, graphite electrodes, sole leather	FRUS, *Japan: 1931–1941*, vol. 2, pp. 248–51.
4 Mar 41	Same.	borax, cadmium, carbon black, coconut oil, copra, cresylic acid and cresols, fatty acids, glycerin, jute, lead, palm kernel oil and palm kernels, petroleum coke, phosphates, pine oil, shellac, titanium	FRUS, *Japan: 1931–1941*, vol. 2, pp. 253–54.
4 Mar 41	Same.	anything related by manufacture, design, description, technology, or possible adaptation to any of the items subject to export licensing	FRUS, *Japan: 1931–1941*, vol. 2, p. 254.
27 Mar 41	Same.	acetic aldehyde, acrylonitrile, alkyd resins, aniline, animal fats, arsenic trichloride, bristles, butadiene, butylene, carbon electrodes, chloroacetyl chloride, chloropicrin, chloroprene, cork, cuprous oxide, detonators and blasting caps, dibutyl phthalate, dicyanodiamide, diethyl phthalate, dipropyl phthalate, ethylene chlorhydrine, explosives, fatty acids, formaldehyde, guanidine nitrate, hexamethylenetetramine, iodine, kapok, monochloroacetic acid, naphthalene, nitroguanidine, nux vomica, nylon, omega chloroacetophenone, pentaerythrite, petrolatum, phenol, phthalic anhydride, Rochelle salts, sodium chlorate, strychnine, styrene, sulfur chlorides, tartaric acid, thiodiglycol, various nitro-derivatives, various polymers and copolymers, vegetable oil seeds, vegetable oils, vinylidene chloride, wood pulp	FRUS, *Japan: 1931–1941*, vol. 2, pp. 258–59.
14 Apr 41	Same.	all machinery, caffeine, calcium cyanide, casein, manufactures, sodium cyanide, theobromine, vegetable fibers	FRUS, *Japan: 1931–1941*, vol. 2, pp. 260–61.
28 May 41	Above trade restrictions to be applied in the Philippines, the Panama Canal Zone, and the District of Columbia.	all of the above	FRUS, *Japan: 1931–1941*, vol. 2, pp. 261–62.
14 Jun 41	German and Italian assets in the United States frozen.	all trade with Germany and Italy under U.S. government control	FRUS, *Japan: 1931–1941*, vol. 2, pp. 266–67.
25 Jul 41	Japanese assets in the United States frozen.	all trade with Japan under U.S. government control	FRUS, *Japan: 1931–1941*, vol. 2, pp. 266–67.
1 Aug 41	Revocation of all valid export licenses except to the Western Hemisphere, the British Empire, Egypt, the Dutch East Indies, unoccupied China, and the Belgian Congo.	all petroleum products	FRUS, 1941, *Far East*, vol. 4, p. 850.

The Japanese Response to the U.S. Embargo

Once Japan had taken the territories accessible via the Chinese railway system (mainly accomplished by 1939), its military and strategic paradigm had reached the limits of its manpower constraints. So Japanese strategy turned from trying to dislodge the Nationalist government from its mountainous redoubt in Sichuan Province to preventing it from spending its foreign loans on the matériel necessary to stay in the fight. Having called on Britain to sever the Burma Road supply route in July 1940, on 22 September the Japanese pressured the French governor of Indochina to allow their troops to land in Haiphong, which they did the following day.[36] Japan intended thereby to cut the last important supply line to China—the route across the Indochinese border. Three days later, on 26 September, the United States began retroactively revoking steel-scrap export licenses issued after 26 July 1940 and permitting future unrestricted iron and steel scrap exports only to Britain and the Western Hemisphere.[37] This meant no more U.S. iron or steel for Japan.

The Department of State took very seriously the Imperial Japanese Navy's plans for a resource grab throughout the South Pacific, the so-called Southward Advance policy.[38] The Japanese government was well aware that the likely American response would be a trade embargo.[39] On 17 February 1940 Ambassador Grew had reported that the previous day Foreign Minister Nomura Kichisaburō had discussed with Diet members the growing support in Congress for a trade embargo but that rather than taking it seriously Nomura had optimistically predicted that U.S. implementation of an embargo "would require a considerable length of time."[40]

On 8 October 1940, when Ambassador Horinouchi lodged an official protest against the iron-and-steel-scrap "virtual embargo," characterizing it as an "unfriendly act," Secretary of State Hull replied that given the "constant and repeated Japanese depredations against American rights and interests in the Far East, the Japanese Government was in no position to characterize a national defense measure as an unfriendly act."[41] Hull asserted that "those who are dominating the external policies of Japan are, as we here have believed for some years, bent on the conquest by force of all worthwhile territory in the Pacific Ocean area without limit as to extent in the South and in southern continental areas of that part of the world."[42] He concluded, "I reiterated the view that it was unheard of for one country engaged in aggression and seizure of another country, contrary to all law and treaty provisions, to turn to a third peacefully disposed nation and seriously insist that it would be guilty of an unfriendly act if it should not cheerfully provide some of the necessary implements of war to aid the aggressor nation in carrying out its policy of invasion."[43] The exchange impressed neither side.

On 15 October 1940, President Roosevelt authorized the requisitioning of war matériel.[44] On 27 November, following his reelection on 5 November, the United States restricted machine tool exports; soon afterward, it loaned China a hundred million dollars and began augmenting its forces in the Philippines—an archipelago that lay astride Japan's sea lines of communication between the home islands and the oil fields of the Dutch East Indies.[45] On 30 December, Roosevelt made his arsenal-for-democracy speech, promising that America would arm democracies beset by aggressors. His next key piece of legislation interpreted "democracy" broadly to include China and the Soviet Union: on 11 March 1941, he jettisoned the old strategy of neutrality by signing the Lend-Lease Act, which allowed massive aid to nations beset by invaders. He extended military aid initially to Great Britain and soon to Russia and China.[46] Like the abandoned neutrality strategy, Lend-Lease produced no discernible mitigating effect on Japanese expansion. This left a freeze of Japanese assets as the last remaining economic tool.

Back in May 1939, the British ambassador to Japan, Robert Craigie, had raised the possibility with the U.S. ambassador, Joseph C. Grew, of a retaliatory trade embargo should Japan act against the International Settlement in Shanghai. Grew had not been enthusiastic.[47] Meanwhile, the British had pressured the United States to halt the flow of natural resources being transshipped from the Japanese empire to Germany via the Trans-Siberian Railway.[48] On 26 July 1940, when President Roosevelt announced his intent to subject petroleum products, tetraethyl lead, and steel and iron scrap to licensing procedures, the British feared that this move would propel the Japanese to take control of Dutch East Indies oil fields.[49] By October 1940 the United States, Canada, and Britain were planning future trade restrictions on Japan.[50] The British were pushing for a coordinated trade policy among Britain, the United States, and the Netherlands severe enough to prevent Japan from stockpiling strategic materials yet not so severe as to provoke a declaration of war.[51]

On 23 November 1940, the Council on Foreign Relations issued a confidential study on Japan's vulnerability to American sanctions concluding that combined action by the United States, Britain, and the Netherlands would withhold "essential imports," deprive Japan of the foreign exchange to buy elsewhere, and strain its merchant marine capacity, which was already insufficient for stockpiling. Also, most critically for U.S. naval strategy, "Japan would have to operate outside of Japanese waters, far from her home bases." In the event of war, these long sea lines of communication would make the Japanese fleet vulnerable to attack, especially from the U.S. Navy's robust submarine force. Nevertheless, as the report presciently predicted, sanctions alone "would not necessarily stop her war machine."[52]

The Freeze of Japanese Assets

On 14 June 1941, the United States froze German and Italian assets. A week later, on 22 June, Germany invaded Russia, and Japan redoubled its efforts to sever outside support to China. Between 24 and 27 July 1941 Japan occupied southern Indochina. The United States immediately retaliated, freezing on 25 July Japanese assets in the United States worth five hundred million yen, thereby putting "all financial and import and export trade" involving Japanese interests under U.S. government control. On 14 July the United States had decoded a Japanese military communication indicating that "after the occupation of French Indo-China, next on our schedule is . . . the Netherlands Indies."[53]

On 25 July 1941, the Chief of Naval Operations, Adm. Harold R. Stark, and the Chief of Staff of the U.S. Army, Brig. Gen. George C. Marshall, sent a joint dispatch to their subordinates in Hawaii, the Philippines, the Panama Canal Zone, and Great Britain alerting them that the United States would embargo all trade with Japan, save through a licensing system, and that all Japanese assets in the United States would be frozen: "It is not repeat not expected that Japanese merchant vessels in United States ports will be seized at this time. United States flag merchant vessels will not at present be ordered to depart from or not to enter ports controlled by Japan."[54] Wakasugi Kaname, special aide to the Japanese ambassador to the United States, Nomura Kichisaburō, requested assurances from the U.S. government that it would not seize or detain Japanese ships wishing to enter American ports—at that time, these ships were remaining out at sea. The United States, notwithstanding Stark and Marshall's provisional guidance—refused to provide such assurances.[55]

On 26 July, on the second anniversary of the American renunciation of its commercial treaty with Japan, Britain followed suit, freezing Japanese assets in Britain and the empire. It also notified Japan of an intent to abrogate Japan's 5 May 1911 Treaty of Commerce and Navigation with the United Kingdom of Great Britain and Ireland, the British Dominions beyond the Seas and India, as well as Japan's 12 July 1937 trade and commerce treaty with India and its 7 June 1937 trade and commerce treaty with Burma. All these abrogations would go into effect six months later in January 1942.[56] Also on 26 July the United States appointed Gen. Douglas MacArthur as commander in chief of U.S. forces in East Asia and made plans to improve defenses in the Philippines.[57] On 27 July, the Dutch government too froze Japanese assets.[58]

Britain had been urging the United States to ramp up economic pressure on Japan (but to do so with great care). On 3 March 1941, the British ambassador to the United States, E. F. L. Wood, first Earl of Halifax, had called on Secretary of State Hull, who later reported of their conversation, "He brought up the question of an embargo on exports of gasoline to Japan" and provided a document from his embassy that began, "One of the main weapons which the Democracies hold against Japan is her dependence on them for many of the materials without which she would be unable to maintain her war effort." The British document continued, Japan had used "the last twelve months to import quantities of these materials far in excess of her current consumption needs." Given that a "large proportion of these excessive imports has undoubtedly gone to build up strategic reserves," the British recommended a denial of just "*excess* supplies."[59] According to a second enclosed document, "in the last six months of 1940 more than one million barrels of aviation grade spirit went to Japan, compared with 560,000 barrels in the twelve months of 1939. In 1941, 180,000 barrels have already gone, and orders for an additional 250,000 barrels are reported." The British did not recommend a complete embargo, simply a curtailment sufficient to prevent further Japanese stockpiling.[60]

Then, on 1 August 1941, Acting Secretary of State Sumner Welles revoked all valid licenses allowing the export of petroleum products to any country outside the Western Hemisphere, the British Empire, Egypt, the Dutch East Indies, unoccupied China, and the Belgian Congo.[61] This meant no exports to Japan. Some believe that the oil embargo was made total not by intention but by mistake, through a bureaucratic snafu.[62] In any case, it put Japan in dire straits. At the time Japan had reserves of 9.4 million kilotons and consumed 450,000 kilotons per month, giving it about a year and a half's supply at stable consumption rates.[63] Japanese leaders construed this period as defining a deadline for making alternate supply arrangements.

The escalating embargoes, far from deterring Japan, appear to have acted as an accelerant as Japanese leaders put the finishing touches on their plans to expand the war throughout the Pacific. Within a week of the total oil embargo, just as the British had predicted, the Imperial Japanese Army favored going to war in the Pacific. The total oil embargo meant that Japan's Greater East Asia Co-prosperity Sphere had to be expanded to include the oil fields of the Dutch East Indies. In September the cabinet and thereafter an imperial conference confirmed the Imperial Japanese Army and Navy's recommendation for the "Southern Advance" war plan to take over European colonies in Asia during the window of opportunity opened by the war in Europe, when neither the colonial powers nor Russia could interfere. The navy, but not the army, added Hawaii to the list of targets.[64] Both services wanted to complete their conquests before the window began to close: Japan's relative naval strength would peak in late 1941 at near parity with the U.S. Navy and thereafter decline rapidly in relative terms as a result of the American building program under the Two-Ocean Navy Act.[65]

On 10 November 1941, Foreign Minister Tōgō Shigenori warned Ambassador Grew, "The freezing by the United States of Japanese assets had stopped supplies of many important raw materials to Japan. Economic pressure of this character is capable of menacing national existence to a greater degree than the direct use of force."[66] With Japan's power diminishing with each passing day, Prime Minister Tōjō and other leaders had concluded, "If Japan could not solve the fatal situation by means of diplomacy then there would be no way remaining to her but to take up arms and break through the military and economy barrier flung around her."[67]

As the postwar trials made clear, in the estimation of the Imperial Japanese Army high command "there was but a faint prospect of a successful conclusion of the negotiations, and . . . Japan would therefore eventually have to go to war." It was convinced that while negotiations dragged on, Japan was being subjected to gradual exhaustion of natural resources as the economic warfare of the Allied powers began to take full effect; that the nation was losing its power to fight; and that hostilities should therefore be commenced while Japanese fighting power was still relatively strong compared with that of the potential enemy. The Naval General Staff believed that if "war was to be inevitable, it should be determined upon promptly."[68]

On 26 November 1941, the United States delivered another ultimatum to Japan—the "Hull Note," for U.S. Secretary of State Cordell Hull. It required Japan to evacuate Indochina and China, including Manchuria, and to repudiate both its puppet government in China under Wang Jingwei and its Tripartite Pact with Germany and Italy. Within the fortnight Japan attacked Pearl Harbor—clearly not the desired outcome of a strategy of deterrence. In the end, the United States succeeded in deterring a Japanese attack not against itself but against Russia—the Imperial Japanese Army finally gave up its long-standing war plan to invade Russia as relations with the United States deteriorated.[69]

The U.S. Navy Fleet-in-Being at Pearl Harbor

U.S. military and economic deterrents were supposed to work hand in hand. The embargo strategy accurately identified and targeted a key Japanese strategic vulnerability: Japan could not sustain military operations in China, let alone across the Pacific, without a long shopping list of imported natural resources. In October 1941, Ambassador Nomura informed the foreign minister, Adm. Toyoda Teijirō, "If the United States continues to carry on economic warfare against Japan, a measure just short of armed warfare, the United States will be able to attain the objectives of a war against Japan without firing a shot."[70] Nomura warned President Roosevelt, "People in my country take the freezing of assets as an economic blockade and they go even so far as to contend that the means of modern warfare are not limited to shooting. No nation can survive without the supply of material vital to its industries."[71]

Yet the embargo failed in its primary objectives either to roll back or deter further Japanese conquests. Instead, it succeeded only in its third objective, of limiting Japanese resource stockpiles for future military operations. The problem lay not in the strategy's

understanding of an enemy critical vulnerability but in Japan's reaction to the strategy. In 1938 analysts in the State Department warned that an oil embargo would risk
"Japan's forcibly taking over the Netherlands East Indies."[72] On 7 June 1940 Maxwell
M. Hamilton, chief of the Division of Far Eastern Affairs, accurately predicted that a
"restriction or prohibition of the exportation of petroleum products . . . would tend to
impel Japan toward moving into the Dutch East Indies."[73] On 19 July 1941 the director of the War Plans Division provided the Chief of Naval Operations, Admiral Stark,
with a "study of the effect of the embargo of trade between the United States and Japan"
that predicted, "An embargo would probably result in a fairly early attack by Japan on
Malaya [a key source of iron] and the Netherlands East Indies [a key source of oil], and
possibly would involve the United States in early war in the Pacific." The report recommended not embargoing all trade with Japan at that time lest the United States become
overextended in a possible two-front war.[74]

The trick would be to deter such a Japanese escalation. This is where forward basing
of the U.S. Navy came in. The stationing of the Battle Fleet in Hawaii was considered
essential for the implementation of an embargo and as a deterrent against a Japanese
seizure of the Dutch East Indies oil fields.[75] Despite the risks of military escalation, from
1938 to 1941 Stanley K. Hornbeck, who served as chief of the State Department's Division of Far Eastern Affairs (1928–37) and subsequently adviser on political relations to
Secretary of State Cordell Hull (1937–44), supported the strategy of increasing economic
pressure so that American exports would not facilitate Japanese aggression or, even
worse, allow Japan to stockpile resources that it would one day use against the United
States.[76]

On 24 July 1940, Hornbeck reported that

> the possibility of substantial embargoes by this country is linked closely with the question of the
> existing location and the possible alteration of the location of the U.S. Battle Fleet. So long as we
> have the Fleet in the Pacific, and especially while we have it at Hawaii, the Japanese have reason to
> fear what we may do in the field of embargoes. The Fleet stands as the defensive and shielding arm
> behind which and screened by which there is the potential striking power of the other arm, em-
> bargo. If and when our Fleet leaves the Pacific and moves into the Atlantic, Japan will have reason
> to be very little fearful that we will go in extensively for embargoes. Thus, our present setup—with
> authority for embargoes and with the Fleet in the Pacific—contributes greatly to the maintenance of
> the negative equilibrium in Japanese political thought.

Hornbeck believed that forward basing was the best available strategy to ensure that
"there will be no abrupt and drastic change in [Japan's] foreign policy in the immediate
future."[77] Sixteen months later the abrupt and drastic change occurred anyway.

At the postwar International Military Tribunal of the Far East, defendants such as
former prime minister Gen. Tōjō Hideki, former vice chief of the Naval General Staff
Adm. Kondō Nobutake, and former minister of the navy Adm. Shimada Shigetarō listed

the factors that had driven Japan to attack the United States. Quite ironically, the factors they cited had been the main elements of the American strategy of deterrence, which according to them, far from deterring further aggression had actually propelled it. Specifically Tōjō listed six major points: first, the American renunciation of its Treaty of Commerce and Navigation in 1939, followed by growing numbers of embargoed items; second, skyrocketing U.S. military appropriations, most notably for naval and air assets; third, peacetime conscription; fourth, growing military coordination among the United States, Britain, and the Netherlands; fifth, the strengthening of U.S. defenses in the Philippines; and sixth, capping them all off, the Allied freeze of Japanese assets.[78]

To this list Admiral Kondō added the forward basing of the U.S. Fleet at Hawaii, Japan's deadlocked negotiations with the Dutch East Indies and French Indochina in pursuit of alternative sources for supplies, and the growing Allied aid to the Nationalist government of China. According to Admiral Kondō, this aid made Chiang Kai-shek "confident of victory" and undermined Japan's ability to win the war in China, which was "Japan's greatest concern at that time."[79] Rather than deterring Japan's attack, as intended, the U.S. Navy's fleet-in-being in Hawaii invited attack by offering a poorly defended, lucrative target.

The Boomerang Effect

Far from deterring a Japanese attack, then, escalating U.S. military and economic pressure did not even delay but apparently precipitated one. General Tōjō listed in his opening statement before the military tribunal the tightening trade embargo against Japan as the first of three causes of the Pacific War, causes that together forced "Japan to invoke the right of self-defense."[80] He highlighted the effectiveness of the American freeze of Japanese assets: "Japan was quite unable to keep its population alive by the products raised within the Empire alone. Japan had to obtain the necessary commodities by trade. By the freezing of assets by the United States, Britain and the Dutch East Indies, more than half of Japan's foreign trade disappeared and the toil of eighty years' standing [to become a great power] was wiped out." With the oil embargo, "Japan's navy was thus to lose mobility after her oil stock was exhausted; solution of the China Incident [Japan's euphemism for its war against China] was made practically impossible; Japan's defense was emasculated."[81]

The Imperial Japanese Navy too saw the American embargoes not as deterrence but as a looming deadline for war. According to the testimony of Admiral Shimada, "These embargoes and freezing orders were deliberately designed to paralyze, and in themselves were capable of paralyzing within a short space of time, the entire economy of Japan. They were designed to force Japan's capitulation in China from sheer industrial and raw material exhaustion. One of the principal commodities vitally affected was oil. Without it [her] civilian economy and her entire national security would be strangled."[82]

At the root of the failure of the U.S. strategy of deterrence was the enormous value Japanese civil and military leaders placed on the attainment of their objectives in China. Prior to Pearl Harbor, Japan had suffered 600,000 casualties in China, a sunk cost of stupendous proportions that its leaders found difficult to justify to the Japanese people.[83] The domestic and political costs, not to mention "loss of face," associated with a unilateral withdrawal from China would have been simply too great to bear. Ambassador Grew warned that an embargo alone would not force Japan to abandon its "adventure in China."[84]

At an imperial conference in September of 1941 the prime minister, General Tōjō, argued that together the American oil embargo, its Lend-Lease aid to Russia, and its increasing military aid to Chiang Kai-shek constituted an attempt to encircle and destroy Japan. General Tōjō and Japan's other leaders—civil, army, and navy—who rarely agreed on much, concluded that peace on American terms, entailing a withdrawal from China, would lead to the gradual impoverishment of Japan and undo the efforts of generations of Japanese to transform their country into a modern power. War with the United States, on the other hand, offered a fifty-fifty chance of success. Finance Minister Kaya Okinori alone repeatedly raised economic concerns indicating the unfeasibility of Tōjō's plans. The others ignored him.[85] On 5 November Tōjō predicted, "America may be enraged for a while, but later she will come to understand [why we did what we did]."[86] He argued that risking war with the United States was better than "being ground down without doing anything."[87] His and his colleagues' misreading of the American psyche also failed to deter, and like America's deterrence strategy, produced for Japan a strategic boomerang, delivering precisely the kind of war Japan could never win and that ended with atomic bombs on Japanese cities.

As it turns out, Japanese leaders did not perceive the U.S. strategy as one designed to deter. They concluded that American demands put at risk the survival not only of their country but of themselves personally, responsible as they were for Japan's China policy, leaving them a stark choice between fighting or perishing. Americans would have disagreed that their demands threatened Japanese survival. They did not perceive the tremendous value that the Japanese attached to stability in China or the extreme fear the Japanese leadership had of the spread of communism. Americans would have argued that the Japanese invasion greatly exacerbated Chinese instability, to which the Japanese would have responded by pointing to the rapid economic development of Manchuria as proof of what was possible if only the Chinese would cooperate.

Conclusions

Because the United States faced aggressors in both Europe and Asia, it had to devise a cost-effective and politically feasible method to deal with both. Its economy had not come close to recovering from the Great Depression, world trade remained hamstrung by protectionism, and American voters remained devoutly isolationist until the Japanese attack on Pearl Harbor on 7 December 1941 changed everything. Until then, isolationist voter sentiment severely constrained American policy choices.

So the United States settled for a "Europe first" strategy, which meant adopting in Asia a shoestring strategy of economic embargo in combination with a forward-based fleet-in-being, in the hope that the two together would slow if not deter further Japanese expansion. This strategy, far from deterring Japan, apparently hastened its military operations. At the root of this strategic boomerang was the enormous value the Japanese civil and military leadership placed on their version of a stable China. They equated it with national survival. Little could deter those who already considered their very survival at stake.

For a trade-dependent nation like Japan, embargo was a lethal strategy. But because the stakes were so high, rather than backing down Japan escalated, and this escalation then required an expensive boots-on-the-ground solution for the United States. It turns out that there was no cheap deterrent strategy that would set Japan right, only a very costly one bought at the price of tens of thousands of American lives.

Notes

The thoughts and opinions expressed in this essay are those of the author and are not necessarily those of the U.S. government, the U.S. Navy Department, or the Naval War College.

1. I have covered these issues in detail in S. C. M. Paine, *The Wars for Asia 1911–1949* (New York: Cambridge Univ. Press, 2012), see esp. chap. 2.

2. Secretary of State Henry L. Stimson to U.S. Ambassador to Japan W. Cameron Forbes, 7 January 1932, in U.S. State Dept., *Papers Relating to the Foreign Relations of the United States: Japan: 1931–1941* (Washington, D.C.: U.S. Government Printing Office [hereafter GPO], 1943) [hereafter FRUS, *Japan: 1931–1941*], vol. 1, p. 76.

3. Department of State, Division of Far Eastern Affairs, "Manchuria Situation," 6 December 1931, p. 2, Stanley K. Hornbeck Papers, box

369, file "Sanctions, Economic," Hoover Institution Archives, Stanford, Calif.

4. Covenant of the League of Nations, 29 April 1919, art. 16, available at cil.nus.edu.sg/.

5. Herbert C. Hoover, interview, 10 April 1942, p. 3, Payson J. Treat Papers, box 45, file "Herbert C. Hoover Interviews," Hoover Institution Archives, Stanford, Calif.

6. FRUS, *Japan: 1931–1941*, vol. 2, p. 201.

7. Drew Pearson, "Washington Merry-Go-Round," *New York Mirror*, 22 July 1942, Stanley K. Hornbeck Papers, box 155, file "Embargo, May Act," Hoover Institution Archives, Stanford, Calif.

8. FRUS, *Japan: 1931–1941*, vol. 2, p. 201.

9. Bradford A. Lee, *Britain and the Sino-Japanese War 1937–1939* (Stanford, Calif.: Stanford Univ. Press, 1973), pp. 90–91.

10. Steven T. Ross, *American War Plans 1890–1939* (London: Frank Cass, 2002), pp. 164–65.

11. David C. Evans and Mark R. Peattie, *Kaigun: Strategy, Tactics, and Technology in the Imperial Japanese Navy 1887–1941* (Annapolis, Md.: Naval Institute Press, 1997), pp. 235, 296; George W. Baer, *One Hundred Years of Sea Power: The U.S. Navy, 1890–1990* (Stanford, Calif.: Stanford Univ. Press, 1993), pp. 130, 134.

12. FRUS, *Japan: 1931–1941,* vol. 2, p. 222.

13. 宓汝成 [Mi Rucheng], "抗战时期的中国外债" [The Foreign Loans to China during the War of Resistance], 中国经济史研究 [Research in Chinese Economic History], no. 2 (1998), pp. 55, 59; FRUS, *Japan: 1931–1941,* vol. 2, pp. 222, 326; 吴景平 [Wu Jingping], "抗战时期中美租借关系述评" [Sino-American Lend-Lease Relations during the War against Japan], 历史研究 [Historical Research], no. 4 (1995), pp. 53, 59–60, 64; Arthur N. Young, *China's Wartime Finance and Inflation, 1937–1945* (Cambridge, Mass.: Harvard Univ. Press, 1965), pp. 114–15; Arthur N. Young, *China and the Helping Hand 1937–1945* (Cambridge, Mass.: Harvard Univ. Press, 1963), p. 350; Academia Sinica, Institute of Modern History Archives, 431.4/0004, 清理中美戰債 [Settling Accounts for Sino-American Military Debts], pp. 62–81, 11-NAA-06283, 30 June 1945; idem, 431.4/0007, ibid., pp. 74–78, 11-NAA-06286.

14. Baer, *One Hundred Years of Sea Power,* pp. 134–37, 149–51; Sadao Asada, *From Mahan to Pearl Harbor: The Imperial Japanese Navy and the United States* (Annapolis, Md.: Naval Institute Press, 2006), pp. 240–41; David Isaakovich Goldberg, *Внешняя политика Японии (сентябрь 1939 г.–декабрь 1941 г.)* [The Foreign Policy of Japan (September 1939–December 1941)] (Moscow: Издательство восточной литературы [Eastern Literature Publishing], 1959), pp. 120–21, 282–85.

15. U.S. State Dept., *Foreign Relations of the United States Diplomatic Papers 1940: The Far East* (Washington, D.C.: GPO, 1955) [hereafter FRUS, 1940, *Far East*], vol. 4, pp. 605–606; Chinese Council for Economic Research, "Sale of War Materials by the United States to Japan, First Eight Months, January–August, 1939, Compared with Corresponding Periods of 1938 and 1937," *Bulletin No. 16,* 10 November 1939, Arthur N. Young Papers, box 99, "Folder: Embargo—Japan 1939," Hoover Institution Archives, Stanford, Calif.

16. Richard L. Stokes, "Survey Shows Loss of U.S. War Exports Would Cripple Japan," *Star,* 13 October 1940, Stanley K. Hornbeck Papers, box 155, file "Embargo," Hoover Institution Archives, Stanford, Calif.

17. Thomas W. Burkman, *Japan and the League of Nations: Empire and World Order, 1914–1938* (Honolulu: Univ. of Hawai'i Press, 2008), p. 107; Akira Iriye, *The Cambridge History of American Foreign Relations,* vol. 3, *The Globalizing of America, 1913–1945* (Cambridge, U.K.: Cambridge Univ. Press, 1993), pp. 162–64, 166, 180; 江口圭一 [Eguchi Kei-ichi], 十五年戦争小史 [A Short History of the Fifteen-Year War] (Tokyo: 青木書店, 1996), p. 40; Michael A. Barnhart, *Japan Prepares for Total War* (Ithaca, N.Y.: Cornell Univ. Press, 1987), p. 144.

18. Stokes, "Survey Shows Loss of U.S. War Exports Would Cripple Japan."

19. 安部彦太 [Abe Hikota], "大東亜戦争の計数的分析" [A Statistical Analysis of the Great East Asian War], in 近代日本戦争史 [Modern Japanese Military History], vol. 4, 大東亜戦争 [The Great East Asian War], ed. 奥村房夫 [Okumura Fusao] and 近藤新治 [Kondō Shinji] (Tokyo: 同台経済懇話会, 1995), p. 825.

20. Dr. Ben Dorfman, "Japan Gains Little in Her Manchurian Adventure," *San Francisco Chronicle,* 6 August 1933, p. F5, Diplomatic Records Office, E.1.2.0-XI-MAI, vol. 4, 各国財政経済及金融関係雑件満州国ノ部 [Miscellaneous Papers on Various Countries' Public Finance and Credit, Section on Manchukuo], July–December 1933, Foreign Ministry, Tokyo, Japan.

21. Michael A. Barnhart, "Japan's Economic Security and the Origins of the Pacific War," in *Imperial Japan and the World, 1931–1945: Critical Concepts in Asian Studies,* ed. Antony Best (London: Routledge, 2011), vol. 2, p. 227; Stokes, "Survey Shows Loss of U.S. War Exports Would Cripple Japan."

22. FRUS, *Japan: 1931–1941,* vol. 2, pp. 201–204.

23. Stokes, "Survey Shows Loss of U.S. War Exports Would Cripple Japan."

24. FRUS, *Japan: 1931–1941,* vol. 2, p. 189; "Treaty of Commerce and Navigation between the United States and Japan," in "Official Documents," supplement, *American Journal of International Law* 5, no. 2 (April 1911), p. 105.

25. FRUS, *Japan: 1931–1941,* vol. 2, p. 190.

26. Ibid., pp. 191–92.

27. Ian Cowman, *Dominion or Decline: Anglo-American Relations in the Pacific, 1937–1941* (Oxford, U.K.: Berg, 1996), p. 172.

28. Irvin H. Anderson, Jr., "The 1941 De Facto Embargo on Oil to Japan: A Bureaucratic Reflex," *Pacific Historical Review* 44, no. 2 (May 1975), p. 201.

29. Cowman, *Dominion or Decline*, p. 173.

30. FRUS, 1940, *Far East*, vol. 4, pp. 572–73.

31. Ibid., pp. 573–75.

32. Ibid., pp. 576–80, 587–90, 596–99, 608–10, 617–18, 620–25; FRUS, *Japan: 1931–1941*, vol. 2, pp. 205–207, 218–19, 223–30, 237, 269, 537–39.

33. FRUS, *Japan: 1931–1941*, vol. 2, pp. 211–12; FRUS, 1940, *Far East*, vol. 4, p. 579.

34. Iriye, *Globalizing of America*, pp. 162–64, 166, 180; Eguchi Kei-ichi, *Short History of the Fifteen-Year War*, p. 140.

35. FRUS, 1940, *Far East*, vol. 4, p. 569.

36. F. C. Jones, *Japan's New Order in East Asia: Its Rise and Fall 1937–1945* (London: Oxford Univ. Press, 1954), p. 230; Cowman, *Dominion or Decline*, p. 172.

37. FRUS, *Japan: 1931–1941*, vol. 2, pp. 222–23.

38. FRUS, 1940, *Far East*, vol. 4, pp. 1–250.

39. Ibid., p. 3.

40. Ibid., p. 567.

41. Ibid., p. 608.

42. FRUS, *Japan: 1931–1941*, vol. 2, pp. 226–27.

43. Ibid., p. 227.

44. Ibid., p. 228.

45. FRUS, 1940, *Far East*, vol. 4, pp. 617–18.

46. Eguchi Kei-ichi, *Short History of the Fifteen-Year War*, p. 154.

47. U.S. State Dept., *Foreign Relations of the United States Diplomatic Papers 1939: The Far East, the Near East, and Africa*, vol. 4 (Washington, D.C.: GPO, 1955), p. 53 [hereafter FRUS, 1939, *Far East, the Near East, and Africa*].

48. FRUS, 1940, *Far East*, vol. 4, pp. 569–70.

49. Ibid., pp. 589–91.

50. Ibid., p. 610.

51. Ibid., pp. 613–14.

52. William Diebold, Jr., "Japan's Vulnerability to American Sanctions," *Studies of American Interest in the War and the Peace, Economic and Financial Series*, no. E-B 24, preliminary confidential memorandum first draft, 23 November 1940, p. 3, Stanley K. Hornbeck Papers, box 369, file "Sanctions #2," Hoover Institution Archives, Stanford, Calif.; Anderson, "1941 De Facto Embargo on Oil to Japan," pp. 212–14.

53. FRUS, *Japan: 1931–1941*, vol. 2, pp. 266–67; Wu Jingping, "Sino-American Lend-Lease Relations during the War against Japan," pp. 53, 59–60, quoting from Anderson, "1941 De Facto Embargo on Oil to Japan," p. 218.

54. Chief of Naval Operations, Adm. Harold R. Stark, and U.S. Army Chief of Staff, Gen. George C. Marshall, joint secret dispatch to the commanding generals of Hawaii and the Philippines; army subordinates; Commander-in-Chief United States Pacific; Commander-in-Chief United States Atlantic; Commander-in-Chief U.S. Asiatic Fleet; Commander Fifteenth Naval District, headquartered in the Panama Canal Zone; and Special Naval Observer in London, Rear Adm. Robert L. Ghormley, 25 July 1941, in International Military Tribunal for the Far East, *The Tokyo War Crimes Trial*, comp. R. John Prichard and Sonia Magbanua Zaide (repr. New York: Garland, 1981) [hereafter IMTFE], vol. 11, pp. 25319–21. I have taken the liberty of changing the punctuation, replacing *x* with periods.

55. FRUS, *Japan: 1931–1941*, vol. 2, p. 266.

56. William Logan, Jr., American associate counsel for Kido Koichi, in IMTFE, vol. 15, pp. 36970–72.

57. Herbert P. Bix, *Hirohito and the Making of Modern Japan* (New York: HarperCollins, 2000), p. 400; Mark A. Stoler, *Allies and Adversaries: The Joint Chiefs of Staff, the Grand Alliance, and U.S. Strategy in World War II* (Chapel Hill: Univ. of North Carolina Press, 2000), p. 59.

58. Wu Jingping, "Sino-American Lend-Lease Relations during the War against Japan," pp. 53, 59–60.

59. British Embassy to the Department of State, 3 March 1941, in U.S. State Dept., *Foreign Relations of the United States Diplomatic Papers 1941: The Far East*, vol. 4 (Washington, D.C.: GPO, 1956) [hereafter FRUS, 1941, *Far East*], pp. 788–90 [emphasis in original].

60. Ibid., pp. 790–91.

61. Sumner Welles, Acting Secretary of State, to the Collectors of Customs, 1 August 1941, in FRUS, 1941, *Far East,* vol. 4, p. 850.

62. Anderson, "1941 De Facto Embargo on Oil to Japan," pp. 201–31.

63. Eguchi Kei-ichi, *Short History of the Fifteen-Year War,* p. 162; 近藤新治 [Kondō Shinji], "物的国力判断」" [An Evaluation of National Material Strength], in *Great East Asian War,* ed. Okumura Fusao and Kondō Shinji, pp. 212–18.

64. 糸永 新 [Itonaga Arata], "開戦前の日米戦争計画" [Prewar Japanese and U.S. War Plans], in *Great East Asian War,* ed. Okumura Fusao and Kondō Shinji, pp. 280–84.

65. Baer, *One Hundred Years of Sea Power,* pp. 134–37, 149–51; Asada, *From Mahan to Pearl Harbor,* pp. 240–41; Goldberg, *Foreign Policy of Japan,* pp. 120–21, 282–85.

66. Ambassador Joseph C. Grew, report of meeting with Foreign Minister Tōgō Shigenori, 10 November 1941, in IMTFE, vol. 11, p. 25936.

67. Gen. Tōjō Hideki, testimony, 29 December 1947, in IMTFE, vol. 15, pp. 36277, 36281.

68. Ben Bruce Blakeney, American associate counsel for Umezu Yoshijirō, in IMTFE, vol. 11, pp. 25656–57.

69. 幕内光雄 [Maku'uchi Mitsuo], 満州国警察外史 [An Unofficial History of the Manchukuo Police] (Tokyo: 三一書房, 1996), p. 147.

70. Ambassador to the United States Nomura Kichisaburō to Foreign Minister Adm. Toyoda Teijirō, 23 October 1941, in IMTFE, vol. 11, p. 25844.

71. Ambassador Nomura Kichisaburō, statement to President Franklin D. Roosevelt, 10 November 1941, in IMTFE, vol. 11, p. 25981.

72. Quotation from Anderson, "1941 De Facto Embargo on Oil to Japan," p. 203.

73. FRUS, 1940, *Far East,* vol. 4, p. 576.

74. Director, War Plans Division Richmond K. Turner to Chief of Naval Operations Harold R. Stark, "Study of the Effect of an Embargo of Trade between the United States and Japan," 19 July 1941, in IMTFE, vol. 11, pp. 25341–50; Adm. Harold R. Stark, testimony before the Senate, 4 January 1946, in IMTFE, vol. 11, pp. 25335–36.

75. FRUS, 1940, *Far East,* vol. 4, pp. 582, 589.

76. Michael Barnhart, "Hornbeck Was Right: The Realist Approach to American Policy toward Japan," in *Pearl Harbor Reexamined: Prologue to the Pacific War,* eds. Hilary Conroy and Harry Wray (Honolulu: Univ. of Hawai'i Press, 1990), pp. 67, 70.

77. Adviser on Political Relations Stanley K. Hornbeck to Under Secretary of State Benjamin S. Welles, 24 July 1940, in FRUS, 1940, *Far East,* vol. 4, pp. 588–89.

78. Tōjō Hideki, testimony, 29 December 1947, in IMTFE, vol. 15, pp. 36196, 36271–76.

79. Adm. Kondo Nobutaka, testimony, 25 August 1947, in IMTFE, vol. 11, pp. 26567, 26664, 24666–68.

80. Kiyose Ichirō, Japanese chief counsel for Tōjō Hideki, in IMTFE, vol. 7, pp. 17089–90. The other two were U.S. aid to Chiang Kai-shek and the encirclement of Japan by the United States in cooperation with Great Britain and the Netherlands.

81. Kiyose Ichirō, Japanese chief counsel for Tōjō Hideki, in IMTFE, vol. 7, p. 17094.

82. Takahashi Toshitsugu, Japanese chief counsel for Adm. Shimada Shigetarō, in IMTFE, vol. 10, pp. 24791–92.

83. Edward J. Drea, *In the Service of the Emperor: Essays on the Imperial Japanese Army* (Lincoln: Univ. of Nebraska Press, 1998), p. 30; David P. Barrett, "Introduction: Occupied China and the Limits of Accommodation," in *Chinese Collaboration with Japan, 1932–1945,* ed. David P. Barrett and Larry N. Shyu (Stanford, Calif.: Stanford Univ. Press, 2001), pp. 3–4.

84. Quotation from Anderson, "1941 De Facto Embargo on Oil to Japan," p. 203.

85. David J. Lu, *Japan: A Documentary History,* vol. 2, *The Late Tokugawa Period to the Present* (Armonk, N.Y.: M. E. Sharpe, 1997), p. 427; Meirion Harries and Susie Harries, *Soldiers of the Sun: The Rise and the Fall of the Imperial Japanese Army* (New York: Random House, 1991), p. 295; Nobutaka Ike, trans. and ed., *Japan's Decision for War: Records of the 1941 Policy Conferences* (Stanford, Calif.: Stanford Univ. Press, 1967), p. 223.

86. Nobutaka Ike, *Japan's Decision for War,* p. 239 [brackets inserted by translator].

87. Quotation from Alvin D. Coox, "The Pacific War," in *The Cambridge History of Japan,* ed. John W. Hall, Marius B. Jansen, Madoka Kanai, and Denis Twitchett, vol. 6, *The Twentieth Century* (Cambridge, U.K.: Cambridge Univ. Press, 1988), p. 329.

CHAPTER FIVE

After the Fall of South Vietnam
Humanitarian Assistance in the South China Sea
JAN K. HERMAN

The nature of the 1975 humanitarian crisis in South Vietnam, which was the result of the Vietnam War's chaotic conclusion, was not altogether unfamiliar to those who had witnessed the aftermath of the first Indochina war in 1954.[1] Perhaps the greatest humanitarian assistance mission accomplished by the U.S. Navy in the latter half of the twentieth century occurred at the end of the first Indochina war, during which the communist Vietminh, based in northern Vietnam, overthrew French colonial rule. Under the Geneva terms that ended that war in 1954, the Vietnamese could decide where they wished to settle. Few in the south chose to go north, but with the collapse of French rule, hundreds of thousands of refugees streamed south to escape the communists.

On that occasion the U.S. Navy was called on to conduct Operation PASSAGE TO FREEDOM, a mission that also had an important medical component. Navy physicians and hospital corpsmen provided medical care for the refugees in camps set up near Haiphong, the port of embarkation for the refugees. Those camps were complete with tents, potable water, food, and medical care. Preventive medicine teams worked diligently to control the rodent and insect populations, spray for malarial mosquitoes, and purify water. By the time PASSAGE TO FREEDOM was completed, Navy ships had evacuated more than 860,000 refugees to South Vietnam.[2]

In 1975, the U.S. Navy was tasked yet again, this time to assist many thousands of South Vietnamese intent on leaving communist Vietnam, often permanently. Some commentators have compared the U.S. Navy operation in 1954 to the events that unfolded in the spring of 1975, but this comparison only goes so far. The mass exodus from North Vietnam in 1954 occurred after hostilities had ended. In addition, the evacuation from north to south on board Navy ships took place during a period of three months and went relatively smoothly.[3] By contrast, the rapid demise of the South Vietnamese government during the spring of 1975 and the ensuing refugee crisis occurred during an active conflict, and the U.S. Navy was given little or no warning that its services would be required to assist fleeing Vietnamese military personnel and civilians.

Background to the Crisis

On 27 January 1973, the United States, the Democratic Republic of Vietnam, the Republic of Vietnam, and the Provisional Revolutionary Government (i.e., the Vietcong) signed what became known as the Paris Peace Accords. The agreement called for a cease-fire in place, allowing both the North and South Vietnamese armies to hold the positions they already occupied. The terms also allowed for those armies to resupply during the cease-fire. Other provisions spelled out terms for the release of American prisoners of war, repatriation of the dead, and future negotiations between North and South Vietnam for eventual reunification.

Up until 1975, that document provided the United States a face-saving solution to what had become the longest war in American history. But the Paris Peace Accords merely delayed the inevitable and offered a "decent interval," in the phrase of a former chief analyst of North Vietnamese strategy for the Central Intelligence Agency, Frank Snepp.[4] The cease-fire gave the North Vietnamese an opportunity to rebuild their strength in areas they occupied in northern South Vietnam, to stockpile munitions and other supplies, and to construct a vast network of roads, oil pipelines, and radio networks in preparation for what was to be their final offensive.[5]

On 1 March 1975 the communists struck with a ferocity that staggered the South Vietnamese defenders. By the close of the month the Army of the Republic of Vietnam was hard pressed on all fronts. The People's Army of Vietnam now fought a conventional war with tanks and artillery, this time without the threat of B-52s and U.S. troops to slow its advance. Three North Vietnamese divisions captured the Central Highlands town of Banmethuat, then sliced eastward, effectively cutting South Vietnam in two. North Vietnamese tanks also rolled south along coastal Route 1. Names that had etched deep scars in the American psyche after years of war now took the headlines again: Chulai, Hue, Danang, Quinhon, Cam Ranh Bay, Nhatrang.

The fall of South Vietnam's second-largest city, Danang, portended a humanitarian crisis of unprecedented dimensions; it was a dress rehearsal for what in a few weeks would become commonplace. Mobs of refugees sought escape at Danang's port. Fleeing men, women, and children crawled over docks like ants, some wading into the harbor in pursuit of ships, tugs, fishing boats, and barges that had already left their piers. Many Vietnamese drowned in the attempt.

The Humanitarian Crisis Unfolds

On 25 March 1975, the U.S. Navy alerted ten auxiliary transports to stand by for refugee evacuation—SS *American Racer,* SS *Green Forest,* SS *Green Port,* SS *Green Wave,* SS *Pioneer Commander,* SS *Pioneer Contender,* SS *Transcolorado,* USNS *Greenville Victory,* USNS *Sgt. Andrew Miller,* and USNS *Sgt. Truman Kimbro.*[6] Some refugees managed to escape Danang by sea, some in barges towed by tugs supplied by the Navy, others on board the transports named. The relentless communist advance sparked a chain reaction, as port after port fell to the invaders. Chaotic radio intercepts from the evacuation ships told of South Vietnamese army deserters selling scarce water supplies to refugees. On some of these vessels, firefights between rival soldiers broke out over food and water. The refugees were often caught in the cross fire, many being killed and thrown into the sea.

Conditions were almost indescribable, according to Lt. Cdr. Daniel Daly, an aide to Rear Adm. Donald Whitmire, commander of the Seventh Fleet's Task Force 76 and in overall charge of the evacuation: "[They] were armed government deserters or Vietnamese soldiers somehow separated from their units among the refugees. We were afraid that fights would break out on those ships. We had visions of soldiers machine-gunning someone with a thousand people standing behind the targets being hit by the bullets that missed. There was no place for anyone to go."[7]

Daly recalls that fatalities on those ships were becoming unacceptable. When Vietnamese army deserters hijacked USNS *Greenville Victory* on 3 April, Whitmire put squads of U.S. Marines on board the merchant ships to protect the crews. Daly recorded a radio exchange between Whitmire and one of those Marines on board the contract ship SS *Transcolorado:*

Admiral: "Son, this is Admiral Whitmire. I want you to tell me what conditions are really like in your ship."

Marine: "Begging your pardon, sir, but I am currently standing in two inches of shit. There are no latrines on this ship for the refugees. They just squat where they are. The stench is unbelievable.

"About two hours ago I saw a baby being born. As its head came out of the mother, it plowed a furrow in the shit on the deck. About ten minutes ago, I saw the bodies of both the baby and the mother thrown overboard. Someone gets thrown overboard about every fifteen minutes."

Daly vividly remembers watching "tears flow down Admiral Whitmire's face as he listened. We all knew we were witnessing a world-class tragedy."[8]

By the third week of April, the enemy had effectively neutralized what remained of South Vietnamese forces and was approaching Saigon from all directions. Days prior to the fall of the capital, the thousands of panicked refugees attempted to flee the country in anything that would float or fly.

Lt. Robert Lemke was on board USS *Kirk* (DE 1087), a 438-foot destroyer escort. *Kirk* was part of Task Force 76, cruising just off the South Vietnamese coast. As the war reached its tragic climax in the last week of April, that task force of U.S. Navy ships received a new mission: to support the evacuation of an estimated six thousand Americans, mainly embassy personnel and military advisers. But the task force was also assigned the job of securing the escape of "sensitive" South Vietnamese who had worked for the United States during the war. Their very survival would be in question once the North Vietnamese took control. Their numbers were estimated to be in the thousands, not counting their dependents.

Lemke one morning wandered into the ship's Combat Information Center (CIC) before breakfast to catch up on the operations. A large radar screen that consolidated information from the other radar displays was prominent and hard to miss. One look put everything into perspective—distance to the coast and the positions of other ships and their movements. Each green blip was a ship or floating object. One glance enabled the observer to mark these ships' locations on a master grid.

What seemed odd to Lemke was the shoreline, which appeared fuzzy and out of focus. He went topside to the flying bridge and through large binoculars scanned the brightening horizon. The mystery of the blurry radar screen instantly cleared up. Hundreds of boats were heading out to sea in *Kirk*'s direction. Lemke later recalled, "The radar looked a little fuzzy only because there was so much activity on the water."[9]

As the vessels approached, he noted every type of watercraft from small fishing boats to rubber rafts. The lieutenant was shocked to see a small wooden dugout to which a man, woman, and two children clung for dear life. "On that dugout were all the family possessions, including a small motorbike. These people were simply paddling out to sea hoping to get to the rescue ships," he remembers.[10]

By this time, *Kirk*'s commanding officer, Cdr. Paul Jacobs, had made his way to CIC and was looking at a radarscope in utter amazement. The screen was overwhelmed by tiny images flowing together into a single blob. "There were so many contacts that the screen was becoming white as small boats were heading out to sea. It looked like Dunkirk in reverse."[11]

Lemke and the crew of USS *Kirk* were not the only Navy personnel to witness the unfolding humanitarian disaster. Up and down the coast, boats, rafts, and even canoes loaded to the gunwales fogged many a radar screen. On board USS *Cook* (DE 1083), *Kirk*'s sister ship, the executive officer, Lt. Cdr. Ray Addicott, beheld a sea dotted by small boats. He noted that several contract ships from the Military Sealift Command were already taking refugees on board. Within hours, the sky would also be smeared with the exhausts of countless South Vietnamese air force and army helicopters, packed with refugees fleeing their homeland. Hospital Corpsman Second Class (HM2) Randy Hudson, a crewman of the carrier USS *Hancock* (CVA 19), later commented that he was surprised there were no midair collisions: "They were coming from all over and from every direction, and so frequently that the sky was dark from jet exhaust."[12] How would the men of Task Force 76 provide food, water, medical care, and comfort to dispirited people who had just lost everything, including their homeland?

Operation FREQUENT WIND

The evacuation of noncombatants from South Vietnam was not well organized. The ambassador to South Vietnam, Graham A. Martin, had long observed a policy of not preparing for an evacuation, arguing that closing the embassy or making other visible preparations for withdrawal would only panic the South Vietnamese government and that the beleaguered nation would then descend into chaos. Despite pleas from both civilian and military advisers to devise an effective evacuation plan, Martin greatly complicated the situation by refusing even to consider the contingency.

With the North Vietnamese armies now at the gates of Saigon, the very chaos Ambassador Martin had hoped to avoid had come to pass. Enemy rockets and mortars rained down on Tan Son Nhut Airport at dawn on 29 April, rendering most runways unusable. Plan B—Operation FREQUENT WIND, a backup plan (hastily put together by Task Force 76 with Pentagon and presidential concurrence and approved at the last minute by the ambassador) that entailed the use of Navy, Marine, and Air Force helicopters—became the only viable option. That strategy called for CH-53 and CH-46 helicopters, staged from carriers and amphibious support ships offshore, to fly into Saigon and land at predetermined rendezvous sites such as soccer fields, racetracks, and parks. Those helicopters would then embark Americans and "sensitive" Vietnamese. After each load of evacuees had been safely delivered to the task force ships, the helicopters would refuel and return to Saigon until all had been safely transported out of the city.

Despite Ambassador Martin's failure to prepare or to keep in close contact with the naval task force offshore, the shuttle mission began quickly, on the morning of 28 April. Bing Crosby's hit song "White Christmas," broadcast over a Saigon radio station, was the signal for evacuees to assemble at predetermined rendezvous locations. As American helicopters headed back out to sea with their human cargoes, Navy, Marine, and Air Force pilots suddenly noted the sky behind them dotted with other helicopters. South

Vietnamese air force and army "Hueys" (Bell UH-1s) packed with refugees were heading out to sea, seeking any deck that would offer them refuge. It was these aircraft that were now showing up on radar screens throughout the task force.

USS *Kirk*'s chief engineer, Lt. Hugh Doyle, saw the situation for what it was: "A pilot had a Huey fully loaded with fuel. His family is standing next to him, and out on the horizon he knows there are U.S. ships. It doesn't take a genius to put it all together and say, 'Kids! Get in the airplane. We're going!' We had no advance warning. They just started coming."[13]

Just before 11 AM on 29 April, sailors in *Kirk*'s CIC reported to the bridge an inbound South Vietnamese helicopter, which then flew overhead and out of sight. *Kirk*'s crew noted that the Vietnamese helicopters passed up their relatively small ship looking for bigger decks to land on. Nevertheless, some of the officers saw the possibilities of getting directly involved in the action and bringing home a trophy or two. Doyle recalls, "Wouldn't it be great to grab a helicopter? Wouldn't it be great to take part in this?"[14]

With the captain's permission, a member of *Kirk*'s crew who spoke rudimentary Vietnamese began broadcasting an invitation to Vietnamese fliers looking for a place to land. As an antisubmarine platform, the destroyer escort had a small flight deck for its Light Airborne Multipurpose System (LAMPS) helicopter, which was now out of order and housed in its retractable hangar.

"Be careful what you wish for" might have crossed someone's mind as Vietnamese Hueys suddenly began swarming above the flight deck. More than one Huey circling the ship had as many as twenty people crammed together; the aircraft was designed for fewer than half that number. Following one landing, a crewman observed that four or five people were grasping with one finger a single D ring attached to the aircraft's deck.

After taking two helicopters on board, the destroyer escort's small flight deck was at capacity. Jacobs made an instant decision. "Over the side," he ordered, and crew members quickly began dragging the aircraft to the deck edge and dumping them overboard to make room for more landings. This exercise of jettisoning helicopters became routine throughout the task force as South Vietnamese Hueys descended on the fleet and—without authorization—began landing on their decks. Many other choppers, once they were out of fuel, ditched in the ocean, with great loss of life.

As the Hueys landed on board *Kirk* and the refugees disembarked, many crewmen at first felt uneasy and suspicious. No one could be absolutely sure that all the "guests" were harmless refugees. Perhaps Vietcong or North Vietnamese infiltrators lurked among the refugees, bent on taking over the ship. The crew had already heard horrifying stories of murder and mayhem that had occurred on overcrowded transports.

With the arrival of each successive aircraft and the disembarkation of its passengers, men assigned to a security detail relieved the Vietnamese of their weapons. Although the evacuees seemed to pose no threat, armed guards remained alert. Access to certain parts of the ship was curtailed, and, when necessary, refugees were assigned escorts. But most of these people were not peasants from the countryside or the poor refugees Lemke had recently seen escaping in a dugout. They were fairly well-off and from South Vietnam's upper classes. Many were families of aircraft's pilots. The uneasiness soon dissipated as the crew recognized the scope of the tragedy that had befallen these people now without a country.

"You could tell they were scared," Aircrewman (Mechanical) Third Class (AW3) Donald Cox later recalled. "They were almost in shock as you looked at their faces. The children, of course, were crying and scared. The women were just following along and basically would do whatever was needed. The men were trying to protect their families. They were doing everything they could to try to survive."[15]

In the blink of an eye, officers and men began converting their man-of-war into a humanitarian-assistance ship. With ten to twenty people on board each helicopter, the refugee population grew rapidly. The ship's heads were made available for their sanitary needs, and the mess crew soon provided water and hot food on deck to the new arrivals. Very quickly, officers and men set up a holding area on the second level above the main deck where the refugees could rest and take a breather after their recent ordeal. Crewmen spread blankets and mats on the steel decks and set up lean-tos, canvas tarps, plastic sheeting, and awnings to shade them from the oppressive sun and tropical rain. Many sailors, trained as warriors, comforted distraught mothers and babies and brought them refreshments and other sustenance. Young sailors tenderly held babies or aided their mothers in diapering the infants and toddlers, bringing smiles and laughter to refugees who faced uncertain futures.

Not far away from where *Kirk* was operating, other refugees were being received as well. On board the carrier *Hancock,* HM2 Hudson heard from one of the senior medical officers that the refugees would be coming from a plague-endemic area. As a safety precaution, members of the crew received shots if they had not yet had plague immunization. When the refugees came on board, they were dusted with the insecticide lindane. As Hudson later recalled, "That was my first encounter with these folks when they came off the helicopters and into the superstructure. Prior to that, we were given some rudimentary Vietnamese lessons. I don't know whether we were speaking gibberish or we were actually speaking the language. *Yamaki,* which means 'Cover your eyes, and then turn around so we can spray you down.' In retrospect, I wonder if any of that spraying was very effective or even necessary. It was kind of a dignity issue to me. I looked at it several years later and said, 'What a welcome to America!'"[16]

Like the refugees who had landed on board *Kirk,* these former citizens of South Vietnam appeared to be from its upper classes. Hudson noted that "they weren't in wretched condition. They were from Saigon, a big city. If you compared them to us, they were mostly middle class. None of them were in rags. I suspect that many were pretty frightened having taken a helicopter ride. They had just left their country—their home. I don't know if anyone had an outright panic attack, but there was definitely an air of excitement and urgency. 'Come on! Get out of the helicopter! Get on down here!'"[17]

By late afternoon of 29 April, helicopter activity on board *Kirk* had slowed considerably, but not before fifteen helicopters had landed, discharging a total of 157 men, women, and children. The following morning a far more dramatic sight awaited the crew. Hundreds of Vietnamese vessels were now fleeing South Vietnam. Nearby, larger evacuation ships stood by to embark some of the refugees. One of them had already taken on board hundreds of refugees, reminding *Kirk*'s chief engineer of a Hershey bar lying on a summer sidewalk and just crawling with ants.[18]

The contrast between these refugees and those on the various helicopters was remarkable. "The helo people were relatively calm," Doyle noted. "The Vietnamese fishermen and peasants who were coming out in these boats, on the other hand, were just in a frenzy."[19] By this time *Kirk* had received orders not to rescue any of the new boat refugees but instead to stand by and protect the freighters assigned to take on these now-displaced persons. At midday the destroyer escort rendezvoused with the contract SS *Green Port* and transferred all of its 157 refugees to that freighter.

Mission Creep: Saving the South Vietnamese Navy

Many thought their job was done, but at 9:30 on the night of 30 April, *Kirk*'s captain received a strange order from Rear Admiral Whitmire—to approach the flagship, USS *Blue Ridge* (LCC 19), to pick up a civilian passenger. Whitmire told Jacobs that USS *Kirk* had been chosen for a special mission and that Jacobs would be taking his orders from Richard Armitage, an agent working for the Secretary of Defense. Armitage, when he arrived on board, explained the mission and its importance. He briefly recounted how he had earlier been ordered to save or destroy as much sensitive material and technology as possible so it would not fall into the hands of the North Vietnamese. But South Vietnam's sudden collapse had shortened the timetable. Most of the Vietnamese army had already surrendered. But the South Vietnamese navy was a different story. This young agent explained that senior South Vietnamese naval officers had no intention of surrendering their ships.

Kirk would now rescue those vessels, and Armitage outlined how. Steaming alone, the ship would rendezvous with the remaining South Vietnamese ships at Con Son Island, more than 120 miles southwest of Vung Tau, where he and the South Vietnamese Chief of Naval Operations would supervise their escape to the Philippines. Faced with skepticism from *Kirk*'s officers, Armitage emphasized that the gamble was worth taking. If they didn't carry out this mission, the ships could not be saved and their personnel would most likely be slaughtered by the North Vietnamese. Jacobs immediately ordered a new course set for Con Son Island. Another chapter of USS *Kirk*'s adventure was about to begin.

Planning for the new mission had actually begun several days earlier in an office at the South Vietnamese navy's headquarters on the Saigon River. By then the North Vietnamese army was at the city's gates. At South Vietnamese navy headquarters, Capt. Kiem Do, deputy chief of staff for operations, met with his old friend Armitage. The two had worked together on many other missions during the war. Armitage told him that he wanted to discuss evacuating the South Vietnamese fleet before the communists took over Vietnam. They agreed to gather the fleet at Con Son, strategically located relatively close to Saigon and the Mekong Delta.

The arrival of communist troops, however, moved up the schedule. Armitage again met with Captain Do and other officials of the Vietnamese navy and told them that rather than leaving on 3–4 May, the original plan, they would have to evacuate that very evening, 29 April. Armitage would meet them at Con Son Island. Armitage advised Do that the Vietnamese should send all the major ships they had not destroyed to Con Son with as many people on board as possible. Armitage then boarded a helicopter to get out to USS *Blue Ridge* to inform Rear Admiral Whitmire of what he had just arranged.

Armitage's "deal" with the South Vietnamese, in which the U.S. Navy would "rescue" what remained of their fleet, had not been authorized by his superiors back at the Pentagon. The plan was conceived by Armitage and Do alone: "When I showed up on the *Blue Ridge*, I had nothing. I had no wallet. I had no passport. I had no identification. And I looked around when I came off the helo and saw the flag lieutenant. I said, 'Lieutenant. This is going to be hard to believe but I'm on a mission from the Secretary of Defense and I need to speak to Admiral Whitmire.'"[20] Now this thirty-year-old was on board *Kirk* and calling the shots. It was Wednesday, 30 April 1975.

When *Kirk* approached Con Son Island as dawn broke, the crew saw scores of Vietnamese ships, their decks packed with refugees. Jacobs would recall the sight: "As we approached we could see their fleet there . . . and swift boats [fast patrol craft] just milling around dead in the water. Some of them were anchored, some were not. They were adrift. You could look over and see the ships just loaded with people all the way up to the bridge. I would estimate 2,000 or 3,000 people on one of these Coast Guard

WHECs [high-endurance cutters]. I said, 'Oh, my God!' . . . no water, no food—and this is going to be an insurmountable problem. How are we going to pull this off?'"[21]

Operations Specialist Second Class James Bongaard, one of Kirk's radarmen, was overwhelmed by what he saw. "There were just thousands of people on top of this deck. I can't really describe the look on their faces. I can only imagine what they might be going through. Elation that they got away. And number two, where are they going? They have no idea where. They're fleeing so in one way they're happy. But in another way they don't know where they're going. It's sort of a blank, odd stare."[22]

"They were just crammed in there just as tight as you could get," Machinist's Mate Fireman Kent Chipman remembers. "I don't know how many people were on each ship below deck. But above deck, there were just thousands of people, as many as you could get on board. And they were sitting, standing. They were just overloaded to the max."[23]

Armitage later recalled, "[I saw] 29 or 30 ships and about 31,000 people on board them. So the Kirk for me was ideal. They [Kirk] could communicate with the rest of the U.S. fleet. They would go with us across to the Philippines and be able to rescue any folks who might be in harm's way. Some had been wounded. Some were pregnant. All were sick after a while and I needed some way to take care of those folks. And the Kirk for me was perfect."[24]

Jacobs immediately briefed the crew on Kirk's impending mission. But he wondered how he and his small ship would be able to provide humanitarian assistance to an estimated thirty thousand people, as well as lead them safely across nearly a thousand miles of the South China Sea to the Philippines.

The immediate goal was to make order out of chaos. Kirk began corralling the ships and shuffling them into various positions. The first task was to transfer Armitage to the Vietnamese flagship so he could confer with the South Vietnamese Chief of Naval Operations and his staff. Then several members of Kirk's crew, including enginemen, electricians, machinist's mates, and the chief hospital corpsman, went from ship to ship to determine which of the Vietnamese vessels required assistance. Jacobs remembers the sorry state of some of those ships. "Sometimes we couldn't even pull the anchor up. We'd have to slip it—break it loose and let it drop. Some of them got under way without any anchor."[25] A number of ships could not start their engines, and Kirk's mechanics worked to remedy those situations.

Some of the vessels leaving Vietnam jammed with refugees were barely seaworthy. Several fishing boats had never before even ventured far from land. One landing ship had defective bow doors that would not close completely and was taking in water faster than its pumps could expel it. Before it sank, its passengers were transferred to the South Vietnamese flagship, *Tran Nhat Duat.*

The outcome of *Kirk's* mission was anything but certain. How would the North Vietnamese victors react to the potential escape of what remained of the South Vietnamese navy? The destroyer escort was well equipped to fight Soviet submarines but with its single five-inch deck gun was virtually defenseless against hostile aircraft. And that threat was very real. By now most South Vietnamese airfields, along with fighter aircraft, were in the hands of the communists. Moreover, some South Vietnamese pilots had already defected and were flying missions against their former countrymen. "We were like sitting ducks," recalls Jacobs. "They could have taken the planes off, taken the *Kirk* out and all the Vietnamese ships."[26] To emphasize the point, an unidentified low-flying jet appeared off *Kirk's* starboard bow. Fortunately, the aircraft flew on; the crew refocused its attention on the task at hand—aiding refugees.

Kirk finally got under way with its sister ship USS *Cook,* which had joined the effort. *Kirk* now led a very long formation of warships and fishing boats in two parallel columns, about a mile apart, sixteen ships in each. The formation extended five miles, the destroyer escort in the lead. The convoy could steam only as fast as the slowest vessel, a speed that would seldom exceed five knots. All ships—no matter what their condition—sought *Kirk's* and *Cook's* protection and were completely dependent on those ships' generosity for food, water, and fuel.

The Mission Changes

As the procession of ships moved eastward across the South China Sea, the entire idea of having to defend it against attack quickly evaporated. There were no attacks. The mission now evolved into taking *Kirk's* chief hospital corpsman, Stephen Burwinkel, on house calls and delivering water, rice, and medicine. His responsibility for the well-being of an estimated thirty thousand Vietnamese was unheard-of in U.S. Navy history. But this hospital corpsman was no amateur.

Before becoming part of *Kirk's* commissioning crew in 1972, Burwinkel had seen duty at a U.S. Navy hospital in Morocco, served on two ships, and tended wounded Marines in Vietnam. The thirty-four-year-old Cincinnati native was beloved by his crew, not only for his cool, even temperament and wry sense of humor but also for the consummate skill he brought to his profession. Burwinkel was an independent-duty corpsman—that is, a highly trained health-care professional able to run the medical department on any Navy vessel without an assigned physician. "Chief Burwinkel was just tireless," Doyle would recall. "He was a country doctor making house calls. But he had 30,000 patients and he didn't have a little jeep to drive around in. He had a boat."[27]

Doyle was referring to a swift boat, which *Kirk*'s crew sent up and down the columns of Vietnamese ships. Burwinkel would go on board each ship to hold sick call and provide whatever health care he could. Besides his medical kit he wore a pistol on his hip, not knowing whether any of those vessels harbored North Vietnamese who might do him harm.

Following a long day of making rounds, Burwinkel would return to the destroyer escort, grab a bite and a catnap, replenish his supplies, and head back out. "How he did it is beyond me," Doyle would recollect. "In short, he's a wonderful man and a wonderful doctor, and he was absolutely what we needed at that time. He's not a doctor, of course. We call[ed] him 'Doc.' He's a hospital corpsman but he's an independent duty hospital corpsman and very capable. I would have anointed him doctor right after we got into Subic because of what he did."[28]

Operations Specialist James Bongaard reflected the feelings of many fellow crew members. "A lot of people like myself who saw these people up close that one day early on knew that we had to do everything possible to help them. For a lot of us who had been in the Navy just a couple of years, we had never really done anything. We'd go out and play war games and circle around, but we never really did anything of any accomplishment. Now, all of a sudden, we had someone to take care of. We were doing something special. We weren't hunting people down. We weren't trying to shoot anybody. We would give up sleep, give up our off-time to do anything we could to haul rice, give them water, do whatever we could."[29]

But making a difference was indeed difficult. Despite his skill and limitless energy and the assistance of a junior corpsman, Hospital Corpsman Third Class Mark Falkenberg, Chief Burwinkel was hard pressed. Dehydration and diarrhea ran rampant on board the overcrowded and unsanitary ships. Because of overtaxed and often nonworking toilets, refugees relieved themselves in communal buckets, on the deck, or over the side. Both *Kirk* and *Cook* sailors found it necessary to come alongside many of these ships and train their fire hoses on decks besmeared with feces.

Lt. Cdr. Ray Addicott, *Cook*'s executive officer, vividly remembers the squalor that greeted his ship as it moved among the fleet: "The people were almost on top of each other. It was nasty. Our sanitation team would come in and hose down all the decks. A lot of people would spread their clothes out so we could also hose the clothes down."[30]

Cook's skipper, Cdr. Jerry McMurry, later recalled the conditions on one of the Vietnamese landing ships: "The ship was loaded with what I estimated were 4,000 people, and the decks were just running with urine. We used fire hoses to wash down those decks, and then we tried to get enough freshwater on board because it was hotter than hell during the day—up to 110."[31]

Conjunctivitis, also called "pinkeye," was epidemic. "I saw many cases of conjunctivitis caused by the unsanitary conditions and exposure to the sun," Burwinkel later lamented. The combination of tropical sunlight and contaminated water sent the highly contagious disease raging among the flotilla. Burwinkel recalls, "I was very much afraid of that conjunctivitis spreading because it is a very virulent illness. I was afraid that if I caught it, that would be the end of it."[32]

Before four days had passed the corpsman had gone through his supply of antibiotic ophthalmic ointment to treat the eye disease. He had also expended all his Kaopectate and Lomotil, which he had used to stem the diarrhea epidemic. Burwinkel was out of other drugs and dressings too, as well as two other essential items—diapers and baby formula. Without emergency resupply, Doc Burwinkel and his helpers would be out of business. *Kirk*'s skipper quickly radioed an emergency appeal for medical supplies, and within a day the U.S. Air Force responded. Soon a specially equipped C-130 arrived on the scene from Clark Air Force Base in the Philippines and dropped two fully loaded fifty-five-gallon drums suspended from parachutes. Burwinkel was soon back making his rounds.

Those rounds also meant seeking out near-term pregnant women and taking them on board a commandeered swift boat. Burwinkel had located five women who seemed on the verge of childbirth and brought them on board *Kirk,* where he could monitor their condition. To accommodate the pregnant women the crew had converted a crew's lounge into a maternity ward. Each morning Jacobs visited the women to deliver a pep talk and encourage them to get busy and start having their babies. One of those women, seventeen-year-old Lan Tran, later remembered the morning ritual: "He came every day to our room. He always smile. He told us he want at least one baby to be born on the ship and named after the USS *Kirk*."[33] Despite the captain's cheerleading, none of the women gave birth. Their babies would arrive later.

The motley flotilla plodded steadily eastward across the South China Sea, a body of water notorious for frequent storms and rough seas. Sailors and passengers alike observed the uncharacteristic calm and commented on how fortunate that was. Lemke noted that "some of the ships were not very seaworthy and the mild conditions allowed them to transit safely. The flat seas also enabled *Kirk* to continue using its small boats in transferring people and material back and forth."[34]

Mission Finale

Feeding and providing water to more than thirty thousand refugees were too big a job for *Kirk* and *Cook* alone. Soon other Navy vessels joined the flotilla to lend a hand. Swift boats, motor whaleboats, and a number of landing craft scurried about among the Vietnamese vessels, delivering food, water, fuel, and assistance. USS *Mobile* (LKA 115), an amphibious cargo ship, provided not only rice but the temporary loan of four corpsmen, a physician, and medical supplies. The stores ship USS *Vega* (AF 59) and the tank landing ship USS *Tuscaloosa* (LST 1187) also pitched in, as did *Barbour County* (LST 1195). With their small boats, these ships transferred tons of stores and rice to *Kirk* and *Cook*.

During that first week of May, *Kirk*'s gig (the captain's boat) and motor whaleboat shuttled back and forth among the fleet. Its crew delivered food and water, Chief Burwinkel held sick call, and engineers and machinist's mates repaired cranky diesel engines and bilge pumps. The other American vessels also maneuvered around the formation, providing engineering, medical, and logistical support.

As the fleet finally approached Philippine territorial waters on Monday, 5 May, a diplomatic crisis developed, one that threatened the entire plan and the welfare of the refugees. Ferdinand Marcos, president of the Philippines, suddenly declared that since the Republic of Vietnam no longer existed, the South Vietnamese vessels could not enter Subic Bay or any other port in the Philippines. The dictator was torn between his alliance with the United States and a desire to be an integral part of the new reality in Southeast Asia. Marcos perceived a weakening commitment on the part of the U.S. government to deter communist expansion. If the leader of the free world had abandoned an ally, South Vietnam, what guarantee did he have that it would not leave his nation to the same fate? The changing political landscape meant normalizing relations with communist governments in Cambodia, Laos, and Vietnam. He would not offend the North Vietnamese by allowing the remnants of the South Vietnamese navy into his nation.

As William Sullivan, ambassador to the Philippines, tried to get Marcos to change his mind, the flotilla killed time by tracing a circuitous course off the Philippine coast. Jacobs and the other participating U.S. Navy commanding officers faced a dilemma. Conditions on board the Vietnamese vessels were steadily deteriorating despite their own best efforts. Many refugees had been at sea for more than a week. Some were demoralized, not only by the death of their nation, but by the loss of family members. Others were despondent over having left spouses and children behind. More than a few were reaching the ends of their ropes.

Finally, Marcos and Sullivan reached an agreement. Most of the South Vietnamese vessels had once been American, and now that the South Vietnamese government no longer existed they could be returned to U.S. ownership. Naval personnel, mostly from *Kirk*'s crew, would board the vessels, replace South Vietnamese flags with U.S. flags, and take command. The vessels would then enter Subic Bay as U.S. Navy ships. Shortly after 10 AM on 6 May, personnel transfers to the Vietnamese vessels began. By day's end thirty-nine *Kirk* crewmen had been embarked on board the ships. Lieutenant Lemke was told to deliver orders to each of the Americans on those ships, along with an American flag.

Lt. Rick Sautter, officer in charge of *Kirk*'s LAMPS detachment, would recall the events on the South Vietnamese warship he boarded. "A boat came by and delivered the packet with the American flag. And the ceremony was to be done with as much dignity as possible. It was kind of a feeling of finality. That was the final step in the fact that South Vietnam no longer existed."[35]

Capt. Kiem Do recalls the observance with great emotion: "A young officer came on board our ship and said, 'You'll have to lower the flag and hoist the American flag up and sail in.' I said to him, 'We lost our country. We lost our pride. We lost everything. But please. A last favor. Try to have a ceremony of down the flag and raise the flag up. A ceremony that would save us some face, particularly those people aboard the ship, thousands of them.' Finally we got the approval. Every ship would have a ceremony of change of authority to return those ships to the American Navy. We had a very emotional ceremony. It was right at sunset, 6 or 7 of that day. All the people flocked to the deck and sang the national anthem, crying at the same time to lower their flag and then raise the American flag ceremoniously. So the dignity is there. Even though it is a big loss for us, at least it saved our face and also our dignity."[36]

Once on board the ship Lemke was to command, he later observed, "The ship was silent. . . . Then, as a South Vietnamese officer prepared to lower the South Vietnamese flag, his crew sang a capella the national anthem of their former country. It was a very moving time. As the yellow and red colors were slowly brought down, the refugees joined the crew in singing their national anthem . . . and then in silence the American flag was raised."[37]

At 12:27 PM on Wednesday, 7 May, *Kirk*'s log recorded a Filipino aircraft flying over to check the vessel's identity. Two hours later *Kirk* passed just under a mile to starboard of Grande Island in Subic Bay. AW3 Cox observed that many of the refugees seemed elated once they realized "they finally were safe and that they had a new life ahead of them. And the new life was going to be much better than anything they could have imagined under communist rule."[38] Two and a half hours later the destroyer escort moored at Subic Bay, Republic of the Philippines, ending its five-day, thousand-mile odyssey across the South China Sea.

The refugees did not remain long at Subic Bay. Following the terms of the diplomatic agreement, they boarded vessels either operated or contracted by the Military Sealift Command and within two days were on their way to Guam. In a hastily assembled tent camp, the first of several sites the United States would provide for the Vietnamese, Navy medical personnel again offered their services until the refugees were moved to other

camps in California, Arkansas, Florida, and Pennsylvania—way stations on their jour-
neys to permanent settlement in the United States.

Conclusions

USS *Kirk's* humanitarian accomplishment and those of the other Navy ships that assisted went virtually unnoticed for many years. The mood of Americans in 1975 was that
the long Vietnam nightmare was over; they just wanted to move on. Moreover, the men
of *Kirk* and of the other ships participating in that massive rescue in the South China
Sea never thought they had done anything extraordinary. Feeding refugees and diapering infants were not war-related feats that warriors felt worth sharing with old buddies
in American Legion or Veterans of Foreign Wars halls, and many did not discuss these
humanitarian experiences with family or friends.

For the officers and men of USS *Kirk,* however, those events of forty years ago and
their role in rescuing the South Vietnamese refugees have had a profound impact. Cox
observes that they had gone to Vietnam with expectations of being in combat and had
been trained and prepared for it. But when they got there they found out that combat
was not what was needed: "It was a heart and hand that was needed. We didn't recognize
it at first. We just did our jobs. It was after that that we realized that our Vietnam experience was totally different from our brothers who had walked in the field in combat.
We recognized that it was going to be a positive experience for the rest of our lives. We
were there to save life and not to destroy it."[39]

The architect of the rescue, Armitage, added another perspective regarding the mission:
"Seeing the men—and it was only men then—of the USS *Kirk,* and realizing how much
a part of their lives and what a great capstone this was to their careers, that moved me
that they could feel so good about their involvement in that rescue. I envied them. They
weren't burdened with the former misadventure of Vietnam."[40] Another player in the
drama, Erich von Marbod, who was then a high-ranking official of the Department of
Defense and Armitage's superior, points out the story's real impact. After the war, President Gerald Ford's task force for the resettlement of Indochina refugees relocated more
than 130,000 evacuees from Laos, Cambodia, and Vietnam in communities around
the United States. It was not long before almost all of them became American citizens.
Since *Kirk* and its sister U.S. Navy vessels had saved more than thirty thousand South
Vietnamese refugees, a quarter of Vietnamese refugees resettled in the United States by
Task Force 76 can trace their new beginnings in this nation to that very successful and
unusual humanitarian mission.[41]

Notes

1. This chapter is based largely on Jan K. Herman, *The Lucky Few: The Fall of Saigon and the Rescue Mission of the USS* Kirk (Annapolis, Md.: Naval Institute Press, 2013).

2. Jan K. Herman, *Navy Medicine in Vietnam: Oral Histories from Dien Bien Phu to the Fall of Saigon* (Jefferson, N.C.: McFarland, 2009), p. 9.

3. Stanley Karnow, *Vietnam: A History* (New York: Viking, 1983), p. 666.

4. That phrase became the title of Snepp's controversial 1977 memoir.

5. Karnow, *Vietnam,* p. 65.

6. Edward J. Marolda, *By Sea, Air, and Land: An Illustrated History of the U.S. Navy and the War in Southeast Asia* (Washington, D.C.: Naval Historical Center, 1992), p. 357.

7. Daniel Daly, telephone interview, 10 August 2011.

8. Ibid.

9. Robert Lemke, telephone interview, 29 April 2009.

10. Ibid.

11. Paul Jacobs, interview, Fairfax, Va., 29 December 2006.

12. Randy Hudson, telephone interview, 16 January 2007.

13. Navy Medicine Support Command, *The Lucky Few: The Story of USS* Kirk (U.S. Navy, Bureau of Medicine, Visual Information Directorate, 2010), documentary.

14. Ibid.

15. Ibid.

16. Hudson interview.

17. Ibid.

18. Hugh Doyle, *Edited Transcript of Lt. Hugh J. Doyle's Vietnam Evacuation Tapes,* 2 May 1975–6 May 1975, in Hugh Doyle's collection.

19. Ibid.

20. Navy Medicine Support Command, *Lucky Few.*

21. Ibid.

22. Ibid.

23. Ibid.

24. Ibid.

25. Jacobs interview.

26. Navy Medicine Support Command, *Lucky Few.*

27. Ibid.

28. Ibid.

29. Ibid.

30. Ray Addicott, telephone interview, 27 August 2010.

31. Jerry McMurry, telephone interview, 7 September 2010.

32. Stephen Burwinkel, interview, Pensacola, Fla., 16 December 2008.

33. Navy Medicine Support Command, *Lucky Few.*

34. Ibid.

35. Frederick Sautter, Jr., telephone interview, 2 March 2009.

36. Herman, *Lucky Few,* p. 112.

37. Ibid.

38. Ibid., pp. 113–14.

39. Ibid., p. 122.

40. Richard Armitage, interview, Arlington, Va., 31 October 2008.

41. Erich von Marbod, interview, Gainesville, Va., 25 August 2011.

CHAPTER SIX

Continuing to Serve
Deploying Naval Vessels as Artificial Reefs
TOM WILLIAMS

Naval vessels that are close to the end of their useful lives as part of a fleet or that have already served their full terms of duty can still find important and honorable ways to contribute to the common good. Historically, ships can be sunk as part of gunnery exercises, can be sunk on purpose during wartime to form blockships, or can be turned into naval museums, some of which appear to be strategically placed near major waterways to act as potential blockships in times of war.

On 25 November 2003, President George W. Bush signed into law the National Defense Authorization Act (originally HR 1588, sec. 1013), allowing decommissioned ships to be donated for use as artificial reefs. The first ship in the program was the aircraft carrier USS *Oriskany* (CV 34), which was sunk on 17 May 2006 approximately twenty-four miles south of Pensacola, Florida.[1] This program is intended to reduce the inactive-ship inventory in a "cost-effective and environmentally sound manner."[2]

This chapter will begin by summarizing briefly the historical use of blockships and on-going U.S. Navy programs for sinking ships, during both times of war and peace. Most of this chapter, however, will focus on sinking naval vessels to form artificial reefs. This innovative use of naval ships can play an important economic role for coastal communities by increasing maritime tourism and fishing, even while playing a positive ecological role by boosting local marine life.

Blockships

A "blockship" is a vessel deliberately sunk to prevent the use of a river, canal, or harbor. It may be sunk by a navy defending the waterway, to prevent the ingress of attacking forces, or it may be brought by enemy raiders and used to prevent the waterway from being used by the defenders. This practice goes back many centuries. In the eleventh century, around 1070, five Skuldelev ships were sunk at Roskilde Fjord to prevent the northern Vikings from landing at Roskilde.[3] The ships were excavated in 1962 and identified as vessels of different types, ranging from cargo ships to warships; they are now on display in the Viking Ship Museum in Roskilde, which is the Danish national museum for ships, seafaring, and boatbuilding in the medieval period. Another example of early blockships can be found in the Dutch raid on the Medway and Thames Rivers during the Second Anglo-Dutch War (1665–67), when the Royal Navy sank a number of merchant ships and warships to block attacking forces.

During World War I, on the night of 23 April 1918 British naval forces sank blockships to neutralize the port of Bruges-Zeebrugge, Belgium. Older British ships were sunk in the canal entrance to prevent German ships from leaving port. The port was used by the German navy as a base for submarines and light shipping; the latter was of critical importance, especially in the English Channel. The raid was intended to sink three old cruisers to block the flow of traffic into and out of the port, but the execution did not go as planned. Of the three ships, which were all filled with concrete, only HMS *Intrepid* and *Iphigenia* made it to their destination, which was the narrowest point of the canal; HMS *Thetis* was scuttled prematurely.[4]

Another example of the strategic use of blockships occurred at Scapa Flow, in the Orkney Islands, off the coast of Scotland, where the British placed a naval base in 1904. Scapa Flow has a shallow sandy bottom less than two hundred feet deep and is a natural anchorage for ships. Following Germany's defeat in World War I, its fleet was relocated to Scapa Flow, pending a final decision on its fate by the Paris Peace Conference. On 21 June 1919, after eight months of waiting, Rear Adm. Ludwig von Reuter made the decision to scuttle the German fleet at Scapa Flow; he was not aware that there had been a last-minute extension to finalize the details of the peace treaty.[5] He ordered all seventy-four ships scuttled; the British were only able to save four ships from sinking—*Baden, Nürnberg, Emden,* and *Frankfurt.* According to one estimate, "Over 400,000 tons of modern warships were sunk, the largest loss of shipping in a single day in history."[6]

During World War II, the British again used Scapa Flow as a naval base. However, the defenses constructed during World War I had not been maintained, and on 14 October 1939 a German submarine penetrated the roadstead and sank HMS *Royal Oak,* after which HMS *Iron Duke* was sunk by Luftwaffe bombers. The base was closed in 1956 in recognition of the deferred maintenance, operating cost, and general obsolescence. The assemblage of ships on the bottom of Scapa Flow is now a popular destination for scuba divers and provides a substantial amount of trade and income for the local economy. Divers must first obtain a permit from authorities; they are allowed to enter the wrecks but not to retrieve artifacts located within three hundred feet of any wreck. The wrecks of *Royal Oak* and the dreadnought HMS *Vanguard,* which exploded at anchor during World War I, are war graves protected under the Protection of Military Remains Act of

1986. Another protected site is the wreck off Marwick Head, Orkney, of HMS *Hampshire*, which while carrying Lord Kitchener on 5 June 1916 hit a mine and sank. The 10,850-ton armored cruiser went down in a heavy storm four days after the battle of Jutland; only twelve survived from its crew of 655. It lies in 210 feet of water a mile and a half off Marwick Head, on which the Kitchener Memorial now stands. Only divers of the British armed forces are permitted to visit any military sites.[7]

In China, it was a longtime tactic of the Chinese navy to block any maritime threat to China's rivers and canals by clogging harbors with log booms and chains strung from rows of floating junks. Following Japan's 1937 invasion of China, the Nationalist navy proved inadequate to counter the Imperial Japanese Navy, so the vast bulk of the Chinese naval ships were eventually sunk in the Yangzi River. This effort to block Japan's invasion upriver proved futile. In 1940, Chiang Kai-shek ordered that the Navy Ministry be dissolved.[8] A Chinese naval force that had taken decades to build was quickly disbanded and destroyed to ensure it would not fall into enemy hands.

Beginning in the 1930s, conflict over the use and control of the Suez Canal escalated. By the 1950s the Egyptian government was planning to construct the Aswan High Dam. To help pay for the project, Egypt seized and nationalized the canal, so as to charge higher passage fees. Israel invaded Egypt on 29 October 1956, followed by Britain and France, on the grounds that passage through the canal should be free. In retaliation, the Egyptian blockship *Akka* was towed into place and scuttled, "together with another forty-seven concrete-filled ships, effectively closing the waterway."[9] Eventually Egypt sank a total of fifty ships in the canal to block passage.[10]

Nevertheless, since World War II, with the decrease in naval warfare, there have been fewer instances of the use of blockships. During March 2014, however, a Soviet-era warship, decommissioned in 2011 and designated for scrapping, was sunk with two other Russian naval ships at the entrance to Lake Donuzlav, on Crimea's western coast. The three vessels were sunk so as to fill a gap between two spits of land, in an effort to block the Ukrainian navy from leaving port. Rather than gaining international support for the Russian invasion of Ukraine, this action—plus the land-based invasion of Ukrainian territory by pro-Russian "volunteer" forces—has been widely condemned both in Europe and in the United States.

Many older naval vessels continue to function as museums. The historic preservation of naval vessels can provide economic benefits to communities through increased tourism. Currently there are approximately 187 ships registered in the Historic Naval Ships Association and open to visitors. Examples of U.S. Navy ships that continue to serve in this capacity are *Arizona, Lexington, Midway,* and *Missouri*. Many of these ship museums are located along important channels and in strategic harbors, where if needed they could be quickly relocated to serve as blockships.[11]

Ship-Sinking Exercises

Navies often use old ships for gunnery practice. The U.S. Navy's ship-sinking operations, or exercises, are called SINKEXes, and it conducts most of them at four major locations: north of Kauai, Hawaii; off California; off the East Coast; and off Puerto Rico. The exercises are used to hone "weapons firing skills and proficiency."[12] According to Navy spokesmen, sinking exercises can also enhance fleet readiness by "providing environmentally clean target ships for at-sea live-fire exercises." Chris Johnson, spokesman at Naval Sea Systems Command in Washington, acknowledged in 2012 that 118 ships had been sunk in SINKEXes between 1999 and 2012.[13]

Because of the possibility of severe damage to the environment, these SINKEX activities have been criticized by environmental groups, including the Sierra Club. But the Navy argues that it prepares all vessels used in SINKEXes in strict compliance with Environmental Protection Agency (EPA) regulations. According to a document provided by Lt. Cdr. Paul Macapagal, a Navy spokesman at the Pentagon, "Fleet sink exercises are conducted in compliance with the Marine Protection, Research and Sanctuaries Act (MPRSA). . . . Each ship provided is put through a rigorous cleaning process, which includes the removal of all PCB [polychlorinated biphenyl] transformers and large capacitors, all small capacitors to the greatest extent practical, trash, floatable materials, mercury or fluorocarbon containing materials, and readily detachable solid PCB items."[14]

The problem with these preparations, environmentalists have argued, is that in 1999 the Navy was granted a general permit from the EPA that exempted it from the strictest federal standards governing ocean dumping under MPRSA. According to Colby Self, a member of the Seattle-based Basel Action Network, which has sued to stop the SINKEX program, "They are 'cleaned,' but when you look at the requirements of the cleaning, it's not sufficient. They're not removing anything that's not 'readily detachable.' No scraping, no use of machinery, no removal of machinery. They are not going to open up bulkheads to get at asbestos."[15]

The Navy's response is that SINKEX ships are sunk in deep, remote waters, in at least six thousand feet of water at least fifty nautical miles from land. The Navy conducts its own environmental surveys of the area before any sinkings are authorized to ensure that no humans or marine mammals are harmed. The program has carried out the sinking in 2005 of the forty-year-old aircraft carrier USS *America,* which was sunk in a SINKEX about three hundred nautical miles southeast of Hampton Roads. At this writing in

2012, four ships have been sunk, three off Hawaii in July, and one off Guam in September. But according to Chris Johnson, "No more are planned for 2012."[16]

Historical Use of Artificial Reefs

Artificial reefs have been used for enhancement of commercial fishing in two ways. First, almost immediately after the artificial reef deployment fishermen can target specific species of fish. Second, there is an expectation that over time artificial reefs will resemble local natural reefs, as assemblages including sessile organisms associate with a reef's surface, structure, and surrounding water column and eventually increase biomass at the site. This aspect has led to a redefinition of the use of artificial reefs in the last decade from the historic one of simply fish attractors to a more expansive one that includes the role of ecosystem developers, which provides recreation for scuba divers and other visitors.

Reef making is not new. As discussed previously, blockships have been used since ancient times. The Greek geographer Strabo recorded the use of artificial reefs by the Persians across the Tigris River to obstruct the passage of naval pirates from India.[17] The Roman historian Polybius later recorded that the Romans built a reef across the mouth of the Carthaginian harbor in Sicily during the First Punic War to trap Carthaginians there.[18] Obstructing harbors with sunken ships, logs, or other structures was a common naval tactic. As arsenals got more sophisticated, rocks and logs were replaced by mines and other more destructive devices.

In the United States, the first documented artificial reef was built in 1830, when log huts were sunk off the coast of South Carolina to improve fishing. However, it was not until the latter part of the twentieth century that artificial reefs were supported by community efforts; artificial reefs before this time were built by ad hoc volunteer groups. Most reefs constructed off U.S. coasts have used materials of opportunity, relying on volunteers and materials that were readily available and free, or nearly so.[19]

Ship sinkings not only benefit local communities but can also benefit the government, in terms of disposal of retired military vessels. In 1994, the Atlantic States Marine Fisheries Commission reported that at least 666 steel-hulled vessels had been sunk for reefs since 1974. Forty-one of these ships had been donated to the states by the Maritime Administration (MARAD) pursuant to the Liberty Ship Act (Public Law 92-402, 1974), amended in 1984 by PL 98-623 to include ships other than Liberty ships. Although MARAD ships account for only 6 percent of the total inventory of vessels, they constituted by 1994 almost all the forty-four sinkings of large ships, defined as those over three hundred feet long.[20] Nearly half the 666 ships were very small fishing boats or tugboats no more than seventy-five feet long. There is today a reported demand among

Atlantic and Gulf Coast states for between five and six hundred additional ships just to meet the increasing need for improved fish resources.[21]

MARAD and the Navy have jointly responded to the value of "reefing" retired vessels by establishing an Artificial Reef Program. MARAD maintains the National Defense Reserve Fleet (NDRF) as a reserve of ships for defense and national emergencies. There are three fleet sites: the James River Reserve Fleet, at Fort Eustis, Virginia; the Beaumont Reserve Fleet, in Beaumont, Texas; and the Suisun Bay Reserve Fleet, at Benicia, California. When ships are no longer considered useful for defense or aid missions, MARAD arranges for their responsible disposal.

In 2001, Congress passed the Floyd D. Spence National Defense Authorization Act.[22] This act authorized MARAD to use appropriated funds for the procurement of ship-dismantling and recycling services. Since that time, MARAD's Ship Disposal Program (SDP) has utilized vessel sales and ship-recycling services as the primary means of disposing of obsolete NDRF vessels. The SDP includes reefing as a disposal option and accepts applications from coastal states, U.S. territories and possessions, and foreign governments. This legislation also allows MARAD to provide financial assistance for specific domestic reefing projects.

Using Naval Ships to Create Artificial Reefs

An important nonmilitary use of navies is in reef building. As mentioned above, the 2003 National Defense Authorization Act (originally HR 1588, sec. 1013) allows appropriate decommissioned ships to be donated for use as artificial reefs. This legislation calls on the Navy to accomplish the overall process for artificial reefing to deliver a cost-effective transfer of available naval vessels. This process also provides a viable alternative available to the Navy's Inactive Ships Program, administered under the Naval Sea Systems Command and MARAD, under the Department of Transportation, to reduce the inventory of unneeded vessels.

The Navy's program to sink ships is also known as "Ships 2 Reefs." Its main objective is to reduce the size of the inactive ships inventory in a cost-effective and environmentally sound manner. The program is a partnership of agencies, localities, and the various applicants. The Navy prepares the vessel as an artificial reef through several steps, including environmental remediation in accordance with the EPA's best management practices. Other costs, including the towing and sinking of the ships, are considered as part of cost-sharing proposals from applicants. MARAD coordinates federal agency solicitations and applications for obtaining vessels for use as artificial reefs.[23]

Donation and transfer applications for Navy and MARAD ships for use as artificial reefs may be submitted only by states, commonwealths, territories, and possessions of the United States, and municipal corporations, or political subdivisions thereof. Foreign countries, except by Navy policy, and other foreign applicants are ineligible to apply for or receive obsolete warships, defined as aircraft carriers, battleships, cruisers, destroyers, frigates, and submarines. This policy specifies that applications can be submitted only by local governments, either on their own behalf or in support of private industry. For example, both the *Spiegel Grove* and *Vandenberg* projects were proposed by local entrepreneurs but were applied for by local governments—Florida's Monroe County for *Spiegel Grove* and the City of Key West for *Vandenberg*. The Navy is currently accepting only one application from each state per vessel available for reefing. The first warship offered for donation by the Navy for sinking as an artificial reef was *Oriskany*.

The other ships sunk for reefs have all been MARAD vessels. MARAD recently has updated its own program in two ways: first, MARAD will no longer consider for reefing vessels built before 1985; second, vessels that are within twenty-four months of a more expeditious method of disposal, such as recycling, will not be included. The 1985 date reflects the agency's concerns about PCB products or components in the supply stream used in vessel construction or repairs. If these amendments to the program are continued, there will certainly be a negative impact on the availability of ships for artificial reefs.

These policy amendments were announced to the public in a memorandum dated 13 April 2012. A recent casualty of this policy change is USS *Kawishiwi,* a fleet oiler that was scheduled to be sunk just off Dana Point Harbor, California. Fortunately, a replacement has been found in the same MARAD vessel source, Suisun Bay. USS *Willamette* will be scuttled at the proposed site, while *Kawishiwi* will be placed in MARAD's recycling program.

Major Examples of Naval Ships as Artificial Reefs

There are four primary disposal options for retired naval vessels: they can be placed in the "mothball fleet," sold for alternate use, such as to a foreign navy or as a service vessel, recycled or scrapped, or used as artificial reefs. Reefing provides an economic benefit not only for the U.S. government but also for the state or foreign destination of the vessel. The examples below illustrate the potential benefits in terms of disposal costs to the government and tourism or recreational value.

The two most recent reefings of naval vessels illustrate the economic benefits. The Navy had estimated the cost of scrapping *Oriskany* at twenty-four million dollars, but it cost only nineteen million to scuttle the ship off Pensacola. A 2007 report from the University of West Florida states that the sinking of *Oriskany* generated nearly four million dollars for Pensacola and Escambia County, receiving over 4,200 visits that year. In

addition, a Florida State University study estimates that *Oriskany,* the world's largest
artificial reef at the time of its sinking, could generate up to ninety-two million dollars annually from tourists, divers, and sportfishermen. Even if this attraction does not
generate that much money, utilizing the ship as an artificial reef seems to make good
financial sense. In the case of the destroyer *Radford,* the net savings to the Navy were
several million dollars, aside from immediate profits to the tristate participants.

The following sections discuss the most significant naval vessels used for artificial reefs.
USS *Spiegel Grove* was the first vessel of its size to be procured as an artificial reef by
private industry. USNS *General Hoyt S. Vandenberg* was the first artificial reef to have
the specific purpose of education. The Canadian destroyer HMCS *Yukon* established
the largest artificial reef of its time, still the largest on the West Coast. USS *Kittiwake*
was the first U.S. naval vessel donated to a foreign country for an artificial reef. USS
Oriskany was the largest naval vessel sunk as an artificial reef and the second largest was
USS *Radford,* sunk in 2011. These examples help illustrate the benefits of using retired
naval vessels as artificial reefs.

USS Spiegel Grove *(LSD 32)*

The dock landing ship *Spiegel Grove* spent the greater part of its active service participating in amphibious exercises along the eastern seaboard and in the Caribbean. *Spiegel
Grove* was deployed to the Sixth Fleet from January to June 1964; from 3 November
1966 to 11 May 1967; and from 17 April to 9 October 1971. This ship was deployed as
an artificial reef on 17 May 2002, on which occasion it unintentionally sank ahead
of schedule, leaving a portion of its bow exposed above water. A month later, *Spiegel
Grove* was rolled onto its side. It was opened to the public, for recreational divers, on
26 June 2002.

Spiegel Grove had been proposed to Monroe County, Florida, as an artificial reef by
local dive industry entrepreneurs, with the primary objective of determining whether
scuba diving on adjacent natural reef sites could be reduced through the placement of an
artificial reef. The secondary objective was to stimulate the local economy of Key Largo
through increased diving-related tourism.[24] It was the first proposal of this magnitude
in size, cost, and potential impact. The proposal, after meeting the preliminary requirements of the Florida Keys National Marine Sanctuary, the Army Corps of Engineers,
and other agencies, was reviewed by Monroe County and submitted for approval con-
secutively with a request for funding.

This proposal lacked any empirical data to support its conclusions. Rather, it relied
on the data of a 1998 National Oceanic and Atmospheric Administration (NOAA)
study for validation. Several creative debt-recovery strategies were described in the

entrepreneurs' business plan. The narrow scope of use limited the project's scientific potential; also, it was in need of a postdeployment data-collection strategy. The decision-making process appeared to be primarily political, with the intent to stimulate the economy of Key Largo and the Upper Keys. However, in the event, preliminary postdeployment data seem to have supported the project's hypothesis that the artificial reef would relieve use pressure on the surrounding natural reefs and stimulate new populations of reef fish.[25]

Given the perceived success of the project, Monroe County appears to have been content with its decision-making process. However, since the applicants for *Spiegel Grove* used a primarily volunteer deployment workforce, they encountered several significant problems, resulting in delays and miscalculations of revenue needs. The problems of the *Spiegel Grove* deployment were not lost on Monroe County later, when the *Vandenberg* proposal came up for review (see below).

The Reef Environmental Education Foundation (REEF) conducted a fish-monitoring study from April 2001 through August 2007, to evaluate the impact *Spiegel Grove* was having on fish populations.[26] The overall objective of the study was to assess any changes in fish community structure over time—changes not just to the *Spiegel Grove* site but to the surrounding natural reef sites as well. A central biological question about the merits of artificial reef deployments is whether they add fish species, in terms of both numbers of fish (biomass) and numbers of fish species (biodiversity), to the artificial reef and the surrounding natural reef sites. Ultimately, resource managers and other stakeholders hope that artificial reefs not only add fish to the targeted site but seed surrounding reefs with the reproductive output from the resident fish population.

The scope of REEF's monitoring study did not address all of these long-term impacts, but it is important to understand the concepts behind sinking ships as artificial reefs. The method of surveying used by REEF in its study involved the Roving Diver Technique (RDT), which is specifically designed to produce a list of the frequency and abundance of species found by divers swimming throughout the site. REEF conducted seventy-six RDT surveys on the *Spiegel Grove* site and 445 on seven surrounding reference sites. There were forty-six fish species documented on *Spiegel Grove* during the first month of surveying, April 2001, and by August the number of species had grown to sixty-six; the average number of species rose to seventy-six per monitoring event thereafter. During each of the monitoring periods individual REEF members added 138 surveys to the scheduled number. Approximately three years after deployment, the persistence in species composition at the *Spiegel Grove* site through time had increased to levels close to those of the surrounding reefs. A total of 191 species have been documented at *Spiegel Grove*, of which forty-one were not documented during the monitoring but rather during individual survey efforts by volunteers.

Another aspect of the use of naval vessels for artificial reefs is socioeconomic impact on a community. Although this was not addressed in REEF's work, it is valuable to inquire how much extra tourist revenue is generated by the addition of such a destination feature as a naval vessel redeployed as an artificial reef. As demonstrated by the *Spiegel Grove* reef site, the biological and socioeconomic impacts can reach beyond those directly associated with the vessel and spread to indirect impacts, such as relief of pressure by scuba divers and other users on nearby sites, and the economic benefits to ancillary businesses in support of tourist uses from the artificial reef. Finding answers to these socioeconomic questions is critical for guiding future marine resource-management decisions on whether to deploy artificial reefs of this type.

USNS General Hoyt S. Vandenberg *(T-AGM 10)*

On 1 July 1964, *General Hoyt S. Vandenberg* was acquired by the Navy and designated as a missile range instrumentation ship. It was one of ten such ships transferred from the Commander, Air Force Eastern Test Range to participate in the Global Atmospheric Research Experiment. Formerly named *General Harry Taylor* and used for a time as a U.S. Army Transport Service vessel, *Vandenberg* was refitted with extremely accurate and discriminating radar and telemetry equipment. On 27 May 2009, *Vandenberg* became the largest artificial reef in the Florida Keys National Marine Sanctuary and the second-largest artificial reef in the world at that time.[27]

The *Vandenberg* sinking was proposed to Monroe County, Florida, by an entrepreneur interested in creating an artificial reef with a comprehensive list of uses—scientific, educational, recreational, and economic. This project offered Monroe County an expanded socioeconomic base that could involve colleges and universities, the scientific community (such as Mote Laboratories, which has a field facility in the Lower Keys), and unique economic opportunities for the community. The 1998 NOAA study was used to validate the conclusions and projections of the project.

In addition, the *Vandenberg* team could refer to the success of the *Spiegel Grove* site in Key Largo for its proposal. The most significant difference in strategy for *Vandenberg* was the use of professionals in project development. From cleaning to sinking, the *Vandenberg* directors proposed using experienced companies, so as to avoid the costly mistakes of the *Spiegel Grove* project. However, even though they submitted an improved project development plan, the backers could not shake off the negative experiences of the *Spiegel Grove* sinking. Monroe County refused to sponsor another artificial reef project until debt recovery and postdeployment data could be analyzed. Monroe County did agree to provide some badly needed funding for the project after the first year's debt-recovery data demonstrated that the *Spiegel Grove* reef was ahead of projections.

HMCS Yukon *(DDE 263)*

In 1996, the San Diego Oceans Foundation (SDOF) began a precedent-setting program to create a Master Plan for Habitat Enhancement (MPHE) for California state waters off San Diego County. The intent was to create a broad framework to fulfill the desires of fishermen, divers, and scientists for more places to explore, more fish to catch, and specific sites reserved for habitat enhancement research. The MPHE envisioned four types of zones, designed to serve different user needs: six Kelp Enhancement Zones, three Research Zones, three Deep Water Economic Zones, and one Shallow Water Economic Zone. The concept of an economic zone and underwater recreation area was developed to meet these goals for recreational diving, fishing, and scientific research.[28]

The destroyer HMCS *Yukon* of the Canadian Forces Maritime Command (today the Royal Canadian Navy), scuttled off San Diego during July 2000, is the largest ship ever sunk on the West Coast as an artificial reef. It is resting on its port side in a hundred feet of water just 1.85 miles west of Mission Beach. It is in a location accessible to divers and fishermen, which makes it a favorite recreational area. An estimated ten thousand recreational dives were made on it in the first year of its new life as an artificial reef. As a result, this facet of the tourism industry in San Diego has flourished since the sinking. Most of the divers visiting the *Yukon* reef are from out of town and spend money locally, and by doing so they have increased civic revenues.[29]

In the fall of 2002, the SDOF proposed a study to determine what effects the *Yukon* sinking had had on tourism in San Diego. It was earlier reported that *Yukon* had resulted in increased recreational use of the artificial reefs in the area known as "Shipwreck Alley" by 30 to 40 percent.[30] But specific goals and objectives still must be evaluated to determine the level of success the project achieved.

The SDOF received in 2005 an ecological assessment from the Scripps Institution of Oceanography, in the Integrative Oceanography Division of the University of California, San Diego, in La Jolla.[31] The assessment utilized a volunteer-based monitoring program to determine the colonization of marine life on the ship to gauge its ecological effects. The assessment covered four years, from 2000 to 2004. The data were found to be difficult to rely on, provided as they often were by volunteers with differing levels of experience in conducting fish counts, taking photographs, and collecting other data necessary for the assessment. The report established, however, that the initial colonizers of the ship were species that had moved from nearby artificial and natural habitats. Secondary colonization was ongoing, and consisted of fish that were residential elsewhere and have migrated to the ship. These species are generally smaller than the initial colonizers, and abundances vary. The *Yukon* reef provides habitat for adult species of commercial and sport fish, including sheepshead and bocaccio, and also provides nursery habitat for these species. The SDOF intends to continue the monitoring indefinitely.

Shipwreck Alley is a network of artificial reefs that appear to display "synergistic beneficial effects by increasing forage area," which gives mobile species the opportunity to go from one site to the next.[32] However, this assessment indicated that compared with the natural habitat in waters off La Jolla, the *Yukon* fish populations were significantly less diverse. However, diversity was increasing and should continue to do so—at least in the short term. The stationary communities, such as anemones and filter feeders, were abundant but not mature. The algal community was not prolific, likely owing to the antifouling paint on the substrate of *Yukon*'s hull. The assessment did not have the resources to address such bigger questions as whether artificial reefs increase the regional fish production or lead to more concentrated fish stocks. The assessment concluded that determining whether artificial reefs in Shipwreck Alley are beneficial or detrimental to natural habitats will require additional comprehensive studies of artificial reefs.

USS Kittiwake (ASR 13)

Kittiwake was a 1945-vintage submarine rescue ship. The 251-foot, 2,200-ton vessel was originally built to rescue sailors from damaged submarines. *Kittiwake* was the first vessel the U.S. Navy donated to a foreign country for an artificial reef. The ship, which assisted U.S. submarine operations around the globe for decades, had been anchored in recent years among the rusting vessels of the James River Reserve Fleet, commonly known as the "Ghost Fleet," near Fort Eustis, Virginia.

Tourism authorities in the Cayman Islands noted the growth in popularity of scuba diving on wrecks, especially those from World War II. Noticing the draw of wreck diving at Truk Lagoon (Micronesia) and Scapa Flow (Scotland), they desired to see whether the same economic benefit could make the Cayman Islands into a diving mecca. They requested *Kittiwake* to join MV *Captain Keith Tibbetts,* a renamed Koni-class frigate built for Cuba by the Soviet Union in 1984 and sunk off Cayman Brac in 1996, now decorated with a thick coating of sponges and corals.

Kittiwake was decommissioned on 30 September 1994 and stricken from the Naval Vessel Register on the same day. Its title was transferred in November 2008 for an undisclosed amount to the government of the Cayman Islands. *Kittiwake* was sunk on a sandy bottom off Grand Cayman's Seven Mile Beach on 5 January 2011. The ship, forty-seven feet (fourteen meters) tall, is at a depth of sixty-two feet (nineteen meters), so the top deck is fairly close to the surface, easily accessible for snorkelers and divers.

USS Oriskany (CV 34): "The Mighty O"

On 15 April 1976, with defense budget cuts looming and the aircraft carrier showing wear and tear, *Oriskany* was designated for mothball fleet; it was decommissioned on 30 September of the same year. Towed to Bremerton, Washington, the aircraft carrier remained in reserve until stricken from the Navy list on 25 July 1989 for use as a museum ship or scrapping. Initially intended for possible sale to Japan as a museum ship, the vessel was eventually ordered scrapped and was towed to the Gulf of Mexico. Three dismantling contracts were canceled owing to high cost and environmental concerns.

In May 2003, *Yukon* and *Spiegel Grove* having been successfully reefed, competition for a reef site for *Oriskany* commenced. On 5 April 2004 Pensacola, in Escambia County, Florida, was chosen from among proposed locations that included sites in Florida, Mississippi, and Texas, and a joint proposal from Georgia / South Carolina. Several other destinations in Florida—including the Broward/Miami-Dade County area—also wanted the carrier, but because of its long-term naval-aviation heritage Pensacola seemed the appropriate choice.

Oriskany became the first U.S. warship deployed as an artificial reef under authority granted by the fiscal 2004 National Defense Authorization Act (Public Law 108-136). The Navy announced on 5 April 2004 that it would transfer the former aircraft carrier to the state of Florida for use as an artificial reef. Ultimately, on 17 May 2006, after many years of planning and hazardous-material cleanup, the carrier was sunk as an artificial reef off Pensacola, Florida.

Some ecologists warned that the sinking of *Oriskany* would unnecessarily risk introducing PCBs into the food chain. The Navy worked with the Environmental Protection Agency to create special guidelines allowing the PCBs to stay. A study by the state of Florida is under way to determine whether chemicals are entering the environment. Meanwhile, the wreck is being dived on and fished nearly every day. The *Oriskany* reef has attracted at least thirty-eight species of fish, including goliath groupers, mako sharks, amberjacks, and red snappers.

USS Radford (DD 968)

The *Spruance*-class destroyer USS *Radford* was commissioned on 16 April 1977 and decommissioned on 18 March 2003, after serving twenty-six years. *Radford* was declared a candidate for reefing by the Navy in 2006 and was deeded to the state of Delaware. On 10 August 2011 its hull was scuttled off the coast of Delaware to form part of an artificial reef, at a total cost of $945,000.

The Del-Jersey-Land Inshore Reef, about twenty-five miles out in the Atlantic Ocean equidistant from Delaware, New Jersey, and Maryland, is a joint effort of the three

states. It is made up of subway cars, military tanks, and ships. *Radford,* the latest
addition, is, at 563 feet long and seventy feet high, the largest vessel to become an
artificial reef in the Atlantic Ocean. Delaware, New Jersey, and Maryland divided the
million-dollar cost of stripping toxic and recyclable materials from the ship and sinking
it. *Radford* is the only multistate reefing project in the country.

Asserting the value of adding a prestigious naval vessel to the local economy, the governor of Delaware, Jack Markell, declared in July 2011 that "the Navy destroyer turned
artificial reef will provide a big boost to tourism—both for anglers and divers. And it
will turn a sand-covered section of the ocean floor into a rich, new habitat for sea life
from the bottom of the food chain to the top. He estimated that the reef site will be 400
times richer in marine diversity than the natural bottom and that changes in the species
diversity should take place there within days of the sinking."[33] There are already fourteen artificial reef sites in Delaware Bay and just offshore in the Atlantic Ocean—some
created from ballasted tires, others from concrete culverts, and still others from surplus
vessels. *Radford* is considered the most ambitious reef project Delaware officials have
undertaken to date.

The Artificial Reef Controversy

As soon as a significant interest is shown in a reefing proposal, many articles usually
appear denouncing and opposing it. However, most criticism is less about public interest
than about private gain or loss. There are a few exceptions that merit discussion. One
controversy caused by the use of derelict vessels concerns whether these potential reefs
pollute the environment. Opponents argue that the artificial reefs constructed from
mothballed vessels leak oil and contain hazardous substances, such as asbestos. An artificial reef program requires that preparation for deployment include a comprehensive
cleaning, followed by established measurement to ensure that no contaminants will be
released. Certification that the vessel is "clean" is one of the many steps in the permitting process.

Nevertheless, concern about contamination is justified. For example, the Georgia Strait
Alliance and other environmental groups have warned that oil and other contaminants
remain in inaccessible areas of ships, such as crankcases, fuel tanks, and day tanks
(small tanks that directly supply individual machines). The groups have stated that
ships sunk have also contained such hazardous materials as asbestos and paint made
with tributyltin. Other groups, such as the Artificial Reef Society of British Columbia,
have been more supportive, asserting that the sinking of decommissioned warships
increases biodiversity and supports diving tourism. Environment Canada (equivalent to
the EPA in the United States) found in a study conducted two years after sinking a vessel that there were no elevations in the concentrations of any water-quality parameters

measured.[34] This test has been repeated several times, with similar results. The accepted practices for preparing a vessel for use as an artificial reef are considered safe, and are monitored by the government agencies charged with environmental oversight.

Another issue is the view that artificial reefs are simply a disguise for ocean dumping. Opponents argue that the variety of materials being used in artificial reefs, such as tires and concrete blocks, which are heavily regulated by ocean-dumping agreements and statutes, are not being properly prepared for use as an artificial reef but simply dumped. Strict criteria are needed for creating artificial reefs, including cleaning and proper preparation of the material. The United States and the international community have promulgated regulatory measures designed to prevent the abuse of artificial reefing. These regulations are intended to ensure that fishery habitat enhancement will not be used as a pretext for disguised ocean dumping. The international agreements and accepted principles of international law, however, provide only discretionary protec- tion. Guidance over artificial reefs in U.S. waters comprises international standards and domestic statutes, in conjunction with agency actions that are often seen as inconsistent, thereby creating increased opportunity for disguised ocean dumping.[35]

The benefits to the environment of artificial reefs are widely acknowledged. An example is the case of the Florida Keys. In 1998, the Australian Institute of Marine Science issued a report, *Status of Coral Reefs of the World,* of deteriorating quality in the waters of the Keys.[36] A meeting of the NOAA Coral Reef Taskforce on 4 May 2006 placed two coral species on the Endangered Species List: *Acropora palmate* (elkhorn coral) and *A. cervi- cornis* (staghorn coral).[37] However, the NOAA report also noted that the use of artificial reefs had contributed to the improvement in conditions. Much of the literature specific to the Florida Keys addresses the tendency to "love reefs to death"; this study suggests that the use of artificial reefs has in fact significantly lessened the pressures associated with tourism on the natural reefs.

Many reports describe in positive terms the carrying capacity of the reef system, focus- ing on the lessening of pressure on existing reefs and the establishment of artificial reefs. In addition, the increased number of corals and filter feeders has improved water quality and possibly increased juvenile fish of commercial and sport species, such as groupers, and other valuable reef species, such as lobsters. Artificial reefs provide addi- tional habitats for the development of these and other species that feed the food chain.[38]

Conclusions

Artificial reefs provide one practical solution to the precipitous decline in marine resources. Man-made reefs date back to ancient times. Today, artificial reefs made from sunken Navy ships can play an important role in conservation and restoration of natural reefs by relieving pressure of use and establishing habitats to increase marine life within these miniecosystems. The biological elements necessary to establish and sustain marine ecosystems are present in artificial reefs. With proper planning and employment strategies, artificial reefs can achieve their intended purposes while minimizing unintended consequences. The socioeconomic benefits of artificial reefing are paramount. Savings to the U.S. Navy and MARAD in maintaining vessels and the cost savings of reefing compared with the alternative disposal options make this option increasingly appealing.

In particular, artificial reefs provide an impetus for tourism by supplying alternatives to traditional venues, such as natural reefs. Providing variety helps maintain interest in an area for reef users.[39] The presence of diverse marine life in these areas also provides entrepreneurial opportunities for businesses in such sectors as scuba diving, fishing, education, research, and ecotourism. These activities, furthermore, require ancillary commercial services, such as boat charters, lodging, and food services, all of which assist the primary users of artificial reefs, while generating increased revenues. With economic growth comes increased competition between businesses. As a result, the reef users may benefit from cheaper charter fees.[40]

Recently, there has been a sharp increase in the use of naval vessels as artificial reefs. The cost of scrapping, the low value of salvageable material, and the identified benefits of artificial reefing underlie a demand curve that has prompted MARAD and the U.S. Navy to expand their efforts to reef retired vessels. As the U.S. Navy actively seeks today to reduce the number of inactive ships, more former warships may soon be turned into artificial reefs.

Notes

1. "USS Oriskany (CV 34)," *Unofficial US Navy Site*, navysite.de/.

2. "U.S. Navy Ship Sinking Exercises (SINKEX)," *Unofficial US Navy Site*, navysite.de/.

3. "Roskilde 6," *The Navis I Project*, www2.rgzm .de/navis/.

4. Colin McKenzie, "Albert McKenzie VC," *The Raid on Zeebrugge: 23rd April 1918*, www .mckenzie.uk.com/.

5. Robert K. Massie, *Castles of Steel: Britain, Germany, and the Winning of the Great War at Sea* (New York: Ballantine Books, 2004), pp. 778–88.

6. "Scapa Flow Scuttling of the German High Seas Fleet," *World War 1 Naval Combat*, www .worldwar1.co.uk/.

7. "Wrecks Designated as Maritime Scheduled Ancient Monuments," *Maritime and Coastguard Agency (MCA)*, www.gov.uk/.

8. Bruce Swanson, *Eighth Voyage of the Dragon: A History of China's Quest for Seapower* (Annapolis, Md.: Naval Institute Press, 1982), p. 166.

9. Michael H. Coles, "Suez, 1956: A Successful Naval Operation Compromised by Inept Political Leadership," *Naval War College Review* 59, no. 4 (Autumn 2006), p. 110.

10. "Suez Crisis" (course reading, HIST351: Islam, the Middle East, and the West, Saylor Academy, n.d.), p. 8, accessed 26 December 2012, www.saylor.org/.

11. *Historic Naval Ships Association,* www.hnsa.org.

12. "U.S. Navy Ship Sinking Exercises (SINKEX)."

13. Tamara Dietrich, "Environmentalists Aim to Stop Navy's 'Target Practice,'" *Newport News Daily Press,* 3 October 2012.

14. Ibid.

15. Ibid.

16. Ibid.

17. *National Geographic Education: Reference and News,* s.v. "reef," education.nationalgeographic.com/education/.

18. Ron Hess et al., *Disposal Options for Ships* (Santa Monica, Calif.: RAND, 2001), p. 59, available at www.rand.org/.

19. "Guidelines for Marine Artificial Reef Materials," *Gulf States Marine Fisheries Commission,* no. 38 (January 1997), p. 2, available at www.gsmfc.org/.

20. *The Role of Vessels as Artificial Reef Material on the Atlantic and Gulf of Mexico Coasts of the United States,* Special Report 38 (Arlington, Va.: Atlantic States Marine Fisheries Commission, 1994), pp. 4, 6.

21. Ibid.

22. Floyd D. Spence National Defense Authorization Act for Fiscal Year 2001, Pub. L. No. 106-398, 114 Stat. 1654A-1 (30 October 2000).

23. National Defense Authorization Act for Fiscal Year 2004, Pub. L. No. 108-136, 117 Stat. 1392 (24 November 2003).

24. "Business Plan for the Sinking of the USS *Spiegel Grove,*" Key Largo Chamber of Commerce Artificial Reef Committee, 1997.

25. V. R. Leeworthy, T. Maher, and E. A. Stone, "Can Artificial Reefs Reduce or Alter User Pressure on Adjacent Natural Reefs?," *Bulletin of Marine Science* 78, no. 11 (2006), pp. 29–37.

26. Ibid.

27. "Sinking the *Vandenberg* . . . From Ship to Shipwreck," *Florida Keys & Key West,* www.fla-keys.com/.

28. City of San Diego, California, *Final Programmatic Environmental Impact Report,* LDR No. 98-0686 (San Diego, Calif.: San Diego Underwater Recreation Area and *Yukon* Project, September 1999).

29. See *San Diego Oceans Foundation,* sdof.org.

30. "San Diego Sunken Ship: A Diver's Paradise," *ABC News,* 12 September 2000, www.ABCNEWS.com/.

31. Ed Parnell, *Ecological Assessment of the HMCS* Yukon *Artificial Reef off San Diego, CA (USA)* (La Jolla, Calif.: Scripps Institute of Oceanography for San Diego Oceans Foundation, 7 January 2005).

32. Ibid.

33. "Destroyer Will Be Sunk to Create Artificial Reef off IR Inlet," *StructureSpot,* 31 July 2011, structurespot.com/.

34. Marnie Eggen, "That Sinking Feeling: Do 'Artificial Reefs' in BC Waters Increase Biodiversity or Waste?," *Alternatives Journal* 23, no. 1 (Winter 1997).

35. John Macdonald, "Artificial Reef Debate: Habitat Enhancement or Waste Disposal?," *Ocean Development and International Law* 25 (January–March 1994), pp. 87–118.

36. Judy Lang and Clive Wilkinson, eds., *Status of Coral Reefs of the World* (Townsville, Qld.: Australian Institute of Marine Science, 1998), p. 130.

37. "Elkhorn and Staghorn Corals Listed in Threatened Status," *National Oceanographic and Atmospheric Administration (NOAA),* 5 May 2006.

38. Ibid.

39. J. W. Milon and R. Schmied, "Identifying Economic Benefits of Artificial Reef Habitat," in *Artificial Reef Research Diver's Handbook,* ed. J. G. Halusky (Gainesville: Univ. of Florida, Sea Grant College Program, 1991).

40. Robert A. Collinge and Ronald M. Ayers, *Economics by Design: Principles and Issues* (Upper Saddle River, N.J.: Prentice Hall, 2000), p. 45.

CHAPTER SEVEN

Naval Sonars, Strandings, and Responsible Stewardship of the Seas

DARLENE R. KETTEN

In 1923 Thomas Edison founded what would become the Naval Research Laboratory in Washington, D.C. Today the laboratory has a broadly based program of research and development and satellite centers, aligned with the Navy's systems commands. All these facilities operate under the Office of Naval Research, established in 1946 with the mission of fostering Navy-relevant scientific research. The Office of Naval Research allocates nearly two billion dollars in research funds annually to support a wide range of scientific programs. Many of these are based at civilian institutions and address basic research questions that have little to do directly with immediate mission needs but touch on current and future issues that may impact naval operations and effectiveness. They range from neuroscience and medicine to climate change and ecology.

Since 2000 there has been a dramatic global increase in U.S. Navy–funded research on underwater hearing in marine animals and on the potential for acoustic impacts on them. Although strandings of marine mammals have been reported for over two thousand years, scientific and public attention has become focused by a string of stranding cases related to naval sonar exercises. In 1996, twelve Cuvier's beaked whales beached on the same day, in rapid succession, on the coast of Kyparissiakos Gulf in western Greece. All died. *Alliance,* a NATO research vessel, had been conducting sonar exercises offshore using midfrequency (MFA) and low-frequency (LFA) sonars for several days prior to the beachings. Four years later, in March and May 2000, a mass stranding of beaked whales occurred, first in the Bahamas and then off Madeira, coincident with naval exercises using MFA sonars.[1] Subsequent widely publicized events in the Canary Islands in 2002 and 2004, off Hawaii in 2004, and in Madagascar in 2008 fueled public concern that the use of midrange sonars may be a significant cause of marine mammal strandings.[2]

At present, there are no solid answers about what exactly triggered these whale strandings. Was it the sounds per se, the movements of the ships, a peculiarity of the sound

profiles of those areas, a special sensitivity to some aspect of sonar signals in the species
that stranded, or perhaps a "perfect storm" of some or all of these factors? During the
past fifteen years there has been a major research effort, funded primarily by the U.S.
Navy, to understand the mechanisms behind sonar-related strandings, with the ultimate
goal of preventing future occurrences. The exact relationship between naval sonar and
strandings remains in some ways perplexing, but there has been significant progress.

Historical Background of Strandings

Aristotle noted the phenomenon of marine strandings in his treatise on animals circa
350 BC. In AD 1324, a law in England gave all rights over beached, entrapped, or fished
cetaceans to the Crown.[3] From the fifteenth century onward, there are illustrations of
beached whales in Europe. Clearly, there are abundant natural causes for marine mammals to strand, to die and wash ashore, or to find themselves alive on a beach or in water
too shallow or with currents and tides too strong for them to return to deeper water,
particularly if weakened by disease, age, or injury.

The term "stranding" technically refers to an event in which an animal is found alive or
dead in an "inappropriate" location. Strandings take many forms. One or more animals
may be beached, well up on the shore or simply near shore in water depths or areas that
are atypical, such as the case of a normally pelagic (oceanic) species coming into a bay
or estuary, or they may become entangled in lines or fishing gear at sea. Approximately
four thousand animals strand annually along the U.S. coast and in American territorial
waters. Strandings occur singly and in groups. The number of individuals and species
involved vary widely both by region and by season.[4] A "mass stranding" is defined as
more than two animals, not mother-calf or mother-pup pairs, stranding simultaneously
or synchronously in close proximity. Therefore, a mass stranding can involve as few
as three animals or hundreds, and the animals may be, as is true for any stranding, on
a beach (as in the Greek, Bahamian, and Canary Island cases) or, if normally pelagic,
sighted in a bay or estuary (as occurred in Hawaii and Madagascar).[5] A stranding incident may be declared an "unusual mortality event" on the basis of several factors: the
rarity of the species, the number of individuals involved, the location of the species, and
the numbers stranding and dying in comparison with common patterns for that species.
These definitions are based on the practices of the Marine Mammal Health and Stranding Response Program of the U.S. National Oceanic and Atmospheric Administration's
National Marine Fisheries Service.[6] But this terminology is fairly common in all stranding response networks worldwide.

When a report of a stranding is received, local response network personnel are acti-
vated. They attempt to assist the animal if it is alive. If it is dead or must be euthanized,
they collect the carcass and record "Level A Data"—observations on the animal's

gender, size, and condition, reports of any known perimortem events, and documentation of the physical environment near the stranding. Most such reports do not provide conclusions on a likely cause of death. Rather, a systematic examination of the body, called a necropsy, is performed, on the beach or at an established facility, following an established protocol.[7] The aim of the necropsy—often involving X-rays, histopathology, polymerase chain-reaction studies, and other tests, in addition to gross dissection—is to provide a comprehensive analysis of the animal's condition and obtain and assess any evidence potentially relating to the cause of death.

Because of the inevitable postmortem loss of tissue integrity; the practical limitations on examining large animals under, often, field conditions; and the limited number of personnel fully trained to perform necropsies, especially in remote areas, complete answers are not always possible for every animal. In the last decade, clear causes of death could be assigned only in 30–40 percent of all examined cases. Even for unusual mortality events, in which numerous experts are brought in to examine every case and the large numbers of individuals examined offers a better probability of finding cross correlates, causes of death were determined for only 53 percent of events in the past five years.

Any analysis needs to take into account potential biases from sampling error. Human population distributions impact reporting of strandings, as shown by comparing maps of report locations over time.[8] An overwhelming majority occur in the Northern Hemisphere, although increasingly there are reports from South America and Oceania. As electronic capabilities spread globally, improvements will most likely occur in the spread and speed of reporting, as well as in on-site documentation by both the public and professionals. This will undoubtedly lead to a truer global picture of these events and their causes.

While marine mammals certainly succumb to disease, age, complications in calving, habitat disruption, food shortages, predators, and naturally occurring injuries and toxins, many are impacted by human activities, particularly through bycatch (animals inadvertently caught in nets in large fishing operations), entanglement in lines or debris, collision with ships, or occasionally direct attack, such as shootings. There are also more subtle but equally mortal human-derived risks, stressors that can be acute or cumulative, such as chemical pollutants and noise from boat traffic. Bycatch numbers, estimated to range as high as a hundred thousand annually worldwide, account for the majority of human-related stranding deaths.[9] However, in recent years, as a result of better gear design and the use of acoustic warning devices on nets, estimates have been reduced to less than two thousand annually, on a par with those related to commercial and scientific whaling. Traditional fisheries capture far fewer animals in hunts and drives.

Noise, historically, is the most common method used to drive or herd marine mammals. Aristotle refers to using "a loud and alarming resonance . . . to induce [dolphins] to run in a shoal high and dry up on the beach and so to catch them while stupefied with the noise."[10] Such methods continue today in the Taiji drive fisheries in Japan and traditional hunts in the Faeroe Islands. Depth and fish finders have also been used to bring whales to the surface.[11] Clearly, multiple human activities have potentially significant impacts on whales; human-generated, or anthropogenic, sound is one we are just beginning to appreciate.

Ocean Sound: Natural versus Anthropogenic

The ocean is not naturally silent. Indeed, a quiet ocean is a dead ocean. There are myriads of natural sources of ocean noise, most notably geophysical events—such as earthquakes, seafloor spreading, and volcanic activity—most of which produce sounds in the seismic or infrasonic domain. Substantial noise is generated by wave action, bubbles, and cavitation or is transmitted into the water by ice movements and atmospheric events, notably lightning and storms. Some sources, like hydrothermal vents, particularly the "black smokers" in the deep ocean, produce low-frequency "belches" at frequencies of 5–250 hertz (Hz) that raise ambient sound levels by from 20 to 35 decibels (dB).[12]

By far the largest contributor to natural marine noise, however, is life itself. Marine fauna produce sounds ranging from infra- to ultrasonic frequencies at source levels higher than 200 dB. Most of these sources are concentrated in the continental shelf regions, where 95 percent of all ocean life lives, although there are pelagic and migratory species as well. Virtually all marine fauna produce and rely on sound for a broad range of critical cues and activities—for example, navigation, detection of prey and predators, communication, and mating. The classic Wenz curves provide an excellent summary of the relative contribution of biologic versus geophysical and atmospheric sources, as well as human sources. They demonstrate graphically how animals evolved to exploit less naturally noisy bands for their vocalization frequencies and how human sources are competing in some of those bands.[13]

Atop this background, or "natural ambient," anthropogenic sources are adding to the total noise budget at an ever-increasing pace. According to the findings of a panel convened by the Ocean Studies Board under the auspices of the National Academy of Sciences, humans are adding significant new noise to the marine environment at a rate of 3 dB per decade, although recent data suggest that the rate is slowing as vessel hull designs and propulsive systems improve.[14] Human contributions to the ocean soundscape include vessel noise, industrial operations, sonars (military, navigational, and fisheries), and technologies for research and oil and gas exploration that employ seismic, explosive, and impulse sources. There is no human activity in the ocean, whether in the coastal or blue-water domain, that does not add noise, either intentionally or as a by-product. Many of these activities, including defense and commercial shipping, are not just beneficial but critical for our modern lives.

Military sonars, which are primarily low- to midfrequency sources ranging 100 Hz to 8 kilohertz with source levels over 200 dB, have received to date the greatest attention in the media, although they are estimated to contribute less than 5 percent to the ocean noise budget, according to the Ocean Studies Board.[15] Seismic source technologies constitute the next-largest source. These are the mainstay of oil and gas exploration and include air-gun arrays, impulse sources with peak spectra below 100 Hz. Commercial sonar systems are next, in use as navigational aids and as depth sounders for transport, fisheries, tourism, and recreational vessels. These range from low- to midsonic to ultrasonic. Source levels are difficult to determine, as exact noise specifications are not always provided by manufacturers, but they have been estimated to exceed 230 dB.

Commercial shipping is by far the dominant source of human-generated noise. Virtually all NATO navies have been reduced over the last two decades, by as much as half in all ship categories.[16] At the same time, the global merchant marine fleet has increased exponentially. Shipping alone is estimated to have increased background noise by 15 dB in the last fifty years and now accounts for over 50 percent of the total ocean noise budget in the Northern Hemisphere. The sounds we are adding may be infrequent or constant, narrow or broad spectrum, and they vary in intensity by place and time, raising the issue of how to evaluate not just immediate or acute effects but also long-term, cumulative impacts. In some ocean areas, particularly in fragile coastal habitats, we are effectively creating a noise environment akin to that of industrial workplaces.

Beaked Whales: An Aquatic Canary for Sound Impacts?

Most concerns for sonar impacts have focused on beaked whales, specifically on Cuvier's beaked whales *(Ziphius cavirostris)*, as this is the prevalent species in the majority of beachings associated with naval exercises. Systematic analyses of beaked-whale strandings have determined that the overall number of whales beached in association with any naval activity is relatively low compared with those resulting from all other events but also that there is a striking pattern that should be investigated.[17] From 1874, when international efforts to document beachings began, up to 2004, 136 events involving a total of 539 beaked whales were recorded. Of these, 126 cases, with 486 animals, or 90 percent of all recorded beaked-whale strandings, occurred after 1950, implying a loss equivalent to approximately eight animals per year for the last sixty years.

Echo-ranging devices were first developed in the early twentieth century, and their development gathered momentum to counter submarines in World War I.[18] World War II brought sonar to the fore and saw the introduction of hull-mounted systems. By the 1960s, surface-ship active scanning sonars with longer pings and greater detection ranges were common. This period also saw the development of systems that exploited bottom-bounce and convergence-path rather than direct-path algorithms, again increasing range, followed by systems of different frequencies, notably LFA and MFA sonars.

The first atypical Cuvier's beaked-whale stranding occurred in 1963, near La Spezia, Italy, shortly after a new generation of MFA sonars became available. Several review panels noted increases in beaked-whale strandings following the initiation of NATO LFA sonar trials after 1981.[19] Cuvier's beaked whales were involved in all the cases in which sonars were implicated. Prior to 1950, this species had not commonly stranded, either singly or en masse.

Although the number of sonar-related beaked-whales beachings averages fewer than ten animals per year, it is not the raw number that is important but rather the fact that, as the data demonstrate, at least one species can be seriously impacted to the point of a mortal hazard by naval sonar exercises. Just as in the human workplace, the demonstration of noise hazard led to broader concern for noise in general and its potential for stress and physical damage, in this case not to workers but to threatened or endangered species, many of which rely nearly exclusively on hearing for survival.

While there is a demonstrable association in time and place between sonar activity and beaked-whale strandings, there is as yet no clear explanation of how direct or indirect effects of sonar lead to beached animals. One confounding element, one that argues against sound per se as the culprit, is the fact that these beachings are rare compared with the breadth and number of MFA sonars in use, not only by naval forces, but also as commercial devices. Further, no mass beaked-whale beachings have been reported near any major naval base, worldwide. Lastly, beaked-whale hearing is not known to be exceptionally sensitive at middle to low frequencies in comparison with that of other whales. Why then are other and more abundant dolphin and whale species in the areas of strandings not similarly impacted?

Until a mechanism explaining the beachings is determined, it is impossible to say definitively whether these events represent uniquely a beaked-whale phenomenon. It is reasonable to hypothesize that beaked whales are more susceptible to certain kinds of anthropogenic sound exposure than are other marine mammals, but there have been two other incidents, in Hawaii in 2004 and Madagascar in 2008, in which one other cetacean species, the melon-headed whale *(Peponocephala electra)*, appeared to have been impacted by sound. As with the Greek case, the absence of any other evident cause led the review panels to conclude that exposure to an intense sound source was the likeliest explanation. However, it was later reported that a mass stranding of melon-headed whales had occurred simultaneously with the Hawaiian stranding but several thousand miles away, near Rota, in the Mariana Islands, suggesting some unappreciated trigger, such as prey movement or lunar cycles, had been the true underlying cause.[20]

The lack of clear answers for all cases has led to assertions in the press and in legal suits that the beaked-whale incidents are merely a harbinger of a serious problem of mortalities and broader impacts to a wide range of marine species, potentially at an ocean-wide scale. To date, however, there is no direct evidence of broad species or otherwise broad-scale impacts. There is, however, the possibility of widespread undetected hearing loss among marine mammals from many anthropogenic sources, and that is a legitimate concern.

Noise-Induced Hearing Loss

Noise can cause damage to any ear. But "sound" and "noise" are not the same thing. Sound is a physical phenomenon that animals detect via their auditory systems, which in turn vary in acuity by species. Noise, by contrast, is defined as an aperiodic signal that interferes with sound perception and has a negative physiological or behavioral impact.[21]

In humans, noise-induced hearing loss (NIHL) is common but varies in onset and prevalence across individuals and cultures. Exposure at any age to excessive noise, especially over the long term, produces temporary or permanent hearing deficits in the form of increased threshold—the sound level below which a sound cannot be detected. Approximately 15 percent of people over twenty years old in the United States have high-frequency NIHL. By age forty-five, 2 percent have substantial, broad-frequency NIHL, and by age seventy-five half have extensive, profound hearing loss from long-term noise exposure compounded by presbycusis, age-related auditory system degeneration.[22]

There is no standard method for predicting absolute hearing loss from excess noise exposures, only the probability, based on average hearing abilities. Current U.S. Occupational Safety and Health Administration and European regulations attempt to ameliorate the probability of NIHL by limiting continuous, eight-hour-workday exposures to an ambient sound pressure level (SPL) of 85 dB in air, with a mandatory halving of exposure time for each 3 dB increase in ambient SPL. The principal idea is to lessen the probability of a traumatic loss by avoiding SPLs that could exceed the dynamic range of inner-ear tissues. It is equally important to provide time for recovery from fatigue of critical inner-ear components, particularly membranes and cells.

Sounds change as they travel through air or water. The probability of damage depends on the characteristics of the sound not at its source but when it is received at the ear, including intensity, frequency, duration, whether the signal is impulsive or continuous, and, above all, the subject's sensitivity at that frequency. Collectively these elements result in a physical and physiological response in the middle and inner ear. NIHL is the result of damage to the inner ear's sensory hair cells, which have small fibers that when bent by acoustic stimuli trigger a neural response. Hair-cell overstimulation results in temporary insensitivity (a temporary threshold shift, or TTS), primarily through metabolic exhaustion or tissue fatigue. Permanent hearing loss (permanent threshold shift, or PTS) occurs from irreparable structural cell damage in the inner-ear sensory cells and membranes, and it leads progressively to irreversible retrograde auditory-nerve degeneration. Such damage manifests itself in the inability to hear a given frequency at any sound level and can be seen, in postmortem microscopic examinations of the inner ear, as "dead zones" in the sensory cell array.

There are some commonalities to the basic mechanisms of NIHL across mammals, even though hearing abilities differ. Animals are generally more susceptible to damage at their most sensitive frequencies. At any frequency that they can hear, losses will occur in relation to, first, the power spectrum of the signal and, at some frequencies, one-third octave higher; second, intensity and duration, which can synergistically exacerbate losses; and third, impulse noise, which produces greater impacts than does continuous noise at equivalent levels.

In laboratory experiments with cats, monkeys, and rodents, threshold shifts as large as 50 dB have been produced that returned to normal sensitivity (i.e., TTS), although recovery sometimes required as much as thirty days. Exposures that induced shifts of over 50 dB typically resulted in PTS. To date there is no means of accurately predicting PTS from measures of TTS onsets, particularly for marine mammals, since responses to identical exposures vary widely by both species and individuals. Only in experiments with genetically identical strains of mice has a close response pattern been found across individuals. This suggests that there is a large genetic element for NIHL susceptibility that complicates conclusions when relatively few individuals are tested in any one species.

Hearing curves and TTS data are now available for twelve species of odontocetes (toothed whales) and pinnipeds (seals, sea lions).[23] Although it is still unclear how robust or fragile marine mammal ears are and what their total range is, there is clear evidence that despite adaptations for diving and high-pressure environments, they are not impervious to permanent noise damage. In audiometric tests of captive animals permanent hearing losses have been documented that are consistent with hearing damage from disease, aging, and NIHL. Experiments have also been conducted to determine exposure levels that induce small and fully recoverable TTS. Longitudinal studies on captive animals demonstrate progressive losses with age and, as in humans, steep losses, or "notches," near the best sensitivities in several marine mammal species.[24] Recent postmortem studies of ears from some of these subjects have found evidence of extensive neural losses consistent with long-term profound hearing deficits.[25] Ears from some beachings also show NIHL and age-related changes, as well as other ear pathologies, including labyrinthitis ossificans (a condition in which infections produce bone growth that obliterates the inner ear), and evidence of parasitic infestations and chronic middle-ear disease. All of these are natural hazards for a wild animal, but none are symptomatic of acute noise injury.[26]

Hearing is considered the most important sensory system for most marine species and particularly for marine mammals. Studies to date show that marine mammals, like other mammals, can be impacted temporarily or permanently by excess noise and that the effects may range from mild to profound impairment. Although individual animal health is a concern, the critical issue is biological significance, which means population-level rather than isolated individual impairments. A finding of a single animal with a hearing impairment is not a reliable indicator of a population-level impact. However, a high incidence of NIHL across genders and ages in any one population would be of great concern, as that is not likely to occur through natural processes. Shifting the noise budget of the oceans can result in a significant population-level hazard not only to marine mammals but also to other species, particularly fishes, if the noise spectrum coincides with their best hearing sensitivities. Current data are insufficient to formulate population-level noise-hazard criteria. To achieve that level of understanding, broader species hearing baselines and monitoring systems need to be developed.

The fact that marine mammals sustain natural hearing loss makes demonstrating a direct cause from any anthropogenic source problematic, particularly if few animals are examined. To date there has been no demonstrable evidence of direct acute, traumatic, disruptive, or profound auditory damage in any marine mammal as the result of anthropogenic noise exposure, including to sonar.[27] This does not negate concern that it could happen, but it does underscore the need for a better understanding of the many facets and consequences of sound use. What the examinations of the beached animals do show is that even in the absence of any demonstrable auditory trauma, nonauditory effects can range from behavioral disruption to incidental trauma or even death, and they are an equally important element to consider.

Controversial Theories about Sonar Impacts

The apparent susceptibility of beaked whales to sonar-related stranding triggered a search for mechanisms that could explain why they, of all the marine mammal species, are especially vulnerable. It is unclear whether sonar and ship movements played direct roles in the pathologies documented in the Bahamian, Greek, and Canary Island cases, as opposed to attendant stress and trauma from beaching or some other action the exposures induced. Key questions remain about what to mitigate: direct sound exposure, a behavioral response to sound exposure, a physiological process set in motion by sound exposure, the physical impacts of beaching, or some combination of the above.

Necropsies of beached beaked whales showed blood deposits within the inner ears, hemorrhaging in the subarachnoid space surrounding the brain, the presence of blood in the orbits and oral cavity, and hemorrhages in fatty tissues and in some cerebral ventricles. Some animals in the 2002 Canary Islands incident were reported to have widely disseminated intravascular bubbles.[28] This was also reported in a retrospective study of archived specimens of several species of stranded animals in the United Kingdom.[29] There is a substantial probability that some of these findings are artifacts of a suite of complicated processes including salvage, transport, and storage as well as variable pre- and postmortem environments.

One workshop summarized possible impacts as follows: a behavioral avoidance response to sound leading directly to beaching; maladaptive dive responses (rapid ascent, staying at depth, remaining at the surface) leading to air emboli, hypoxia, hyperthermia, cardiac arrhythmia, hypertensive hemorrhage, or other trauma; and tissue damage or other physiological effects resulting directly from sound exposure (acoustically mediated bubble formation and growth, vestibular responses, tissue resonances, bleeding diathesis, disseminated coagulopathy, or vascular fragility).[30]

At this stage, nothing should be ruled out without a careful, balanced assessment, but it is important to focus on mechanisms consistent with the greatest number of significant observations across cases. For example, there is considerable debate over the suggestion of lethal effects of emboli based on observations of bubbles postmortem. Direct acoustic induction of bubble formation and the possibility of bubbles being related to a decompression-like, or "bends," phenomenon in whales were assessed in a recent workshop of marine mammal and dive physiologists.[31] Diagnosis of decompression sickness requires the presence of several features lacking in the animals examined.[32] The presence of bubbles per se and in isolation is not sufficient to give a diagnosis of decompression sickness.[33] Intravascular air bubbles, or air emboli, in dived animals, including humans, are a common phenomenon and are not in themselves dangerous.[34] They have also been shown to form and increase with postmortem time in experiments with animals "dived" in hyperbaric chambers. Postdiving, air comes out of solution, forming small bubbles in the blood that travel to the lungs and are released via the respiratory process. Bubbles in postmortem animals observed in necropsies are most likely related to the cessation by death of normal off-gassing processes by the lungs, resulting in bubbles that continue to grow in number and size throughout the body. A cascade of bubble formation could be set off in such cases by nicking a vessel, as is common in a necropsy, introducing a small amount of air that sets off an avalanche of bubble formation.[35] Other workshops found that tissue resonances at any sonar frequency are insufficient to produce trauma at even the level of the capillary bed, let alone to account for the hemorrhages reported.

These debates are good examples of how the process of hypothesis, scientific inquiry, and review can work effectively. A number of studies are now under way to monitor blood gases, lung collapse, structural variations in airways, and vasculature of marine mammals.[36] Further, necropsy procedures are being standardized both to regularize reports of presence of bubbles and to introduce procedures that will minimize artifacts.[37] It is not clear, however, when, if ever, the debates will be resolved to the satisfaction of all parties.

One important ongoing area study is on the behavioral effects of sound on beaked whales. The Behavioral Response Study research program is an international consortium of acousticians, engineers, observers, and behaviorists engaged in a series of five-year projects involving field measurements of the response of tagged beaked whales to sonar and control sounds.[38] The studies entail deployment of a vertical-array sound source for controlled sound exposures of tagged focal animals for up to several hours, during which they are subjected to different signals and source levels. Results to date have provided our first glimpse into the highly variable responses across species to the same stimulus under equivalent conditions. It is now clear that beaked whales have a characteristic avoidance response, but it is not specific to sonar—it occurs with any novel sound. By contrast, pilot whales gravitate toward novel stimuli.

Estimating Impacts in the Wild

At present, any activity that may impact marine mammals requires an environmental impact study and estimation of potential "Level A" and "Level B" incidental events, commonly referred to as harassments, or "takes." Level A is defined as activity that has the potential to injure a marine mammal stock in the wild. Level B is the potential to disturb a marine mammal stock by causing disruption of behavioral patterns, including, but not limited to, migration, breathing, nursing, breeding, feeding, or sheltering. Level B in particular is quite broad; it may represent anything from a simple shift of attention, equivalent to noting a car (or ship) passing by, to a substantial disruption of behavior that will endanger several animals. The first National Research Council (NRC) report on the subject, in 1994, commented that as "researchers develop more sophisticated methods for measuring the behavior and physiology of marine mammals . . . , it is likely that detectable reactions, however minor and brief, will be documented at lower and lower received levels of human-made sound." A later NRC report, from 2000, concluded that it "does not make sense to regulate minor changes in behavior having no adverse impact; rather, regulations must focus on significant disruption of behaviors critical to survival and reproduction." The next NRC report concerned with ambient noise, published in 2003, stated that the previous recommendations were still relevant.[39]

The consensus of the successive NRC committees is that the definition should raise the threshold of harassment from detectable individual responses to *biologically significant*—that is, at the population level—events. One consequence of using gaugeless individual responses as a metric is misinterpretation of the number of estimated potential "takes," particularly in the popular press. A recent example of this is a series of articles appearing in the *New York Times* from October through December 2012 that seized on the maximal number of potential incidental takes in a Navy environmental impact study as an indication that millions of animals would be grievously harmed by proposed Navy activities.

One *New York Times* editorial asserted that a weapons training and testing program had a potential for thirty-three million "takes," but it failed to explain that this number derives from a calculation of each possible perception by any single animal for any underwater sound generated in excess of natural ambient levels by the proposed operation, regardless of the level received and absent any observable effect. Nor did the editorial consider that the permitting process rigorously evaluates potential "takes" according to severity, examining carefully the possibility of an animal's being significantly disturbed or harmed, before any permit is issued. The reader is left with an impression of incalculable numbers of ruptured eardrums, extensive hearing loss, resultant ship strikes, and deaths from "sonic chaos."[40]

Popular-press articles like this bolster claims that marine mammal mortalities from sound are underestimated. Several lawsuits have asserted that whales are killed by sound and sink rapidly, disappearing without any indication of the event. This is a denial of the physiology of death. Bodies initially sink, but they typically refloat within a few days. After days or weeks, as decomposition progresses, they expand, lose body-wall integrity, and finally sink again.[41] The timeline varies depending on water temperature, as well as such other factors as gut content, amount of body fat, scavengers, and so on, but there is no reason to expect this process to be substantially different for a whale, which postmortem becomes a well-insulated, warm carcass that fosters bloat and refloating.

Several lawsuits brought against both the military and research institutions have asserted that they are not meeting the requirements of the Marine Mammal Protection Act (MMPA). One sought to halt LFA deployments on the basis of the Bahamian cases of beaked-whale beachings involving midrange sonars. To date there is no evidence of strandings related to use of LFA sonars in isolation. Nevertheless, this lawsuit was successful. Furthermore, much of the suit's discussion centered on the potential for excessive numbers of takes and inadequate appreciation of posited impacts, as well as failure to follow the normal procedures for submission and review of an impact assessment under Endangered Species Act (ESA) and MMPA regulations and definitions.

While such suits are motivated by sincere concerns, their potential impacts are quite broad. The issue of restrictions on sound sources is not simply a military matter. Liabilities and costs related to ESA and MMPA permitting are a common problem for every endeavor, whether currently regulated or not, that involves the use of sound in the seas, including research, exploration, resource development, and commercial shipping.

It is appropriate for any entity operating in the oceans to proceed with care. Sonar exercises have, as the public well appreciates, resulted in serious and regrettable disturbances that led to strandings and deaths of marine animals. High-profile events like the dramatic beachings in the Bahamas are being construed as global events, in terms of both species affected and numbers of harmful sound sources. One recent counterproductive victory was a lawsuit by which an experiment to test the audibility of sonars intended to protect whales from ship strikes was halted, with the result that the project was subsequently abandoned.

Realistically, it is virtually impossible to eliminate all acoustic impacts from all endeavors for all marine mammals. Therefore, the key issues that must be assessed are: What combination of frequencies and sound pressure levels are needed for each anthropogenic acoustic task? What species are present in the area the device will ensonify at levels exceeding ambient? What is the probable severity of any potential impact to exposed marine mammals from the combined frequency-intensity-temporal characteristics of the source? Above all, are these factors likely to produce any biologically significant impact to any marine species?

In the most recent NRC report, published in 2005, a major recommendation was to structure future research on marine mammals to assist predictions of population-level consequences.[42] Individual effects are inputs to the database, but the true issue is biological significance, which implies a species- or population-level effect deriving from impacts that are capable of altering the viability of a significant portion of the population. Just as with injury, biologically significant alterations are the appropriate determinants for behavioral harassment criteria.

Conclusions

There is no denying that anthropogenic noise has the potential to harm marine life. The results from the last decade of intense research efforts on this issue show that anthropogenic noise, intentional or incidental, can be biologically significant, disrupting critical behaviors in ways like abandonment of feeding grounds, corruption of communication signals, and alteration of migration routes, and in some rare cases, causing distress to marine mammals to the point of beaching. It is the responsibility of the media and scientists alike to report events fully and responsibly, to assist in educating the public about the foundations for and extent of legitimate concerns, and to prevent the "media-fueled" rounds of hearings and litigation that were experienced in connection with acoustic testing off Heard Island near Antarctica, the Acoustic Thermometry of Ocean Climate experiments, and now military sonars.[43] At this time, there is no clear demon-stration of a population-level impact on any marine mammal species from any acoustic event; nevertheless, the sonar-related beaching cases have clearly raised valid concerns that warrant a full explanation. As the 2005 National Research Council report stated, "On the one hand, sound may represent only a second-order effect on the conservation of marine mammal populations; on the other hand, what we have observed so far may be only the first early warnings or 'tip of the iceberg' with respect to sound and marine mammals."[44] The remaining uncertainties in these cases is the root cause of much of the fear of dire consequences of noise in the oceans.

Although many questions remain, the research to date has provided some clear answers, and equally important, it has shown how essential a strong, collaborative research pro-gram on sound and its impacts is to protecting marine life and the health of our oceans. Thus far, the research on sonar impacts has been supported nearly entirely by funding from the Marine Mammal Program of the Office of Naval Research, the Energy and Environmental Readiness Division of the Chief of Naval Operations staff, and, recently, the U.S. Navy's newly formed Living Marine Resources Program. Much of this research was directed at assisting the U.S. Navy to understand the core hazards to marine life associated with maritime operations and how to avoid or at the least mitigate those risks. However, the insights and technologies this work has fostered are providing our first clear glimpse of how whales operate at depth and over time. These Navy-funded research programs quickly expanded knowledge of marine mammal hearing and produced innovations in underwater acoustic propagation models, tags for monitoring animals at depth, and increasingly sophisticated operational aids for detecting and pre-dicting movements of individual animals at sea. These innovations assist not only the Navy but also shipping, fisheries, and research to reduce bycatch and ship strikes and to monitor migration patterns, essential behaviors, and population trends. These programs determined critical sound exposure limits and supported development of technologies to test wild stranded animals on-site for hearing loss and injury. Remote sensors now allow us to monitor individual free-ranging animals for changes in dive patterns and physiology in response to sound.

Continuing such broad-based programs of basic and applied research is critical to understanding of not just sonar impacts but a far greater range of potential hazards to ocean life. Parameterizing hazards is essential for the informed risk assessments that are part of this endeavor. There is an undeniable hazard to some marine mammals from any underwater noise at some level and in some location, but the focus must be shifted from the impossible goal of avoiding any possible individual impact to one with a greater perspective. Such a shift, backed by data and implemented with caution and judicious oversight, can prevent stagnation and provide a path forward on the basis of an understanding of what can be achieved without substantive harm and of clear and valid limits for responsible stewardship of the oceans.

Notes

1. D. L. Evans and G. R. England, *Joint Interim Report Bahamas Marine Mammal Stranding Event of 15–16 March 2000* (Washington, D.C.: National Oceanographic and Atmospheric Administration [NOAA], National Marine Fisheries Service, and U.S. Navy Dept., 2001); L. Freitas, "The Stranding of Three Cuvier's Beaked Whales *Ziphius cavirostris* in Madeira Archipelago: May 2000," *ECS Newsletter* 42 (2004), pp. 28–32.

2. A. Frantzis, "Does Acoustic Testing Strand Whales?," *Nature* 392 (1998), p. 29; A. D'Amico and W. Verboom, eds., "Report of the Bioacoustics Panel," SACLANTCEN Bioacoustics Panel, La Spezia, Italy, 15–17 June 1998; D. R. Ketten et al., "Cranial Trauma in Beaked Whales," in *Proceedings of the Workshop on Active Sonar and Cetaceans* (n.p.: ECSN, 2003), pp. 21–27; A. D'Amico et al., "Beaked Whale Strandings and Naval Exercises," *Aquatic Mammals* 35, no. 4 (2009), pp. 452–72; A. Fernández et al., "Last 'Atypical' Beaked Whales Mass Stranding in the Canary Islands (July, 2004)," *Journal of Marine Science Research & Development* 2 (2012), p. 107. See also D. R. Ketten, *Beaked Whale Necropsy Findings for Strandings in the Bahamas, Puerto Rico, and Madeira, 1999–2002*, Technical Publication WHOI-2005-09 (Woods Hole, Mass.: Woods Hole Oceanographic Institution, 2005).

3. Natural History Museum, *Out of the Blue: The UK Whale & Dolphin Stranding Scheme* (London: Dept. of Zoology, 2005), available at www.nhm.ac.uk/.

4. "National Marine Mammal Stranding Program," *Marine Mammal Health and Stranding Response Program*, mmhsrp.nmfs.noaa.gov/.

5. For Madagascar, "Independent Review of a 2008 Mass Stranding in Madagascar," *International Whaling Commission*, [2008], iwc .int/. For Hawaii, "July 2004 Mass Stranding of Melon-Headed Whales in Hawai'i," *NOAA Fisheries Office of Protected Resources*, 2004, www.nmfs.noaa.gov/.

6. "Strandings," *NOAA Fisheries Feature*, www .nmfs.noaa.gov/.

7. N. Young, ed., *Odontocete Salvage, Necropsy, Ear Extraction, and Imaging Protocols* (Washington, D.C.: Office of Naval Research and NOAA Fisheries, 2007), available at csi.whoi .edu/.

8. D'Amico et al., "Beaked Whale Strandings and Naval Exercises."

9. A. Read, P. Drinker, and S. Northridge, *Bycatches of Marine Mammals in US Fisheries and a First Attempt to Estimate the Magnitude of Global Marine Mammal By-catch* (Woking, Surrey, U.K.: WWF-UK, 2006); A. Read, "The Looming Crisis: Interactions between Marine Mammals and Fisheries," *Journal of Mammalogy* 89, no. 3 (2008), pp. 541–48.

10. Aristotle, *The History of Animals*, trans. D'Arcy Wentworth Thompson (Oxford, U.K.: Clarendon, 1910), p. 231.

11. Roger Payne, *Among Whales* (New York: Scribner's, 1995), p. 431.

12. Decibels are a measure of sound pressure and intensity. Pressure and intensity are both calculated with respect to a reference pressure. The reference pressures used in these measures differ in air and water. For airborne sound, the reference is twenty micropascals, written "re 20 µPa." For underwater sound, the reference pressure is re 1 µPa. Consequently,

a sound in air and in water that has the same intensity (acoustic power per unit area) has decibel values that differ by 61.5 dB—that is, a sound measured in air at 100 dB re 20 µPa would have a decibel value of 162 dB re 1 µPa in water.

13. G. M. Wenz, "Acoustic Ambient Noise in the Ocean: Spectra and Sources," *Journal of the Acoustical Society of America* 34, no. 12 (1962), pp. 1936–56.

14. National Research Council [hereafter NRC], *Ocean Noise and Marine Mammals* (Washington, D.C.: National Academies, 2003).

15. Ibid.

16. Bryan McGrath, *Nato at Sea: Trends in Allied Naval Power* (Washington, D.C.: American Enterprise Institute, 18 September 2013), available at www.aei.org/.

17. D'Amico et al., "Beaked Whale Strandings and Naval Exercises."

18. A. D'Amico and D. Pittenger, "A Brief History of Active Sonar," *Aquatic Mammals* 35, no. 4 (2009), pp. 426–34.

19. NRC, *Low-Frequency Sound and Marine Mammals: Current Knowledge and Research Needs* (Washington, D.C.: National Academy, 1994); NRC, *Marine Mammals and Low-Frequency Sound: Progress since 1994* (Washington, D.C.: National Academy Press, 2000); NRC, *Ocean Noise and Marine Mammals*; T. M. Cox et al., "Understanding the Impacts of Anthropogenic Sound on Beaked Whales," *Journal of Cetacean Research and Management* (2005).

20. T. Jefferson et al., "An Unusual Encounter with a Mixed School of Melon-Headed Whales *(Peponocephala electra)* and Rough-Toothed Dolphins *(Steno bredanensis)* at Rota, Northern Mariana Islands," *Micronesica* 38 (2006), pp. 239–44.

21. K. D. Kryter, *Handbook of Hearing and the Effects of Noise* (New York: Academic, 1996); N. Slepecky, "Overview of Mechanical Damage to the Inner Ear: Noise as a Tool to Probe Cochlear Function," *Hearing Research* 22 (1986), pp. 307–21.

22. "Quick Statistics," *National Institutes of Health: National Institute on Deafness and Other Communication Disorders (NIDCD),* www.nidcd.nih.gov/.

23. B. L. Southall et al., "Marine Mammal Noise Exposure Criteria: Initial Scientific Recommendations," *Aquatic Mammals* 33, no. 4 (2007).

24. S. H. Ridgway and D. A. Carder, "Hearing Deficits Measured in Some *Tursiops truncatus* and the Discovery of a Deaf/Mute Dolphin," *Journal of the Acoustical Society of America* 101 (1997), pp. 590–94; R. J. Schusterman, B. L. Southall, D. Kastak, and C. Reichmuth, "Age-Related Hearing Loss in Sea Lions and Their Scientists," *Journal of the Acoustical Society of America* 111 (2002), pp. 2342–43.

25. D. R. Ketten, "Marine Mammal Auditory System Noise Impacts: Evidence and Incidence," in "The Effects of Noise on Aquatic Life," ed. A. Popper and A. Hawkins, special issue, *Advances in Experimental Medicine and Biology* 730 (2012), pp. 207–12.

26. Ketten et al., "Cranial Trauma in Beaked Whales," pp. 21–27.

27. D'Amico et al., "Beaked Whale Strandings and Naval Exercises," pp. 453–72; Ketten et al., "Cranial Trauma in Beaked Whales," pp. 21–27.

28. A. Fernández, "Pathological Findings in Stranded Beaked Whales during the Naval Military Manoeuvres near the Canary Islands," in "Proceedings of the Workshop on Active Sonar and Cetaceans," ed. P. G. H. Evans and L. A. Miller, special issue, *European Cetacean Society Newsletter,* no. 42 (2004), pp. 37–40.

29. P. D. Jepson et al., "Gas-Bubble Lesions in Stranded Cetaceans," *Nature* 425, no. 6958 (2003), pp. 575–76; P. D. Jepson et al., "Acute and Chronic Gas Bubble Lesions in Cetaceans Stranded in the United Kingdom," *Veterinary Pathology* 42 (2005), pp. 291–305.

30. Cox et al., "Understanding the Impacts of Anthropogenic Sound on Beaked Whales."

31. S. K. Hooker et al., "Deadly Diving? Physiological and Behavioural Management of Decompression Stress in Diving Mammals," *Proceedings of the Royal Society B* (2012).

32. A. Brubakk and T. Neuman, *Bennett and Elliotts' Physiology and Medicine of Diving,* 5th ed. (New York: Elsevier, 2002); C. Edmonds et al., *Diving and Subaquatic Medicine,* 4th ed. (London: Arnold, 2002), p. 719.

33. C. A. Piantadosi and E. D. Thalmann, "Pathology: Whales, Sonar and Decompression Sickness," *Nature* 428, no. 6984 (15 April 2004), p. 716ff.

34. Z.-L. Jiang et al., "Flow Velocity in Carotid Artery in Humans during Immersions and Underwater Swimming," *Undersea and Hyperbaric Medicine* 21, no. 2 (1994), pp. 159–67; Edmonds et al., *Diving and Subaquatic Medicine;* M. Ferrigno, "Breath-Hold Diving," in *Bove and Davis' Diving Medicine,* ed. A. A. Bove (Philadelphia: W. B. Saunders, 2004), pp. 77–93.

35. There are a great many other postmortem processes, such as bacterial activity, that produce bubbling and froth. See W. U. Spitz, ed., *Spitz and Fisher's Medicolegal Investigation of Death: Guidelines for the Application of Pathology to Crime Investigation,* 3rd ed. (Springfield, Ill.: Charles C. Thomas, 1993), p. 829; R. S. Cotran, V. Kumar, and T. Collins, *Robbins Pathologic Basis of Disease,* 6th ed. (Philadelphia: W. B. Saunders, 1999), p. 1425.

36. G. L. Kooyman, P. Ponganis, and R. Howard, "Diving Animals," in *The Lung at Depth,* ed. C. Lundgren and J. Miller (New York: Marcel Dekker, 1999), pp. 587–620.

37. Young, *Odontocete Salvage, Necropsy, Ear Extraction, and Imaging Protocols.*

38. B. Southall et al., "Marine Mammal Behavioral Response Studies in Southern California," *Advances in Technology and Experimental Methods, Marine Technology Society Journal* 46, no. 4 (2012), pp. 48–59.

39. NRC, *Ocean Noise and Marine Mammals.*

40. "Marine Mammals and the Navy's 5-Year Plan," *New York Times,* 12 October 2012.

41. Spitz, *Medicolegal Investigation of Death.*

42. NRC, *Marine Mammal Populations and Ocean Noise: Determining When Noise Causes Biologically Significant Effects* (Washington, D.C.: National Academies, 2005), p. 15.

43. W. Munk et al., "The Heard Island Feasibility Test," *Journal of the Acoustical Society of America* 96 (1994), pp. 2330–42; J. R. Potter, "ATOC: Sound Policy or Enviro-vandalism? Aspects of a Modern Media-Fueled Policy Issue," *Journal of Environment and Development* 3 (1994), pp. 47–76.

44. NRC, *Marine Mammal Populations and Ocean Noise,* p. 15.

CHAPTER EIGHT

U.S. Coast Guard Response to the *Deepwater Horizon* Oil Spill

REAR ADM. MARY LANDRY, U.S. COAST GUARD (RETIRED)

Navies and coast guards can respond in nonmilitary ways to natural, and especially man-made, disasters. On 20 April 2010, the BP (formerly British Petroleum) *Deepwater Horizon* offshore oil rig caught fire in the Gulf of Mexico, about 250 miles to the south and east of Houston, Texas. The fire could be seen thirty-five miles away. Eleven of the 126 crew members on board the oil rig perished. From 20 April through 19 September 2010, when the wellhead was finally sealed, an estimated 4.2 million barrels of oil leaked out of the five-thousand-foot-deep well, creating the largest offshore oil spill in U.S. history.

The exact cause of the blowout is still being investigated. One study of the accident was initiated by the U.S. Coast Guard (USCG) and the Minerals Management Service on 22 April 2010, only two days after the accident and the same day the *Deepwater Horizon* rig collapsed into the water and sank to the bottom of the Gulf.[1] It appears, on the basis of this study and other scientific reports, that human error was to blame—technicians on the surface misread the fluid pressure data from the oil well below. Once the accident occurred, the rig's "blowout preventer" refused to close properly, which meant that leaking oil could not be contained. The National Commission on the BP *Deepwater Horizon* Oil Spill and Offshore Drilling report, released on 5 January 2011, blamed the accident on human error, specifically risky decisions based on a desire to save time and money.[2]

USCG ships and personnel were among the first responders to the explosion and oil spill. Not only did the Coast Guard help ensure the safety of the remaining crew members as they evacuated the rig, but it initiated a maritime search for those who were missing. Most important, it became the first point of contact for coordinating disaster-response efforts. Rear Adm. Mary Landry, commander of the Eighth Coast Guard District, headquartered in New Orleans, Louisiana, was the top Coast Guard official coordinating a field response that at its height involved over forty-seven thousand people from federal, state, local, tribal, and private-sector agencies and the international community in what she has described as the largest fully integrated response this country has undertaken using the incident command system. After setting the scene of the accident, this chapter will examine the national response to *Deepwater Horizon,* mainly from Rear Admiral Landry's perspective.

The Blowout, Fire, and Oil Spill on *Deepwater Horizon*

On 2 April 2010, just eighteen days before the *Deepwater Horizon* accident, President Barack Obama stated in a North Carolina speech that offshore oil drilling was "technologically very advanced" and that "oil rigs today generally don't cause spills."[3] While, as noted, the exact circumstances that led to *Deepwater Horizon*'s blowout, fire, and subsequent oil spill are still under dispute—legal wrangling could continue for years, perhaps even decades, to fix responsibility for the accident and to determine appropriate fines and compensation—it is quite clear in hindsight that President Obama was too optimistic, as were the federal regulators overseeing offshore drilling and the companies that were pushing the technological edge in drilling ever farther offshore and at ever deeper depths. The nation had seen fewer spills and vastly improved response actions as a result of *Exxon Valdez* and the subsequent Oil Pollution Act of 1990. But it had become complacent; also, certainly, no containment system had been developed, tested, and proven to secure a blowout taking place a mile below the surface of the Gulf of Mexico.

Before turning to a description of the cleanup effort and the impact of the oil spill on the environment, it will be useful to describe the drilling site, the equipment being used, and the likely causes of the accident. These details are relevant for understanding why the U.S. Coast Guard made many of its later decisions on how best to respond to the oil spill. The *Deepwater Horizon* oil rig was a fifth-generation, deepwater, semisubmersible, mobile, offshore drilling unit. It was designed to drill subsea wells to explore for new oil fields in waters up to eight thousand feet deep; it was one of only a handful of oil rigs in the world capable of drilling at depths of over five thousand feet. *Deepwater Horizon* had been built for R&B Falcon, Inc. (a firm that provides marine drilling-rig services), by Hyundai Heavy Industries in Ulsan, South Korea. Construction began in December 1998, the keel was laid on 21 March 2000, and the platform was delivered on 23 February 2001, soon after the acquisition of R&B Falcon by Transocean Ltd. Transocean then leased the oil rig to BP on a three-year contract for deployment in the Gulf of Mexico; the contract was renewed a number of times, ultimately through 2013. BP paid a daily fee of over $500,000 for the use of this platform.[4]

Deepwater Horizon worked on wells in several oil fields before moving to the Macondo Prospect in February 2010, soon after BP acquired drilling rights there in 2009. This field begins about forty-one miles off the southeast coast of Louisiana and lies under approximately five thousand feet of water. By 20 April, drilling of an exploratory well at this location had been technically "concluded"; engineers were in the final stages of sealing the wellhead when the accident took place.[5]

At 9:45 PM central time on 20 April 2010, a geyser of seawater erupted approximately 240 feet into the air. Such an event is called a "blowout." This one appears to have been caused by human error—engineers, thinking the methane gas pressure in the well was significantly lower than it really was, began to replace the heavier drilling fluid with lighter seawater, which proved insufficiently dense to contain the release of methane. When the blowout occurred, a mixture of water, mud, and methane gas was ejected. After the methane ignited, this caused a series of explosions and then an enormous fireball. Engineers on the rig attempted to activate the blowout preventer, which would normally have cut off the gas flow, but the device failed. The preventer had apparently sustained damage in the initial event—it is not known for sure.

One of the many contractors that had employees working on the rig was Halliburton. One of the main jobs of the Halliburton workers was to seal the wellhead with concrete. Drilling had fallen six weeks behind schedule, however, and when it came time to finish the wellhead the "steps required to form a cement seal in the well were shortened or skipped, and the usual test on the cement was eliminated."[6] In addition, software modeling by a Houston-based Halliburton engineer named Jesse Gagliano showed that twenty-one centralizers needed to be used, and there were only six on board *Deepwater Horizon*: "Installing the extra centralizers would take up to ten hours, considerable time on a rig that was costing BP a million dollars a day to lease and operate."[7] To save time, the extra centralizers were not added. Arguably, it was the combination of these shortcuts that resulted in the blowout.

At the time of the explosion there were 126 crew on board: seven were employees of BP, seventy-nine of Transocean, and many others working for contractors like Halliburton, Anadarko, and M-I SWACO. Eleven workers went missing and "were never found despite a three-day Coast Guard (USCG) search and rescue operation" and so were presumed dead.[8] The eleven who died were two mud engineers, Gordon Jones and Keith Blair Manuel; a driller, Dewey Revette; a toolpusher, Jason Anderson; a crane operator, Aaron Dale Burkeen; two assistant drillers, Donald Clark and Stephen Ray Curtis; three floor hands, Karl Kleppinger, Jr., Shane Roshto, and Adam Weise; and a derrick hand, Roy Wyatt Kemp. Most were young, in their twenties and thirties; Keith Manuel was the oldest, at fifty-six, driller Dewey Revette next, at forty-eight.[9]

The oil rig was immediately evacuated, and numerous injured workers were airlifted to medical facilities. Seventeen of the survivors suffered serious injuries. Investigations into the causes of the accident revealed that senior Transocean officials had authorized safety alarms on *Deepwater Horizon* to be "inhibited," since "they did not want people woken up at three o'clock in the morning due to false alarms." The long-term impact of this decision was that on the day of the accident "visual and sound alarms which should have gone off when sensors detected fire or combustible or toxic gases did not warn workers of impending danger."[10]

After burning for approximately thirty-six hours, *Deepwater Horizon* sank on 22 April 2010, which, coincidentally, was Earth Day. Wreckage from the rig was found resting on the seafloor about 1,300 feet, or about a quarter of a mile, to the north and west. Meanwhile, oil continued to seep out of the wellhead. Several efforts to cap the well failed. The oil spill lasted for eighty-seven days before it was finally capped on 15 July 2010. Relief wells were then drilled so as to seal the well permanently. The well was declared "effectively dead" on 19 September 2010. Although estimates differ, the total spill size was about five million barrels (210 million U.S. gallons), making *Deepwater Horizon* the largest accidental marine oil spill in U.S. history.

Creating the Incident Command System

Rear Admiral Landry responded to this accident by using the Incident Command System (ICS), which had been the doctrine for response in the Coast Guard since the mid-1990s. This system was created to help align federal agencies and enhance coordination with states, local communities, Native American tribes, the private sector, and nongovernmental organizations, so as to improve the nation's ability to respond to crisis. The ICS is based on the premise that the most economical and efficient way to respond to crises of the magnitude of the *Deepwater Horizon* accident is to integrate Department of Defense (DoD) capabilities within the existing domestic response structure. This not only makes fiscal sense but also maintains respect for the governance structures and legal authorities that exist at the local, state, and federal levels. By the time this incident occurred, the expectation for oil spill crisis response was that federal, state, and local authorities and the private sector (in this case, BP, as the responsible party) would operate with unity of effort under the Incident Command System.

Since the nineteenth century the U.S. military has been limited in what tasks it can undertake within the country's borders, under the insurrection statute and *posse comitatus*.[11] But there have been instances where the National Guard, under state authority, has responded to natural disasters as well as human-made events, such as the Los Angeles riots in 1992. The military's support for civil authorities has evolved over time. For example, Public Law (PL) 91-606, commonly known as the Disaster Relief Act of 1970, heavily influenced the modern approach to the military support to civil authorities.[12] This act expanded disaster relief and increased the required coordination of federal relief programs. Up to this time, disaster relief had been provided by numerous agencies in an uncoordinated fashion, making it difficult for individuals, businesses, and state and local governments to obtain assistance being offered. In particular, the Disaster Relief Act encouraged states to develop comprehensive relief plans to prepare for disaster relief operations. The Secretary of the Army was given the lead for all military support in disaster response, and his leadership shaped how the military provided this capability in domestic situations.

The next significant piece of legislation that influenced DoD's support to civil authorities (DSCA) came with the enactment of the Robert T. Stafford Disaster Relief and Emergency Assistance Act, PL 100-707, signed into law on 23 November 1988. While expanding the federal government's ability to provide disaster relief to state and local governments after major natural disasters, the Stafford Act also specifically authorized local military forces to provide an immediate response to save lives, prevent human suffering, and mitigate property damage without prior approval from the Secretary of Defense. The act authorized these missions to last up to ten days without specific funding approval, although the local commander was required to request a mission assignment as soon as possible.

During this time the DoD continued to publish military directives and guidance on how to support civil authorities.[13] In the same way that federal law improved coordination among federal agencies, DoD consolidated its guidance for the DSCA mission. In 1992 the federal government published the Federal Response Plan, which focused on federal roles and responsibilities during a disaster.[14] In 1993, DoD republished its military directive, DoDD 3025.1, consolidating all the policies and procedures into one system to provide military support to civilian authorities. A 1997 directive (DoDD 3025.15) clarified the policy's intent on how state and local authorities could request assistance directly from the military.

While both the federal law and DoD legal authorities and policies had been updated to meet the changing times over the years, the events of 9/11 catapulted this work to a new level as the nation reacted to the first act of war on American soil since World War II. Progress in improving incident management quickened; reforms were implemented, and the new funding and added attention from Congress after the terrorist attacks brought fundamental changes. In 2003, President George W. Bush signed Homeland Security Presidential Directive 5, "Management of Domestic Incidents," to enhance the ability of the United States to manage domestic incidents by establishing a single and comprehensive national incident-management system. The Federal Emergency Management Agency (FEMA) was given responsibility to administer the National Incident Management System (NIMS). There was also a concerted effort to have states adopt the Incident Command System, by making NIMS participation a condition of federal preparedness-grant funding. The NIMS can be applied to incident management of everything from terrorist attacks to natural disasters, and it has become the basis for preparedness and response.

In the wake of 9/11, DSCA has rapidly evolved to meet the threat against the homeland. It continues to be refined in the context of providing capabilities to meet "all hazards," including natural and man-made disasters. The policy and planning work at the federal level has made an important leap from scenario-based planning for each potential type of event (which resulted in reams of planning documents to reflect particular scenarios from pandemic to terrorism), to capabilities-based planning (where capabilities are examined and refined to deliver what is needed under any circumstance).

During 2004, the federal government updated the Federal Response Plan, renaming it the National Response Plan, which was itself updated in 2006; finally in January 2008 it was renamed again as the National Response Framework (NRF).[15] The NRF was released as a national guide to conduct all-hazards response. It was built on flexible coordinating structures to align key roles and responsibilities across the country, linking all levels of government (including federal, state, and local), nongovernmental organizations, and the private sector. Meanwhile, the DoD has continued to update policy regarding the DSCA mission, publishing DoDD 3025.18 on 29 December 2010 and change 1 to that directive on 21 September 2012.[16]

Finally, Presidential Policy Directive (PPD) 8, *National Preparedness,* published on 30 March 2011 is intended to strengthen the security and resilience of the nation through systematic preparation for all hazards. Most importantly, it incorporates the concept of an integrated, capabilities-based approach to preparedness, an approach involving everyone from the local citizen to the largest federal agencies and businesses. It should allow for better tracking of the nation's ability to build and improve the capabilities necessary to prevent, protect against, mitigate the effects of, respond to, and recover from threats that pose the greatest risk to the security of the country. Rather than emphasizing preparedness and response to specific types of incidents, like earthquakes or hurricanes, PPD 8, *National Preparedness,* treats domestic incident response as a system with mutually complementary phases and as one that is as a whole one of the building blocks of a more capable and resilient nation ready to deal with all hazards through an "all of nation" response.

The USCG and the NIMS

The U.S. Coast Guard was particularly well positioned to take charge in a crisis. As far back as 1915, Capt. Ellsworth Price Bertholf, Commandant of the Revenue Cutter Service when it merged with the Life-Saving Service to become today's Coast Guard, stated, "The Coast Guard occupies a peculiar position among other branches of the

Government, and necessarily so from the dual character of its work which is both civil and military. Its organization, therefore, must be such as will best adapt it to the performance of both classes of duties."[17] The U.S. Coast Guard had begun investing in NIMS in the wake of the 1989 *Exxon Valdez* oil spill and continued to improve it as the nation expanded its incident management capabilities.

The Coast Guard, as the fifth armed service, is unique in that it is the only service with federal regulatory and law-enforcement authorities. It has operated as a military service in every war and conflict in our nation's history, even while serving locally in the ports and waterways throughout the nation. When the Coast Guard moved into the newly formed Department of Homeland Security in 2003, it continued to focus on incident management and in that connection often worked side by side with Department of Defense colleagues in making the adjustments necessary to integrate NIMS successfully into domestic crisis response.

Simultaneously with the Coast Guard's work, the other branches of the armed forces were examining better ways to integrate their capabilities into the federal response structure. The Department of Defense assigned permanent Defense Coordinating Elements (DCEs) into the ten Federal Emergency Management Agency Regions across the country. Led by Defense Coordinating Officers (DCOs), the DCEs have tremendously improved the ability of DoD to meet the DSCA mission requirements.

Rather than NIMS, the military uses the Joint Operation Planning and Execution System (JOPES). It emphasizes the chain of command and a very clear command-and-control hierarchy, while NIMS places emphasis on unity of effort and coordination with and among federal, state, and local entities, all of which retain their own authorities and jurisdictions. The DCOs and their teams act as the interpreters of the two "languages" of NIMS and JOPES, thereby ensuring that military capabilities can be integrated as needed in a crisis, with clear lines of authority and chains of command for the military coordination with civil authorities. Synchronization between the military and civil response structures continues to improve among the DCEs, in exercise programs, and in actual responses to major events. It often appears seamless to people both working in and observing from outside the disaster response. That being said, there are always novel aspects to crisis response that challenge unity of effort and coordination. The Gulf oil spill was no exception.

Reacting to the *Deepwater Horizon* Oil Spill

Rear Admiral Landry assumed command of the Eighth Coast Guard District, headquartered in New Orleans, Louisiana, during June 2009. This timing was deliberate, meant to allow her to get in place and oriented to the region prior to the peak of the hurricane season. She gave a high priority to traveling to meet each of the Gulf Coast governors and other key leaders, visit state emergency operations centers, and inspect key Department of Defense commands. The list included the governors of Louisiana, Florida, and Mississippi, and the homeland security leaders and heads of the emergency operations centers of these three states, as well as Texas and Alabama.

Rear Admiral Landry also visited the Army Corps of Engineers, Mississippi Valley Division, with headquarters in Vicksburg, Mississippi, under the command of Maj. Gen. Mike Walsh. The Army Corps of Engineers was a key component, providing critical waterway management of locks and dams throughout the district and heavily involved in building the $14.5 billion hurricane barrier and flood-control project authorized by Congress in the wake of Katrina to protect New Orleans from another flooding crisis.

The 2009 hurricane season passed relatively quietly, but it was merely the calm before the real storm—on 20 April 2010, when the *Deepwater Horizon* accident occurred. The government reaction to this accident was the largest fully integrated response the United States has ever undertaken using the Incident Command System. At its height, tens of thousands of responders were being coordinated from federal, state, local, tribal, and private-sector entities. There were also representatives included from academia, national laboratories, nongovernmental institutions, and the international community.

The response was organized under the National Oil and Hazardous Substances Pollution Contingency Plan (NCP), the Oil Pollution Act of 1990 (OPA 90), and the Coast Guard's Spill of National Significance (SONS) protocol.[18] The NCP had been published in 1968 in the wake of a massive oil spill from the tanker *Torrey Canyon* off the coast of England, and it outlined a process for a comprehensive and coordinated spill response. The NCP continued to be updated to reflect best practices and lessons learned from various worldwide incident responses; the latest update was completed in 1994 after the passing of OPA 90 legislation following the *Exxon Valdez* oil spill in Alaska. The SONS protocol was the Coast Guard's published policy doctrine, continuously exercised.

Legislation and doctrine clearly outlined the structure of the response under the Incident Command System and laid out a unified command construct wherein the federal and state agencies and responsible party would work together to minimize the environmental impact from the spill. But it soon became clear that the scale and scope of the *Deepwater Horizon* incident would eclipse what had been envisioned in the OPA 90 legislation and would test the doctrine and practices of all involved. Every tanker, every barge, every coastal marine oil terminal that transferred oil from the waterway to shore, and every mobile offshore drilling unit, such as *Deepwater Horizon* itself, had to have a plan to respond to a worst-case discharge of oil. In other words, the responsible party had to provide its own resources on the basis of what it identified as the worst-case-scenario discharge. The oil companies, in turn, relied on contracts with companies called "oil-spill-response organizations," which had both locally based resources and access to resources around the world.

In terms of natural resources, the Eighth Coast Guard District is one of the richest in the United States, by virtue of its extensive shipping, fishing, and offshore drilling. Rear Admiral Landry clearly outlined the "worst case scenario parameters" during the first hours of the response. As she repeatedly stated in her first news conferences to the *Today Show,* "The potential scale and scope of this spill was going to be immense and require the full capacity of response companies, federal agencies, states, local communities, and even the Department of Defense."

It is hard to describe the sense of urgency everyone felt after the accident—it was like being in a vortex where everyone was totally consumed by the task at hand and what drew us all together was a full sense of what was at risk. The intensity can be compared to that of the Coast Guard work in port security post-9/11. Just as 9/11 required us to protect our nation and way of life from terrorism, the responders to *Deepwater Horizon* were focused on saving an ecosystem and a way of life along the Gulf Coast.

Immediate Decisions after the Accident

The role of the Department of Defense under its DSCA mission was enormous. During the first week of the incident an important meeting and conference call was held that would set the tone and direction for the response by federal agencies, including the Department of Defense. As District Commander, the author assumed the role of Federal On Scene Coordinator (FOSC), which meant field coordination of the overall response. The goal for the FOSC was to direct the response, working to gain consensus among all parties with equities in the response: the Gulf Coast states and local communities, the federal agencies such as the Department of Commerce for federal fisheries and the Department of the Interior for federal trust territories and the offshore energy sector, and others.

Rear Admiral Landry directed the responsible party, in this case BP, to meet its legal obligation under OPA 90, which required the responsible party to be ready to respond to the worst-case scenario. In the initial days she was in constant contact up the chain of command, all the way to the Commandant of the U.S. Coast Guard, Adm. Thad Allen, who was briefing senior cabinet officials and President Obama, along with senior officials of the White House team. Admiral Landry was also in contact with governors of the Gulf Coast states, with Louisiana senators Mary Landrieu and David Vitter, and with other senior congressional leaders from the Gulf Coast states. Within that first week several cabinet secretaries and congressional leaders saw the site of the incident by air and arrived in Robert, Louisiana, for a tour of the command post, a briefing, and a press conference. The group included the Secretary of Homeland Security, Janet Napolitano; the Secretary of the Interior, Ken Salazar; the administrator of the Environmental Protection Agency, Lisa Jackson; and the White House Energy and Climate Coordinator, Carol Browner. The governor of Louisiana, Bobby Jindal, accompanied the group and spoke at the press conference.

After this event the cabinet secretaries convened in a room to conduct a conference call with other key leaders in Washington, D.C. The importance of this call should not be underestimated, in that it included the Secretary of Defense, the Chairman of the Joint Chiefs of Staff, and the White House National Security Staff lead for domestic response (Richard Reid). Several of these senior leaders were answering to President Obama and keeping him informed on a regular basis. The Coast Guard and FEMA are both under the Department of Homeland Security, and Secretary Napolitano had options for how best to execute the response to the crisis. The author vividly recalls that Secretary Napolitano agreed that the response was best handled under OPA 90 legislation, leaving the responsible party funding the response, as opposed to declaring a disaster using the Stafford Act, which would require federal funding.

A second important point of this phone call came when the Secretary of Defense offered anything that might be needed as part of the response under the DSCA rubric. He also suggested that the response team bring in the National Guard to support the governors but have DoD pay the National Guardsmen under federal orders so individual states would not be burdened and would not have to struggle with reimbursement. The fact that the Secretary of Defense and the Chairman of the Joint Chiefs both participated so early in the event demonstrated to everyone that this would be a comprehensive response and that we would be supported by the full capacity of the nation.

As the days, weeks, and months unfolded, active-duty service members, reservists, and National Guardsmen all served in the response in various capacities, and DoD equipment was used for everything from logistics to oil skimming. Rear Admiral Landry repeatedly stated, "There is a sense of urgency, and there has been since day one. We have not backed off on this since day one."[19] Reflecting this urgency, Governor Jindal declared a state of emergency for Louisiana on 29 April. The loss of tourist dollars quickly impacted almost all the Gulf states; estimates of lost revenue climbed into the billions of dollars.

At the start of *Deepwater Horizon* cleanup, a Tyndall Air Force Base unit agreed to provide airspace management. The Gulf of Mexico is like a small city; over thirty thousand people work offshore every day. Helicopters fly people and logistical supplies back and forth to and from the oil rigs. At first the goal was to keep the footprint light and not interfere with routine practices of airspace activity, but over time and after a few near midair collisions, the government put in flight restrictions and ramped up its airspace-management capacity.

Because this was a domestic situation, the Air Force took a supporting and advisory role from the very beginning, thus allowing the Federal Aviation Administration (FAA) to exercise its statutory jurisdiction over management of airspace. There were later accusations that press access to the scene of the accident was too restricted. Local and federal authorities were challenged for denying access to members of the press attempting to document the spill from the air, from boats, and on the ground, by blocking access to areas supposedly open to the public. There was one report that the U.S. Coast Guard stopped Jean-Michel Cousteau's boat and another that a CBS News crew was denied access to oil-covered beaches. The Coast Guard readily admitted that the communication of restrictions was not as clear as it could have been and that this had led to misunderstandings. The Coast Guard public-affairs team, turning to DoD public-affairs specialists for additional capacity, worked through the problems of managing the balance between transparency and safety and environmental protection during this massive response. The latter issues included what were labeled "the boom wars." Booms (floating barriers meant to contain oil on the surface and to block sensitive areas) were a scarce commodity. There were incidents of booms being stolen, of people cutting through booms, and of journalists and civilians tramping through oiled areas, further damaging marshes. These were some of the reasons the Coast Guard put restrictions in place.

A suspicious public and media, however, believed the motive behind the restrictions was to deny access. Members of Congress criticized the restrictions placed on journalists' access. The FAA, for its part, argued that all media access had to be arranged through the Coast Guard. The Coast Guard, supported by DoD, worked hard to overcome the misunderstanding, allowing as many as four hundred journalists to embed themselves on board boats and aircraft, in this way giving access while maintaining safety and environmental protection.

Oil Spill Response

Another example of Department of Defense capability was the Navy's oil spill response equipment. The primary components of the strategy for addressing the spill were containment, dispersal, and removal. Oil began seeping out of the underwater well almost immediately after the accident. An early estimate by BP authorities suggested a rate of a thousand barrels per day, but on 28 April 2010, Rear Admiral Landry stated that it could be closer to five thousand barrels per day, which soon became the official estimate.[20] Later estimates were as much as ten times higher, at between 52,700 and 62,200 barrels per day. Total estimates of leaked oil were approximately 4.9 million barrels

(210,000,000 U.S. gallons), plus or minus 10 percent. BP challenged these higher figures, saying that not only had the government overestimated the total volume but these higher estimates did not reflect over 810,000 barrels (thirty-four million U.S. gallons) of oil collected or burned before entering the Gulf waters. Notwithstanding, and although the total volume is still in dispute, the amount was significant enough to require the full response capacity of the private sector and government.

The Navy has its own oil-recovery equipment, which it uses on naval installations. BP, trying to mobilize everything that was commercially available in the region, found it necessary to contract the Navy equipment for additional capacity. The National Guard proved especially resourceful, building land berms to protect marsh areas and inlets. The berms absorbed the oil before it entered these sensitive areas, wetlands already at risk from loss of land and coastal erosion. Booms stretching altogether over 4,200,000 feet were eventually deployed, either to corral the oil or to serve as barriers. The booms extended an average of eighteen to forty-eight inches above and below the water surface and were especially effective in relatively calm and slow-moving waters. Adding one-time-use sorbent booms, a total of 13,300,000 feet of booms were deployed.

A good example of DoD logistics capability was demonstrated in the midst of the "boom wars." By the early weeks of the response BP had bought virtually the entire global inventory of ocean booms, but governors of the Gulf Coast states were insisting they be provided with enough booms to outline their coastlines and inlets. BP called every ocean-boom manufacturer in the world trying to satisfy the demands of a particular governor who insisted that deliveries were not coming fast enough. BP found that one of the oil-spill response organizations had extra ocean booms in storage in Alaska and authorized a million dollars to have the military fly the booms to the Gulf Coast overnight.

According to satellite images, despite the use of booms to stop the spread of oil, the spill directly impacted sixty-eight thousand square miles of ocean, an area about the size of Oklahoma. This was frustrating for Rear Admiral Landry, who noticed during one aerial inspection that many boats and much cleanup equipment appeared to be sitting idle just beyond the edges of the oil slick. To put pressure on BP, she announced that the Coast Guard would double its manpower in the Gulf: "There is really no excuse for not having constant activity. . . . Our frustration with BP is there should be no delays at all" in making use of emergency equipment.[21]

By early June 2010, after several early failures by BP to stem the flow from the wellhead, oil had washed up onto about 125 miles of Louisiana's coastline. Thad Allen, who had retired as Coast Guard Commandant in May but was still the national incident commander in the Gulf, compared the spill to a war: "And this is a war, it's an insidious war . . . because it's attacking, you know, four states one at a time, and it comes from different directions depending on the weather."[22] At about this same time, the barrier islands in Mississippi, Alabama, and the panhandle of Florida began to be impacted. By July, tar balls had appeared along the shores of Lake Pontchartrain. By September, a new wave of oil unexpectedly hit sixteen miles of Louisiana coastline and marshes west of the Mississippi River in Plaquemines Parish. By October the oil spill even reached Texas. By some estimates, a total of 1,074 miles of coastline was damaged by oil in Louisiana, Mississippi, Alabama, and Florida.

On 15 July 2010, after many delays and failed attempts, the wellhead was finally capped. One industry expert noted that however frustrated the federal, state, and public stakeholders had been with the time it took, industry had designed and built in three months a solution that would under normal research and development standards have taken two to three years. Everyone now agrees that the optimal situation would have been to have the cap on standby during the drilling process, and that is now a Department of the Interior response requirement for deepwater drilling.

Before the wellhead was capped significant amounts of oil were diverted to containment ships, but most of it escaped into the surrounding waters. There were three basic approaches for removing the oil from the water: combustion, offshore filtration, and collection for later processing. Rear Admiral Landry announced a decision to use "controlled burns" miles from shore, which it was hoped "could reduce the amount of oil collected within fireproof booms by more than half, though she acknowledged that the downside was that a plume of soot and possibly toxic air pollutants would be spewed into the atmosphere."[23] From the end of April to mid-July 2010, 411 controlled in-situ fires destroyed approximately 265,000 barrels (11,100,000 U.S. gallons) of oil, or about 5 percent of the amount leaked. As for filtering contaminated water, in mid-June BP ordered thirty-two machines that could separate oil and water, each capable of extracting up to two thousand barrels (320 cubic meters) of oil per day. After a week of testing, BP began to use this equipment and by 28 June had removed 890,000 barrels of oil. The USCG later calculated that 33,000,000 U.S. gallons of tainted water had been recovered by filtration, extracting five million U.S. gallons of oil (about 2 percent of the leaked oil). Finally, about 3 percent of the oil was skimmed from the surface of the water. In total 2,063 skimmers were used, about sixty of them open-water skimmers.

Within about two weeks of the *Deepwater Horizon* disaster, most of the surface oil appeared to have dissipated. Much of it washed up on shore. By summer 2010, approximately forty-seven thousand people and seven thousand vessels were involved in the cleanup project, which soon became one of the largest on record. Sandy beaches and marshlands were the two main challenges. For beaches, the main techniques included sifting sand, removing tar balls, and digging out tar mats by hand or with mechanical devices. For marshlands, techniques such as vacuuming and pumping, low-pressure flushing, vegetation cutting, and bioremediation were used. As of January 2013, the oil cleanup alone had cost BP over fourteen billion dollars.

Although the majority of visible oil deposits were ultimately collected, an unknown amount of subsurface oil remained unaccounted for. In 2010, the Department of the Interior and the National Oceanic and Atmospheric Administration stated that "75% [of the spilled oil] has been cleaned up by Man or Mother Nature." However, since only about 25 percent of the released oil was collected or removed by BP, this meant that about 75 percent of the oil remained in the environment in one form or another.[24] In 2013, at a meeting of the Gulf of Mexico Oil Spill and Ecosystem Science Conference, some experts suggested that as much as a third of the oil may have mixed with deep ocean sediments, where it could continue to harm ecosystems and commercial fisheries.

The methods used to clean up the spill oil were also notable for the sheer volume of an oil dispersant called Corexit they used. It was estimated that 1,840,000 U.S. gallons were dispersed. Some of the application methods were considered "purely experimental," and "BP's use of chemical dispersant underwater, for example, was the first time this method was attempted."[25] Almost half the total amount of dispersants, or some 771,000 U.S. gallons, was released at the wellhead. In addition, over four hundred airplane sorties to disperse Corexit were flown.

There were many unanswered questions about the use of dispersants, especially in such large quantities. Rear Admiral Landry acknowledged these concerns but pointed out that federal scientists had approved their use: "That threshold we crossed was not done lightly. . . . It was done in cooperation with all the federal agencies. . . . It's all a series of trade-offs. We are really trying to minimize the environmental impact of all these methods being done."[26] On 2 August 2010 the Environmental Protection Agency determined that dispersants had stopped a large amount of oil from reaching the coast by breaking it down. However, outside experts continued to voice concerns about this approach. Two years after the spill, one study found that Corexit had increased the toxicity of the oil by up to fifty-two times.[27]

The Department of Defense was instrumental in support of the overall crisis response, as were many other federal, state, local, nongovernmental, and academic institutions. An employee from BP remarked in conversation with the author months after the event that had someone asked him whether BP would need the federal government's help in a scenario such as *Deepwater Horizon* he would have said no but that this response would have proved him wrong; he now readily admitted that it needed the help.

Conclusions

The *Deepwater Horizon* accident was later blamed on excessive risk-taking by the rig's crew: "On the platform the day of the blowout, tests and sensors showed dangerous pressure levels rising in the well, but the idea of a blowout was unthinkable to workers."[28] Considering the unexpected size of the *Deepwater Horizon* accident and the enormous oil spill that it caused, the USCG did a remarkable job helping orchestrate a response that had to take into account all the many instruments of state power. Once the safety of the survivors among the crew was confirmed, top priorities included protecting beaches, marshlands, and estuaries from the spreading oil by utilizing controlled burns, skimmer ships, floating booms, and well over a million U.S. gallons of Corexit oil dispersant. However, adverse effects from the response and cleanup activities, extensive damage to marine and wildlife habitats and to the fishing and tourism industries, and human health problems continued to have a noticeable impact. For example, in July 2013, more than three years after the spill, the discovery of a forty-thousand-pound tar mat near East Grand Terre, Louisiana, prompted the closure of the local waters to commercial fishing. The Oil Pollution Act of 1990 required the responsible party not only to pay for the response itself but to make restitution for the environmental impact, under a formal natural resource damage-assessment process. That process is still ongoing and could take years. Additionally, in a novel move, Congress passed in June 2012 the Restore Act, which stipulates that 85 percent of the civil penalties collected by the federal government from the responsible parties is to go directly to offsetting environmental and economic impacts to the Gulf states.[29]

This incident shows that oil spill response was inadequate, including how the DoD deploys in support of civil authorities. During *Deepwater Horizon* it took a two-star Coast Guard admiral—Rear Adm. Jim Watson—several days working with the Department of Defense just to get the accounting straight for the military interdepartmental purchase request required to allocate troops and capabilities to the crisis. Something is wrong with a system that tied up that much manpower to figure out the paperwork in the critical first days of the response.[30] Additionally, some units in DoD deploy to domestic situations with the same complements they use going overseas. But when deploying domestically they need to go in lighter, to have more adaptive packages, so as to ensure that the most efficient and effective resources are applied to the situation. DoD resources do not come cheap, but they can be indispensable. The key is to strike the right balance between what is needed for domestic crisis response and what the Department of Defense is uniquely able to provide.

The legal disputes caused by the *Deepwater Horizon* explosion and oil spill are not over. Numerous investigations to determine responsibility for the accident have been conducted. Notably, a U.S. government report on the disaster in September 2011

determined that defective cement on the wellhead was mainly to blame, for which it
faulted BP, Transocean, and Halliburton. Earlier in 2011 a White House commission
had likewise criticized BP and its partners for a series of cost-cutting decisions and
an insufficient safety system. It concluded that the spill resulted from "systemic" root
causes and that "absent significant reform in both industry practices and government
policies, might well recur."[31] In November 2012 BP and the Department of Justice settled
outstanding federal criminal charges, and BP agreed to four years of government monitoring of its safety practices and ethics. In January 2013, Transocean agreed to pay $1.4
billion for violations of the Clean Water Act, and two months earlier BP and the Department of Justice agreed to a record-setting $4.525 billion in fines. As of February 2013,
however, BP had paid a stunning $42.2 billion in criminal and civil settlements, as well
as payments to a recovery trust fund—altogether the largest payout of its kind in history.

Notes

Tragically, eleven souls were lost in the initial explosion of *Deepwater Horizon,* there was damage to the environment, and many people's lives were altered. But the healing continues, and the Gulf Coast was saved.

The thoughts and opinions expressed in this essay are those of the author and are not necessarily those of the U.S. government, the U.S. Navy Department, or the Naval War College.

1. "Coast Guard Confirms *Horizon* Sinks," *Upstream Online,* 22 April 2010, www.upstreamonline.com/.

2. Ayesha Rascoe, "BP and Firms Made Risky Decisions before Spill: Report," Reuters, 5 January 2011, reuters.com/.

3. Glenn Croston, *The Real Story of Risk: Adventures in a Hazardous World* (Amherst, N.Y.: Prometheus Books, 2012), p. 103, citing "Remarks by the President in a Discussion on Jobs and the Economy in Charlotte, North Carolina," *White House: Office of the Press Secretary,* 2 April 2010, www.whitehouse.gov/.

4. Croston, *Real Story of Risk,* p. 103.

5. "Updated: Search Continues for 11 Missing Workers," *Rigzone,* 22 April 2010, rigzone.com/.

6. Croston, *Real Story of Risk,* p. 103.

7. Abrahm Lustgarten, *Run to Failure: BP and the Making of the* Deepwater Horizon *Disaster* (New York: W. W. Norton, 2012), p. 310.

8. Leslie Kaufman, "Search Ends for Missing Oil Rig Workers," *New York Times,* 24 April 2010, p. A8.

9. Tomás Mac Sheoin and Stephen Zavestoski, "Corporate Catastrophes from UC Bhopal to BP *Deepwater Horizon:* Continuities in Causation, Corporate Negligence, and Crisis Management," in *Black Beaches and Bayous: The BP Deepwater Horizon Oil Spill Disaster,* ed. Lisa A. Eargle and Ashraf Esmail (New York: Univ. Press of America, 2012), p. 62.

10. Ibid., p. 69, citing E. Pilkington, "BP Rig's Alarms Were Switched Off 'to Help Workers Sleep,'" *Guardian,* 24 July 2010.

11. The Insurrection Act of 1807, 10 USC §§ 331–35; Posse Comitatus Act, 18 USC § 1385, original at 20 Stat. 152, passed 18 June 1878.

12. Pub. Law No. 91-606, 84 Stat. 1744, 31 December 1970, as quoted by Alice R. Buchalter, *Military Support to Civil Authorities: The Role of the Department of Defense in Support of Homeland Defense* (Washington, D.C.: Library of Congress, February 2007), p. 4.

13. *DoD Issuances: The Official Department of Defense Website for DoD Issuances,* www.dtic.mil/whs/directives/corres/.

14. See www.FEMA.gov. 9230.1-PL Supersedes FEMA 229 (April 1992).

15. "National Response Framework," *Federal Emergency Management Agency,* www.FEMA.gov.

16. This directive with change 1 included superseded DoDD 3025.1 and 3025.15, and it provides the most current DoD policy guiding the DSCA mission. *DoD Issuances.*

17. "United States Coast Guard Historian's Office," *United States Coast Guard,* www.uscg.mil/.

18. See "Emergency Response: National Oil and Hazardous Substances Pollution Contingency Plan (NCP) Overview," *EPA: United States Environmental Protection Agency,* www2.epa .gov/; Oil Pollution Act of 1990, 33 USC § 2701, as amended through PL 106-580, 29 December 2000; U.S. Homeland Security Dept., *Spill of National Significance (SONS) Response Management,* Commandant Instruction 16465.6 (Washington, D.C.: Commandant, United States Coast Guard, 23 May 2012).

19. Mike Magner, *Poisoned Legacy: The Human Cost of BP's Rise to Power* (New York: St. Martin's, 2011), p. 247.

20. John Barnshaw and Lynn Letukas, "Beyond Petroleum in the Gulf of Mexico: The Characteristics and Consequences of Catastrophe," in Eargle and Esmail, *Black Beaches and Bayous,* p. 44.

21. Magner, *Poisoned Legacy,* p. 247.

22. Ibid., p. 256.

23. Ibid., p. 212.

24. Richard A. Kerr, "A Lot of Oil on the Loose, Not So Much to Be Found," *Science* 329, no. 5993 (13 August 2010), pp. 734–55.

25. Sheoin and Zavestoski, "Corporate Catastrophes from UC Bhopal to BP *Deepwater Horizon,*" p. 79.

26. Magner, *Poisoned Legacy,* p. 234.

27. Douglas Main, "Dispersant Makes Oil 52 Times More Toxic," *Science on NBC News.com,* www.nbcnews.com/.

28. Croston, *Real Story of Risk,* p. 104.

29. Bruce Alpert, "Congress Passes Restore Act, Flood Insurance Extension in Massive Transportation Bill," *Greater New Orleans Times-Picayune,* 29 June 2012, www .nola.com/.

30. The author understands that DoD has since improved the military interdepartmental purchase request process.

31. "Obama Oil Spill Commission's Final Report Blames Disaster on Cost-Cutting by BP and Partners," *Daily Telegraph* (London), 5 January 2011.

CHAPTER NINE

Deep Blue Diplomacy
Soft Power and China's Antipiracy Operations
ANDREW S. ERICKSON AND AUSTIN M. STRANGE

For the first time in its modern history China has deployed naval forces operationally beyond its immediate maritime periphery for extended durations, to protect merchant vessels from pirates in the Gulf of Aden. Over a six-year span beginning in December 2008, China has contributed over ten thousand navy personnel in nearly twenty task forces and has escorted over six thousand Chinese and foreign commercial vessels in the process. While it is uncertain how many task forces will be deployed and for how long, China will likely remain in the Gulf of Aden through 2015, and perhaps longer if the United Nations further extends its mandate for navies to fight piracy off Somalia.[1] China's naval antipiracy mission represents an unprecedented instance of conduct by the Chinese People's Liberation Army Navy (PLAN) of sustained long-distance operations. It provides a rare window by which outside observers can see how the naval component of China's "going out" strategy cuts across economic, political, and strategic dimensions. While many of China's other maritime activities damage its international image, antipiracy operations in the far seas project soft power and a positive image.

The Chinese navy's antipiracy missions provide much-needed security for Chinese overseas interests. But the PLAN has also crafted its antipiracy missions to portray blue-water operations positively abroad. Increasingly, the PLAN's antipiracy mandate is oriented toward broader international security objectives. Commercial escort statistics exemplify this trend: initially China's navy was only allowed to escort Chinese-flagged ships through the Gulf of Aden, but now in some cases over 70 percent of ships in given Chinese escort flotillas have been foreign flagged. Similarly, to secure the maritime commons Chinese commanding officers and sailors serving off Somalia have worked increasingly in the framework of bilateral exchanges with other navies as well as in multistakeholder settings.

This chapter explores the soft-power dimension of China's far-seas antipiracy operations. It addresses the extent to which Gulf of Aden deployments might increase the PLAN's prospects for cooperation with other navies and also the impact of these missions on the role the navy plays within China's larger diplomacy. Finally, it assesses how these deployments might relate to future Chinese naval development.

Historical Background

A sharp increase in piracy attacks off Somalia threatened to interfere with China's foreign trade. Several well-publicized pirate attacks prior to the PLAN's antipiracy deployment in 2008 demonstrated Chinese vulnerability. *Tianyu 8,* a fishing boat with twenty-four crewmen, the Chinese tanker *Zhenhua 4,* and the Sinotrans-owned cargo ship *Dajian,* as well as two Hong Kong–registered ships, *Stolt Valor* and *Delight,* were all pirated prior to the PLAN's deployment.[2] Over 1,200 Chinese merchant vessels transited the Gulf of Aden during the first eleven months of 2008, and of this number eighty-three were attacked by pirate groups. Direct threats to China's economic interests and citizens abroad were thus important drivers of the PLAN's first antipiracy deployment.

As the PLAN's initial deployment prepared to set sail in December 2008, Senior Col. Huang Xueping, Ministry of National Defense secondary spokesman and deputy director of the ministry's Information Office, convened a news conference in which he clarified the points that, first, the mission's primary objective was to protect Chinese shipping interests, and that, second, it did not represent a change in Chinese foreign policy or a desire to project greater blue-water naval capabilities.[3] Idealistic and realistic interpretations of China's antipiracy operations differ greatly. The former focuses on China's desire to contribute meaningfully to regional and international security, while the latter includes a "desire to protect Chinese shipping, expand China's influence, and to provide opportunities for realistic training that will enhance the PLAN's capabilities in military operations other than war."[4]

In line with the realists, economic interests in the Gulf of Aden had perhaps the greatest impact on pragmatic Chinese policy makers. As Foreign Ministry spokesman Liu Jianchao explains, "Piracy has become a serious threat to shipping, trade and safety on the seas. . . . That's why we decided to send naval ships to crack down."[5] China's overseas maritime trade is highly dependent on vulnerable sea lines of communication (SLOCs), such as the Bab el Mandeb, Strait of Hormuz, Indian Ocean, Strait of Malacca, Strait of Singapore, and South China Sea. China currently relies on just five SLOCs for roughly 90 percent of its overseas trade. In particular, approximately 60 percent of all commercial vessels that transit through the Strait of Malacca are Chinese flagged.[6]

For China, therefore, the economic benefits of protecting its international trade are abundantly clear. China's leadership continues to emphasize the PLAN's imperative to secure Chinese overseas maritime interests. Specifically, energy supplies transported via international SLOCs will constitute a larger percentage of China's aggregate energy consumption. Having become a net oil importer in 1993, for example, China now relies on seaborne oil imports for over 40 percent of its oil consumption.[7] China's oil import dependence will rise substantially between now and 2030, by some estimates to as high as 80 percent.[8]

Oil and other energy imports constitute just one of many sectors in China that face growing dependence on the sea. *China Daily* reported that as early as 2006, maritime industries accounted for $270 billion in economic output, nearly 10 percent of China's gross domestic product.[9] In 2009, over 260 companies, across various industries, reportedly engaged in international maritime shipping.[10] In 2010 it was reported that each year over two thousand Chinese commercial vessels were transiting the Gulf of Aden.[11] In 2011, more than two years after the PLAN's first antipiracy deployment, a professor at China's National Defense University observed, "From the current situation, ocean lifelines have already become a soft rib in China's strategic security."[12]

China's growth as a sea power has been rapid. It currently has more seafarers, deep-sea fleets, and ocean fishing vessels than any other nation. It has become, in the words of Ju Chengzhi, of the Ministry of Transport, a "maritime shipping power" (海运大国). In 2009 China's merchant maritime fleet reportedly consisted of over 3,300 vessels and forty thousand crewmen.[13] *People's Daily* reported in 2011 that China surpassed South Korea as the world's largest shipbuilder in terms of capacity and new orders.[14]

China's maritime responsibilities are huge, since it has thirty-two thousand kilometers of coastline and claims over three million square kilometers of offshore waters.[15] Public awareness of the importance of maritime issues is increasing. Two Chinese media outlets have reported separate public surveys in which 86 percent and 91 percent of Chinese citizens polled supported the PLAN's antipiracy deployment.[16] Simultaneously, many Chinese "netizens" (frequent Internet users) have criticized their government for its inability to ensure Chinese sailors' safety.[17]

Domestically, in the period before deployments began Beijing faced strong political incentives to intervene decisively to protect its shipping. These political concerns at home paralleled international expectations. Such deployments, it was predicted, would enhance China's image as a "responsible stakeholder" in international society, particularly in the domain of maritime security.[18] In the years since, China's antipiracy operations have already aided the PLAN substantially in developing its blue-water capacity.

Military Development and Blue-Water Aspirations

Beijing's deployment of PLAN antipiracy forces appears to be spurring on Chinese military development. As the Chinese newspaper *Global Times* puts it, over five years of deployments to the Gulf of Aden have transformed PLAN antipiracy forces from "maritime rookies to confident sea dogs."[19] Since China has not fought an actual war since its 1979 conflict with Vietnam, this experience of maintaining multiyear, distant deployments of warships is extremely valuable. In 2011, a PLAN senior captain effectively summarized the multidimensional benefits of distant sea antipiracy operations: "The experience definitely would be unprecedented not only for officers and sailors, but also for the durability and function of the ships."[20]

Furthermore, antipiracy operations have positioned the PLAN as China's most active service. By proving its effectiveness against threats to Chinese overseas interests, the PLAN has ensured that it will continue to procure some of the military's newest and best technology.[21] More broadly, the persistent threat of piracy in international waters has enabled China to expand its far-seas security operations under the umbrella of benign international cooperation.[22]

Close analysis of PLAN antipiracy activities reveals four primary conduits for projecting soft power: the escort of commercial ships and other direct operational aspects of PLAN antipiracy missions; navy-to-navy meetings, combined training, and other exchanges and instances of cooperation with foreign navies; participation in multistakeholder dialogues on land and at sea related to international antipiracy operations; and, perhaps most significantly, a growing number of port visits conducted by PLAN warships for replenishment and diplomatic purposes before, during, and after service in the Gulf of Aden. Exploiting these channels has positioned the PLAN as an important and highly visible player in China's comprehensive quest for international soft power.

Antipiracy services provided by the PLAN to commercial ships have primarily included area patrols, escorts, and on-ship protection.[23] Wang Yongxiang, deputy commander of the tenth escort task force, explains that specific tactics depend on multiple idiosyncratic factors: "the schedules of the merchant vessels to be escorted, their characteristics, and how well our warships have rested. We want to not only ensure the safety of our charges, but also improve the efficiency of escort protection."[24] Area patrol—monitoring certain maritime zones in and around the Gulf of Aden—is the approach least employed by the PLAN. When China's navy does engage in area patrols, it typically maintains two base points 550–600 nautical miles apart—for example, one a hundred nautical miles north of Yemen's Socotra Island and the other seventy-five nautical miles southwest of Aden Harbor.[25] On a normal mission PLAN vessels travel between these points, typically taking two to three days to do so.[26]

Of all the services provided by China's antipiracy forces, the escort of civilian ships is the most common; it has become a daily practice for PLAN task forces in the Gulf of Aden. Task forces consist of two warships—usually a combination of destroyers and frigates—and a replenishment or landing ship. However, since the first task force, two or more warships concurrently stationed in the Gulf of Aden have led separate flotillas of merchant ships, sometimes in opposite directions, through an area west of longitude fifty-seven east and south of latitude fifteen north.[27]

PLAN escort efficiency has improved significantly since 2008. As a 2010 *Liberation Army Daily* article states, "From the first escort to the escort of the 1,000th ship the Chinese naval task force used over 300 days, from the 1,000th to the 2,000th ship used over 220 days, and from the 2,000th to the 3,000th ship only used over 180 days' time."[28] As early as 2011, approximately 70 percent of ships escorted by China's navy at any given time were foreign.[29] In terms of aggregate escorts over the first four years, roughly 50 percent of PLAN-escorted commercial vessels were foreign flagged.[30] *People's Navy* reported in mid-2011 that China had provided escort services to ships from over fifty foreign countries, and this figure has likely increased over the past four years.[31] *People's Daily* emphasizes that escort services are provided gratis for Chinese and foreign commercial ships.[32] That is, PLAN escort services are being provided as a complimentary public good to the international community.

Foreign civilian ships can apply online to join a PLAN escort convoy via the China Shipowners' Association website. Zhai Dequan, deputy secretary-general of the China Arms Control and Disarmament Association, has asserted, "China shoulders responsibility for foreign vessels based on growing national strength and a friendly policy"; many other states do not send escort forces, because of limited interest and the enormous costs. In Zhai's opinion, "such international cooperation and exchanges also help the rest of the world to know more about China and accept it."[33]

Given the international context in which China's antipiracy operations take place, the PLAN has taken steps to professionalize its services. For example, the use of the English language is important while conducting international operations; the twelfth task force had an on-duty translator on board the frigate *Yiyang* to liaise with foreign naval and merchant counterparts.[34] Each PLAN task-force member receives four "pocket books" covering the psychological aspects of deployment, security, international law, and the application of international law to military operations. Also, naval officers specializing in international law provide full-time legal support to officers and crews in meetings with ships of other nations.[35] These efforts have assisted China's internavy exchanges.

Internavy Exchanges and Dialogues at Sea

Chinese and international commentators greatly value the unprecedented exposure of PLAN vessels and crews to foreign navies.[36] Rear Adm. Michael McDevitt, USN (Ret.), articulates the historical significance of the PLAN's deployments in this way: "In terms of international engagement, the first decade of the 21st century should be divided into a pre–anti-piracy operations period and a post-anti-piracy period, because once the PLAN began to conduct anti-piracy operations, the entire nature of its approach to international naval engagement changed appreciably."[37]

The missions have had an undeniable impact on Chinese naval diplomacy; interaction with foreign navies that was novel in 2008 is now routine in the Gulf of Aden and adjacent waterways. In 2011, Han Xiaohu, commander of China's eighth escort task force, visited in March the flagship, a frigate, of NATO's Operation OPEN SHIELD; in May, hosted the Singapore navy's Rear Adm. Harris Chan, then commander of U.S.-led Combined Task Force (CTF) 151, on a PLAN warship; and in June hosted the European Union Naval Force (EU NAVFOR) commander on board the frigate *Wenzhou*.[38] The PLAN and Singapore navy conducted bilateral exchanges in September 2010 in the Gulf of Aden, sending personnel on board each other's ships.[39] China's navy conducted more exchanges with CTF-151 in July 2012 and with NATO in April and July 2012.[40] An article in *People's Daily* stated in 2012 that Chinese naval escort task forces continue to inform the outside world about the "activities of suspicious ships through network mailbox and radio station every day and shared information resources with 50-odd warships of 20-plus countries and organizations."[41]

China's naval diplomacy in the region goes well beyond shipboard interactions with Western antipiracy forces. For example, PLAN task forces off the Horn of Africa have also been active in a variety of bilateral exchanges. The PLAN and the Russian navy executed joint antipiracy escorts for the first time in October 2009, during the PEACE BLUE SHIELD 2009 (平蓝盾—2009) exercise.[42] Similarly, China's navy held extensive joint exercises with Russian navy BLUE SHIELD units in May 2011 and conducted similar antipiracy joint exercises in both 2012 and 2013.[43] Amid comprehensive Sino-Russian joint maritime exercises in 2012, Chinese and Russian naval forces performed extensive piracy-deterrence and rescue joint training off the coast of Qingdao.[44]

The Chinese navy is not interacting only with large navies. During November 2009, PLAN military officials met with Dutch counterparts to perform on-ship inspections and exchanges, and during 2010 PLAN forces collaborated with South Korean naval units in antipiracy exercises in the Gulf of Aden.[45] In 2012, China and South Korea conducted joint antipiracy exercises in which helicopters of the two sides landed on each other's warships for the first time.[46] In April 2011, China's eighth escort task force sent *Wenzhou* and *Qiandaohu* to conduct joint antipiracy exercises with the Pakistani guided-missile destroyer *Khyber*.[47] These combined drills followed the Pakistani-hosted PEACE 11 multinational maritime exercises, which included naval ships from, among other states, China, the United States, Britain, France, Japan, and Pakistan. China sent guided-missile frigates *Wenzhou* and *Ma'anshan,* two helicopters, and seventy special forces commandos.[48] More recently the PLAN conducted joint antipiracy training with the Ukrainian navy in the Gulf of Aden. All of these efforts support China's growing naval diplomacy.

Chinese Naval Diplomacy

At-sea engagements with other navies are crucial for establishing a positive image of China's growing global maritime presence. These engagements are complemented by a growing focus by the PLAN on establishing effective relationships with littoral states in and adjacent to the Indian Ocean region. Indeed, since 2008 the nature and scope of Chinese naval port visits have expanded continuously. Growing port calls bolster China's far-seas soft-power projection by facilitating interaction and dialogue between China and the many countries whose ports and geographic locations heighten the strategic value of these relationships.

The PLAN is increasing port visits (see the table) as its far-seas antipiracy presence matures. A small sample reveals the dynamism with which the PLAN is engaging the navies, governments, and citizens of littoral states in connection with its antipiracy missions. For example, during September 2012, *Yiyang* of the twelfth escort task force arrived in Karachi for a second cycle of rest and replenishment, during which it held seminars and other exchanges with Pakistani naval counterparts.[49] Later that year Rear Adm. Zhou Xuming and members from the twelfth escort task force met with Commo. Jonathan Mead, acting commander of the Australian Fleet, in Sydney on an official visit. The Australian chief of navy, Vice Adm. Ray Griggs, remarked, "I welcome the continued opportunity for our navies to share their experiences today as we exchange lessons learned in the conduct of counter-piracy operations."[50] More recently, in late 2013 the fifteenth escort task force, in addition to holding friendly exchanges with fleets from the EU, United States, and NATO, docked for friendly visits in Tanzania, Kenya, and Sri Lanka.[51]

Clearly, uninterrupted operations in the Gulf of Aden have helped to facilitate PLAN maritime engagement with other countries in the vicinity as well as those strategically situated on the route from China to Somali waters. China has effectively increased the role of naval diplomacy as a component of its antipiracy deployments in a number of world regions. *People's Daily* reports that "since the 2nd Chinese naval escort task force, the Chinese navy has established a new mechanism of organizing escort warships to pay friendly visits to foreign countries, and the Chinese naval escort task forces have successfully paid friendly visits to more than 20 countries, such as India, Pakistan, the United Arab Emirates (UAE) and Singapore."[52]

Selected Port Visits by PLAN Antipiracy Forces

ALGERIA Algiers • 2–5 April 2013, friendly visit **AUSTRALIA** Sydney • 18–22 December 2012, friendly visit **BAHRAIN** Manama • 9–13 December 2010, friendly visit **BULGARIA** Varna • 6–10 August 2012, friendly visit **BURMA** Rangoon • 29 August–2 September 2010, friendly visit **DJIBOUTI** Djibouti • 24 January 2010, replenish/overhaul • 3 May 2010, replenish/overhaul • 13 September 2010, replenish/overhaul • 22 September 2010, replenish/overhaul • 24 December 2010, replenish/overhaul • 21 February 2011, replenish/overhaul • 5 October 2011, replenish/overhaul • 24–29 March 2012, replenish/overhaul • 14 May 2012, replenish/overhaul • 13–18 August 2012, replenish/overhaul • 1–6 December 2012, replenish/overhaul • 6–8 June 2013, replenish/overhaul • 28 July 2013, replenish/overhaul • 7–9 October 2013, replenish/overhaul • 22–26 February 2014, replenish/overhaul • 1–5 April 2014, replenish/overhaul and friendly visit **EGYPT** Alexandria • 26–30 July 2010, friendly visit **FRANCE** Toulon • 23–27 April 2013, friendly visit	**GREECE** Crete • 7 March 2011, replenish/overhaul Piraeus • 9–13 August 2013, friendly visit **INDIA** Cochin • 8 August 2009, friendly visit **ISRAEL** Haifa • 14–17 August 2012, friendly visit **ITALY** Taranto • 2–7 August 2010, joint drills and friendly visit **KENYA** Mombasa • 2–5 January 2014, friendly visit **KUWAIT** Shuwaikh • 27 November–1 December 2011, friendly visit **MALAYSIA** Port Kelang • 6 December 2009, friendly visit **MALTA** • 26–30 March 2013, friendly visit **MOROCCO** Casablanca • 9–13 April 2013, friendly visit **MOZAMBIQUE** Maputo • 29 March–2 April 2012, friendly visit **OMAN** Masqat • 1–8 December 2011, friendly visit Salalah • 21 June–1 July 2009, replenish/overhaul • 14 August 2009, replenish/overhaul • 2 January 2010, replenish/overhaul • 1 April 2010, replenish/overhaul

Selected Port Visits by PLAN Antipiracy Forces, continued

- 8 June 2010, replenish/overhaul
- 10 August 2010, replenish/overhaul
- 8 January 2011, replenish/overhaul
- 19 January 2011, replenish/overhaul
- 10 April 2011, replenish/overhaul
- 8–11 June 2011, replenish/overhaul
- 23 June 2011, replenish/overhaul
- 7–10 November 2011, replenish/overhaul
- 21–24 February 2012, replenish/overhaul
- 1–3 July 2012, replenish/overhaul
- 9 July 2012, replenish/overhaul
- 28–29 March 2013, replenish/overhaul

PAKISTAN
Karachi
- 5–8 August 2009, joint drills and friendly visit
- 7–13 March 2010, joint drills and friendly visit
- 13 March 2011, joint drills
- 8 September 2012, replenish/overhaul

PHILIPPINES
Manila
- 13–17 April 2010, friendly visit

PORTUGAL
Lisbon
- 15–19 April 2013, friendly visit

QATAR
Doha
- 2–7 August 2011, friendly visit

ROMANIA
Constanţa
- 31 July–3 August 2012, friendly visit

SAUDI ARABIA
Jidda
- 27 November–1 December 2010, friendly visit
- 3 September 2011, replenish/overhaul
- 17 June 2012, replenish/overhaul
- 1–6 January 2013, replenish/overhaul
- 5–28 April 2013, replenish/overhaul
- 14–18 September 2013, replenish/overhaul
- 2–6 November 2013, replenish/overhaul

SEYCHELLES
Port Victoria
- 14 April 2011, friendly visit
- 16–20 June 2013, friendly visit

SINGAPORE
Changi
- 5–7 September 2010, replenish/overhaul and joint drills
- 18–20 December 2011, replenish/overhaul and friendly visit
- 5–10 September 2013, friendly visit

SOUTH AFRICA
Durban
- 4–8 April 2011, friendly visit

SRI LANKA
Colombo
- 5–7 January 2010, friendly visit
- 7–12 December 2010, friendly visit
Trincomalee
- 13–15 January 2014, friendly visit

TANZANIA
Dar es Salaam
- 26–30 March 2011, joint drills and friendly visit
- 29 December 2013–1 January 2014, friendly visit

THAILAND
Sattahip
- 16–21 August 2011, joint drills and friendly visit
- 21–25 April 2012, friendly visit
- 12–16 September 2013, friendly visit

TURKEY
Istanbul
- 5–8 August 2012, friendly visit

UKRAINE
Sevastopol
- 31 July–3 August 2012, friendly visit

UNITED ARAB EMIRATES
Abu Dhabi
- 24–28 March 2010, friendly visit

VIETNAM
Ho Chi Minh City
- 13 January 2013, friendly visit

YEMEN
Aden
- 21 February 2009, replenish/overhaul
- 25 April 2009, replenish/overhaul
- 23 July 2009, replenish/overhaul
- 28 September 2009, replenish/overhaul
- 5 February 2010, replenish/overhaul
- 16 May 2010, replenish/overhaul
- 26 July 2010, replenish/overhaul
- 1 October 2010, replenish/overhaul

Whereas in all of 2009 PLAN task forces berthed in foreign ports in just five states, Chinese antipiracy flotillas have, among them, stopped in over ten countries every year since 2010. Moreover, the nature of port calls has evolved dramatically during the past six years. In 2009 and 2010 most Chinese port calls were conducted for replenishment, rest, and relaxation. But by 2012 Chinese antipiracy escort task forces had made eight port calls for friendly visits (i.e., for primarily diplomatic reasons), and this trend has continued over the last two years. This demonstrates a growing share of Chinese naval resources devoted to diplomacy. More importantly, it illustrates the efficiency with which the PLAN is deriving soft-power capital from its contributions to international maritime nontraditional security.

China has also bolstered international exchanges by hosting foreign navies at Chinese ports and cities. In mid-May 2011 China invited twenty representatives from eight African nations, including Algeria, Cameroon, and Gabon, to participate in a twenty-day maritime law enforcement program in Zhejiang Province.[53] At the first International Symposium on Counter-Piracy and Escort Cooperation, in February 2012 at the PLAN Command College in Nanjing, Navy Military Studies Research Institute senior researcher Cai Weidong stated, "The Chinese navy hopes to build up a platform for international cooperation that will allow naval forces of different countries to familiarize themselves with each other. I hope the platform well serves our antipiracy goals."[54]

As these examples illustrate, China has derived incrementally greater soft-power benefits from its antipiracy operations by boosting the number of both midmission port calls and diplomatic and friendly visits en route home. Chinese scholar Wang Yizhou has called for a higher degree of "creative involvement," a foreign policy concept that identifies and adapts creative and flexible modes of foreign engagement on a case-by-case basis.[55] The PLAN seems to be applying Wang's concept in the far seas, perhaps most notably through its antipiracy operations, without changing their fundamental form. Adding more stops before and after antipiracy service in the Gulf of Aden has allowed the PLAN to accumulate larger soft-power gains. This practice reflects the PLAN's greatest lesson from far-seas antipiracy missions: there is no substitute for experience, and six years of continuous operations have allowed China gradually to become more effective in securing its comprehensive interests through the deployment of antipiracy task forces.

Arguably even more than foreign port calls, other nontraditional maritime security operations facilitated by Beijing's Gulf of Aden antipiracy presence contribute to China's "deep blue diplomacy." Escort of foreign vessels carrying Syrian chemical weapons through the Mediterranean and active participation in search and rescue operations during the frantic search for Malaysia Airlines Flight 370 in early 2014 are just two examples of how the PLAN has leveraged antipiracy resources to contribute to international security.[56]

Some commentators are less sanguine about China's attempts to expand its maritime relations; it is important to note that there are objections to the notion that China's antipiracy missions are benign. In that view, self-interested economic and security calculations are arguably the largest drivers of the PLAN's deployment of warships to the Gulf of Aden, and viewing port visits as diplomatic exchanges risks oversimplification, since many states may view them as harbingers of creeping Chinese power projection.[57] For example, the tiny island-state Seychelles is one of several coastal and island African states in which China has actively sought to enhance its soft power.[58] China could be using antipiracy operations to support an aggressive naval development policy, as well as to pursue a more active grand strategy that involves overseas access facilities and a long-term trend toward a greater overall global presence.

Chinese Naval Development

The PLAN is just one of several "independent" providers of antipiracy assets in the Gulf of Aden. While the majority of naval antipiracy forces fight pirates under the aegis of multilateral commands, several states—including China, India, Iran, Japan, Malaysia, and Russia—have primarily operated on a unilateral basis rather than under the command of multinational antipiracy forces such as CTF-151, NATO's Operation OPEN SHIELD, or EU NAVFOR. This posture suggests that China is probably trying to learn as much as it can from other navies without revealing much about its own operations, while also, clearly, maintaining ideological independence in foreign policy.

China's preference to abstain from combined operations is driven by several factors. First, greater independence allows the PLAN to conduct its preferred method of antipiracy operations—relatively low-risk escort operations aimed at deterring, rather than actively searching for, pirates. It also offers China an individual identity as a provider of maritime public goods, rather than as just another state operating within Western-led security mechanisms. Moreover, if China joined the existing security structure, potential frictions might arise that could preclude meaningful integration, such as sensitivities related to information sharing and technology theft. Some Chinese defense experts opposed acceptance of the U.S. Navy's invitation to participate in the 2014 RIMPAC exercises and other joint maritime cooperation activities for such reasons.[59]

These concerns notwithstanding, China's antipiracy operations over the past several years have made meaningful contributions to Gulf of Aden security. In addition, they have achieved unprecedented coordination between China and other antipiracy maritime forces in the region, such as those of the United States. While suspicions abound regarding China's motives, antipiracy cooperation may contribute to more positive outside perceptions of China and its international status. China has been "ready to exchange information and cooperate with the warships of other countries in fighting Somalian pirates" since its inaugural deployment in 2008.[60] One PLAN antipiracy task force commander, Adm. Du Jingcheng, has recalled that he was eager to "facilitate exchanges of information with escort naval vessels from other countries."[61]

In the nearly six-year period beginning December 2008, the PLAN has coordinated information with over twenty nations, including the United States.[62] Li Faxin, associate professor (and lieutenant commander) at the Naval Marine Academy, states that PLAN antipiracy forces have established "high-trust partner relations" (高度信任的伙伴关系) with many nations operating in the Gulf of Aden.[63]

Positive results have also been facilitated by Shared Awareness and Deconfliction (SHADE), a voluntary multistate antipiracy information-sharing mechanism. SHADE meetings occur quarterly in Bahrain and regularly host naval and industry leaders from various states. Willingness on the part of independent navies, China's in particular, to synchronize their antipiracy operations with those of Western forces within the SHADE mechanism is a historic achievement for twenty-first-century maritime commons governance.

China was denied SHADE chairmanship in 2009 but, notwithstanding, coordinates its antipiracy escorts with those of other SHADE members. For example, China has participated in SHADE's Convoy Coordination Working Group and coordinates its monthly escort schedules with other navies providing independent escorts. China, India, and Japan reportedly began coordinating their antipiracy operations as early as 2011.[64] They mutually arranged escort schedules twenty-nine times between January and March 2012, with China acting as the coordinator for ten escorts, India for ten, and Japan for nine.[65]

Conclusions

For six years the PLAN's antipiracy operations in the Gulf of Aden have symbolized China's burgeoning out-of-area naval activity. They also showcase Beijing's growing ability to achieve soft-power objectives while concurrently promoting its overseas interests and military development. Important components of these missions include escort of commercial ships, navy-to-navy meetings, participation in multistakeholder dialogues on antipiracy operations, and, most significantly, the growing number of port visits undertaken by PLAN warships. These position the PLAN as an important and highly visible player in China's recent soft-power diplomacy.

China's ongoing antipiracy operations in its far seas have generated many positive assessments. In contrast to its contentious near seas, where Beijing is consistently embroiled in sovereignty disputes that show no signs of abating, antipiracy missions represent the most significant positive component of China's naval engagement to date, particularly with regard to the degree to which Chinese vessels and sailors are interacting with the outside world. This interaction not only enhances China's maritime image in the eyes of its antipiracy partners but may help alleviate fears that China's naval rise might one day threaten twenty-first-century maritime prosperity in regions beyond the near seas. The United States and China reportedly planned over forty visits, exchanges, and other engagements for 2013, double the number in the previous year, and successfully carried out joint antipiracy exercises in 2012 and 2013.[66] In 2014, China participated in RIMPAC for the first time, the U.S.-hosted forum that is currently the largest naval exercise in the world.

The PLAN's experience fighting piracy in distant seas is a benchmark that can be used by Beijing to cement its positive image in the international arena. Antipiracy operations prove that the PLAN can be a provider—not merely a consumer or, worse, a disrupter—of maritime commons security. International society largely perceives Chinese naval contributions to fighting piracy as positive developments, perceptions that stand in sharp contrast to China's hard-power naval approaches in the East and South China Seas. The nature and perceived efficacy of China's soft power are constantly being scrutinized by scholars.[67] While it is too early to speculate exactly how Beijing's contributions to antipiracy today will bolster its future soft-power influence, the results should be at least moderately positive. More generally, the Gulf of Aden case suggests that China will continue to reap international political benefits commensurate with its contributions to international maritime security.

Notes

The thoughts and opinions expressed in this essay are those of the authors and are not necessarily those of the U.S. government, the U.S. Navy Department, or the Naval War College. An expanded version of this chapter appeared as an article in the Winter 2015 issue of the *Naval War College Review*, pp. 71–91.

1. 陈国全 [Chen Guoquan] and 张新 [Zhang Xin], "海军将继续派兵护航" [Navy Will Continue to Send Troops to Escort], 解放军报 [Liberation Army Daily], 27 December 2013, mil.news.sina.com.cn/.

2. "4艘香港货船申请解放军护航3艘被劫商船2艘已获释" [4 Hong Kong Cargo Ships Apply for People's Liberation Army Escorts, 3 Vessels Have Already Been Hijacked, 2 Vessels Have Already Been Released], 人民网--港澳频道 [People's Net: Hong Kong & Macau Channel], 1 January 2009, hm.people.com.cn/.

3. China Ministry of National Defense News Conference, 23 December 2008, available at military.people.com.cn/ and www.gov.cn/.

4. Erik Lin-Greenberg, "Dragon Boats: Assessing China's Anti-piracy Operations in the Gulf of

Aden," *Defense and Security Analysis* 26, no. 2 (2010), pp. 213–30.

5. Wu Jiao and Peng Kuang, "Sailing to Strengthen Global Security," *China Daily*, 26 December 2008, www.chinadaily.com.cn/.

6. 吴超 [Wu Chao] and 李大光 [Li Daguang], "海上运输线事关中国发展" [Maritime Shipping Lanes Related to China's Development], 海洋热点 [Ocean Hot Spots], 当代海军 [Modern Navy] (October 2011), p. 51.

7. China's dependence on imports as a proportion of total oil consumption had reportedly risen above 55 percent during 2011. See "Experts Warn of China's Rising Imported Oil Dependence," Xinhua, 14 August 2011, news .xinhuanet.com/.

8. See "到2030年中国进口石油依存度将达到 80%" [China's Oil Import Dependence Will Increase to 80 Percent by 2030], 中国资本 证券网 [China Capital Securities Net], 24 September 2011, money.163.com/.

9. "10% of GDP Now Comes from Sea, Says Report," *China Daily*, 10 April 2007, www .chinadaily.com.cn/.

10. 徐菁菁 [Xu Jingjing], "我们为什么要护 航--专访交通运输部国际合作司司长局 成志" [Why We Want to Escort: Interview with Ju Chengzhi, Head of the Ministry of Transportation's International Cooperation Department], 三联生活周刊 [Sanlian Life Weekly], no. 3, 19 January 2009, pp. 92–95, www.zsnews.cn/.

11. Yang Jingjie, "Captains Courageous," *Global Times*, 24 December 2012, www.globaltimes .cn/.

12. 韩旭东 [Han Xudong], "制定国家海洋运 输安全战略" [Formulate National Maritime Transportation Security Strategy], 瞭望新闻 周刊 [Outlook Weekly] 14, 4 April 2011, p. 2, www.zaobao.com.sg/. Original text: "从目前 形势看, 海洋生命线已成为我国战略安全中 的软肋. 这主要是因为: 一是过度依赖外轮 进行海外运输."

13. Xu Jingjing, "Why We Want to Escort."

14. "China Overtakes S Korea as World's Largest Shipbuilder," *People's Daily Online*, 20 January 2011, english.people.com.cn/.

15. "Blue Economy Becomes New Growth Engine for E China," Xinhua, 22 July 2013, www .chinausfocus.com/; Wan Jianmin, "从'沿海'走 向'远海'" [From "Littoral Seas" to "Far Seas"], 经济日报 [Economic Times], 19 August 2011, cpc.people.com.cn/.

16. "网友: 支持中国海军护航树起大国形象" [Netizens: Support Chinese Naval Escorts Establishing the Image of a Great Power], 人民 网 [People's Net], 24 December 2008, military .people.com.cn/.

17. 黄立 [Huang Li], 剑指亚丁湾: 中国海军远 洋亮剑 [Sword Pointed at the Gulf of Aden: The Chinese Navy's Bright Far-Oceans Sword] (Guangzhou: 中山大学出版社出 [Zhongshan Univ. Press], 2009), p. 169.

18. 顾国良 [Gu Guoliang], "中美关系的积极发 展" [The Positive Development of Sino-U.S. Relations], 学习时报 [Study Times], 19 April 2006, www.china.com.cn/.

19. Yang Jingjie, "Captains Courageous."

20. "PLA Navy to Send 11th Batch of Escort Fleets to Somali Waters," *CCTV News Content* (English and Mandarin), 24 February 2012, newscontent.cctv.com/.

21. "中国海军赴索马里军舰雷达系统世界领 先" [Satellite System of Chinese Navy Warship Going to Somalia a World Leader], 3 March 2009, mil.news.sina.com.cn/.

22. Susanne Kamerling and Frans-Paul van der Putten, "An Overseas Naval Presence without Overseas Bases: China's Counter-piracy Operation in the Gulf of Aden," *Current Chinese Affairs* 40, no. 4 (2011), pp. 119–46.

23. 孙自法 [Sun Zifa], "中国海军护航舰艇编 队将以三种行动方式护航" [Chinese Navy Escort Fleet to Adopt Three Modes of Action in Escort], 中国新闻社 [China News Service], 3 January 2009; 责任编辑: 付志伟 [Responsible Editor: Fu Zhiwei], "中国护航编队将 在任务海区设7个巡逻区" [China's Escort Fleet Will Set Up Seven Patrol Zones in the Sea Area to Which It Is Tasked], 中国新闻 网 [China News Net], 4 January 2009, news .xinhuanet.com/.

24. "PLA Navy's Escort Formations Continuously Improve Their Pelagic [Open Sea] Escort Capabilities through Practice in Live Situation," 军事报道 [Military Report], *CCTV-7* (Mandarin), 1130 GMT, 26 December 2011.

25. Sun Zifa, "Chinese Navy Escort Fleet to Adopt Three Modes of Action in Escort"; Fu Zhiwei, "China's Escort Fleet Will Set Up Seven Patrol Zones."

26. Yang Jingjie, "Captains Courageous."

27. Sun Zifa, "Chinese Navy Escort Fleet to Adopt Three Modes of Action in Escort"; Fu Zhiwei, "China's Escort Fleet Will Set Up Seven Patrol Zones."

28. 李建文 [Li Jianwen], "为了黄金航道的和谐平安: 写在海军护航编队护送中外商船总数突破 3000 艘之际" [For the Harmony and Safety of the Golden Waterway: Written at the Time of the 3000th Escort Breakthrough by Naval Escort Task Forces of Chinese and Foreign Ships], 解放军报 [Liberation Army Daily], 4 December 2010, p. 4, www.chinamil.com.cn/.

29. "Number of Ships Escorted by Chinese Naval Escort Task Forces Hits 4,000," *Liberation Army Daily,* 19 July 2011, eng.chinamil.com.cn/.

30. Zhao Shengnan, "Navy Protects Ships from Pirates," *China Daily,* 29 December 2012, europe.chinadaily.com.cn/.

31. 王智涛 [Wang Zhitao] and 侯瑞 [Hou Rui], "走向深蓝的新里程--写在中国海军护航编队护送中外商船总数突破4000艘之际" [A New Course for Moving toward Deep Blue: Written at the Time of the 4,000th Escort of Chinese and Foreign Ships by the Chinese Naval Escort Task Forces], 海军军事 [Naval Military Affairs], 人民海军 [People's Navy], 19 July 2011, p. 4.

32. Cao Jinping and Mo Xiaoliang, "Review of Chinese Navy's Escort Missions in Gulf of Aden in Past 4 Years," *People's Daily,* 27 December 2012, english.peopledaily.com.cn/.

33. Zhao Shengnan, "Navy Protects Ships from Pirates."

34. Cheng Bijie and Hou Rui, "Mercury Net Boosts Exchange between Chinese and Foreign Escort Task Forces," *Liberation Army Daily,* 13 November 2012, eng.chinamil.com.cn/.

35. 刘炎迅 [Liu Yanxun], 陈晓舒 [Chen Xiaoshu], 王婧 [Wang Jing], 何婧 [He Jing], 李郝然 [Li Haoran], and 姚忆江 [Yao Yijiang], "远征索马里背后: 中国海军挺进'深蓝'" [Background of Expedition to Somalia: Chinese Navy Pushes Forward to Blue Water (lit., "Deep Blue")], 中国新闻周刊 [China News Weekly], no. 403, 5 January 2009, pp. 22–27.

36. 孙彦新 [Sun Yanxin] and 朱鸿亮 [Zhu Hongliang], "中国海军首批护航编队开创人民海军历史上多个'第一'" [Chinese Naval First Escort Task Force Achieves Multiple "Firsts" in History of People's Navy], Xinhua, 28 April 2009, news.xinhuanet.com/.

37. Michael McDevitt, "PLA Naval Exercises with International Partners," in *Learning by Doing:*

The PLA Trains at Home and Abroad, ed. Roy Kamphausen, David Lai, and Travis Tanner (Carlisle, Pa.: Army War College Press, 2012), pp. 81–125.

38. "NATO Flagship Welcomes Chinese Naval Task Force Commander," news release, *Allied Maritime Command Headquarters,* 28 March 2011, www.manw.nato.int/; Liu Yiwei and Tang Shifeng, "CTF-151 Commander Visits 8th Chinese Naval Escort Task Force," *Liberation Army Daily,* 9 May 2011, eng.mod.gov.cn/; "EU NAVFOR Force Commander Meets CTF 526 in Salalah," *EU NAVFOR Public Affairs Office,* 27 June 2011, www.eunavfor.eu/.

39. 张鑫鑫 [Zhang Xinxin] and 余黄伟 [Yu Huangwei], "我护航编队与新加坡护航编队互访" [Chinese and Singaporean Escort Task Forces Exchange Visits], 人民海军 [People's Navy], 28 September 2010, p. 1.

40. 吴德春 [Wu Dechun], 胡全福 [Hu Quanfu], and 米晋国 [Mi Jinguo], "第十一批护航编队与美盟151编队指挥官非正式互访" [Commanders of Eleventh Escort Task Force and CTF-151 Hold Informal Exchanges], 人民海军 [People's Navy], 13 July 2012, p. 1; 陈典宏 [Chen Dianhong] and 米晋国 [Mi Jinguo], "第十一批护航指挥员与北约508特混编队指挥官会面交流" [Commanders of Eleventh Escort Task Force and NATO 508 Special Forces Hold Exchanges], 人民海军 [People's Navy], 18 July 2012, p. 1.

41. Cao Jinping and Mo Xiaoliang, "Review of Chinese Navy's Escort Missions."

42. For an interview on the exercise hosted by Li Jie, see 李杰 [Li Jie], "中俄联合护航行动意义非凡" [Sino-Russian Joint Escort Operations Have Profound Meaning], 海上争鸣 [Maritime Schools of Thought Contending], 当代海军 [Modern Navy] (November 2009), pp. 56–58. See also 姚子宝 [Yao Zibao], 余晶俊 [Yu Jingjun], and 张庆宝 [Zhang Qingbao], "和平蓝盾—2009透视: 中俄护航编队联合军演" [Perspective: "Peace Blue Shield–2009" Sino-Russian Escort Task Forces Joint Military Exercises], 海天看点 [Maritime Points], 当代海军 [Modern Navy] (April 2010), pp. 28–33.

43. 王智涛 [Wang Zhitao] and 侯瑞 [Hou Rui], "海军举行'蓝盾11突击-2011A'演练: 旨在为日后营救我被海盗劫持商船奠定基础" [Navy Holds "Blue Shield Assault—2011A": Exercise to Lay Foundation for Future Rescue of Our Merchant Ships Hijacked by Pirates], 人民海军 [People's Navy], 11 May 2011, p. 1.

44. 张庆宝 [Zhang Qingbao], 梁庆松 [Liang Qingsong], and 钱宏 [Qian Hong], "演习科目精彩纷呈 演习取得重要成果 中俄联演海上实兵演习捷报频传" [The Exercise Subjects Are Splendid and Varied, the Exercise Has Produced Important Results: News of Success Keeps Pouring In during the Maritime Actual-Troop Exercise of the China-Russia Joint Exercise], 人民海军 [People's Navy], 27 April 2012, p. 1; "'Maritime Cooperation–2012' Sino-Russian Military Exercise: Main Highlights," 军事报道 [Military Report], *CCTV-7* (Mandarin), 1130 GMT, 23 April 2012.

45. 蔡年迟 [Cai Nianchi], "远洋突击, 我们历练了什么, 人民海军执行护航任务两周军回眸〈二〉[Far Oceans Sudden Attacks, What Have We Experienced and Practiced? A Military Retrospective on the Last Two Weeks of the Chinese Navy's Escort Mission (Part 2)], 人民海军 [People's Navy], 22 December 2010, p. 1.

46. Cao Jinping and Mo Xiaoliang, "Review of Chinese Navy's Escort Missions."

47. "China, Pakistan Navy Conduct First Joint Anti-piracy Drill off Somali Coast," *Naval Today*, 2 May 2011, navaltoday.com/.

48. "'Peace-11' Multinational Joint Maritime Military Exercise Begins," 军事报道 [Military Report], *CCTV-7* (Mandarin), 8 March 2011.

49. "Chinese Naval Escort Task Force Berths at Port of Karachi for Supply and Rest," *Liberation Army Daily*, 10 September 2012, eng.mod.gov.cn/.

50. "Chinese Navy and Royal Australian Navy Share Counter-piracy Lessons," *Australian Government Department of Defence*, 20 December 2012, news.defence.gov.au/.

51. "China's Anti-pirate Fleet Returns from Somali Waters," Xinhua, 23 January 2014, news.xinhuanet.com/.

52. Cao Jinping and Mo Xiaoliang, "Review of Chinese Navy's Escort Missions."

53. "African Officials Study Maritime Law Enforcement in China," *People's Daily*, 11 May 2012, english.people.com.cn/.

54. "PLA Navy Sends Forces to Somalia to Fight Piracy in Gulf of Aden," *CCTV News* (English), 1223 GMT, 27 February 2012.

55. Wang Yizhou, *Creative Involvement: The Evolution of China's Global Role* (Beijing: Peking Univ. Press, August 2013), English excerpt in *China 3.0*, ed. Mark Leonard ([London]:

56. For Malaysia Airlines Flight 370, "17th Chinese Naval Escort Taskforce Departs," *China Military Online*, 25 March 2014, eng.mod.gov.cn/. For Syrian chemicals, "Foreign Ministry Spokesperson Qin Gang's Regular Press Conference on April 25, 2014," *Ministry of Foreign Affairs of the People's Republic of China*, 25 April 2014, www.fmprc.gov.cn/.

57. "UK Commentary Sees 'Commercial Impulses' behind China's 'Empire' of Foreign Ports," Economist.com, in English, 8 June 2013.

58. 钟婷婷 [Zhong Tingting] and 王学军 [Wang Xuejun], "论中国对非洲的软实力外交" [On China's Soft-Power Diplomacy toward Africa], 浙江师范大学学报 (社会科学版) [Journal of Zhejiang Normal University (Social Sciences)] 35, no. 4 (2010), waas.cass.cn/.

59. Dean Cheng, "Countering China's A2/AD Challenge," *National Interest*, 20 September 2013.

60. "Warships to Set Off on Friday for Somalia Pirates," *China Radio International*, 23 December 2008, english.cri.cn/.

61. Bai Ruixue and Zhu Hongliang, "Commander of the Chinese Flotilla for Escort Missions Says: At Present, the Flotilla Does Not Have a Disembarkation Plan," Xinhua, 26 December 2008.

62. "Commander of Chinese Naval Escort Task Force Visits U.S. Guided-Missile Cruiser *Chosin*," *Liberation Army Daily*, 23 November 2009, eng.mod.gov.cn/; "美国151特混编队指挥官访问 '舟山' 舰" [U.S. CTF 151 Commander Visits "Zhoushan"], Xinhua, 2 November 2009, news.xinhuanet.com/.

63. 李发新 [Li Faxin], "第四章: 中国海军护航交流与合作" [Chapter 4: Chinese Naval Escort Exchanges and Cooperation], in 中国海军与海上护航行动 [China's Navy and Maritime Escort Operations] (Beijing: 五洲传播出版社 [China Intercontinental Press], 2013), pp. 87–110.

64. "Indian, Chinese Navies Unite to Tackle Piracy," *Times of India*, 2 February 2012, articles.timesofindia.indiatimes.com/. Japan and China initially agreed to coordinate escorts in March 2009; "Japan, China to Coordinate Moves on Antipiracy Missions off Somalia," *People's Daily Online*, 12 May 2011, english.people.com.cn/.

European Council on Foreign Relations, November 2012), ecfr.eu/.

65. 冯春梅 [Feng Chunmei] and 孝金波 [Xiao Jinbo], "国防部举行例行记者会, 回答海军护航、航母平台、网络黑客攻击等问题: 中印日护航形成统一有序班期" [Ministry of National Defense Holds Routine Press Conference, Answers Questions on Naval Escorts, Carrier Platforms, and Network Hacker Attacks: China, India and Japan Escorts Have Formed Unified Coordinated Schedules], 人民日报 [People's Daily], 30 March 2012, news.163.com/.

66. David Alexander, "China Navy Chief Says Operational Aircraft Carrier a Few Years Away," Reuters, 12 September 2013, www.reuters.com/.

67. Joseph Nye, "Soft Power," *Foreign Policy,* no. 80 (Autumn 1990), pp. 153–71; Trefor Moss, "Soft Power? China Has Plenty," *Diplomat,* 4 June 2013, thediplomat.com/.

Conclusions
Breaking the Mold
BRUCE A. ELLEMAN AND S. C. M. PAINE

Navies are most commonly thought of in terms of warfare, when the primary naval objective is closing the commons to the enemy while keeping it open to friends. In peacetime, the main objective is keeping the commons open to lawful use by everyone. Nonmilitary missions tend to occur in peacetime, and many indirectly concern the protection of the maritime commons through the enforcement of "good order at sea."[1] Such missions include halting the movement of banned cargoes, preventing interference with the movement of legal traffic, and protecting the environment. Many navies and coast guards cooperate with those of other countries to conduct these missions because all nations share a common interest in safe transit and healthy fisheries.

After the end of the Cold War, many military missions no longer fit the standard war-fighting paradigm. A new term, "military operations other than war," or MOOTW, was coined to describe them. Many officers did not like this shift, since it seemed to diminish the military's role. Gen. John Shalikashvili characterized this widely held (and in his mind erroneous) sentiment as the attitude that "real men don't do mootw."[2] But of course, while the term might be new, the missions are not. A RAND study identified no fewer than 846 military operations other than war between 1916 and 1996 in which just the U.S. Air Force, or its Army predecessor, played a role.[3]

As the nine historical case studies in this volume have shown, for well over a century and a half the U.S. Navy has engaged in many nonmilitary missions, dating back to the antislavery patrols of the 1840s. Navies can play a major role in diplomacy, economics, fisheries, humanitarian relief, scientific research, and disaster relief, to name just a few fields. During these historical missions the Navy did not necessarily focus on aiding American citizens but often on assisting allies or simply those in need. These missions affected numerous audiences, ranging from individuals through interest groups to entire nations. Thus, it is important to consider both the targets of these missions and the wide range of audiences observing from the sidelines and to consider how direct and indirect effects impact all stakeholders.

Targets of Nonmilitary Operations

Whereas during wartime the target of a naval force is typically either an enemy or an ally of the enemy, in nonmilitary operations the "target" is quite often one's own citizens or friends; also the goal is rarely destruction, more often being assistance (see table 1). Examples of such missions include freeing slaves, feeding noncombatants in wartime, shutting down one's own commerce by embargo, protecting marine life through research and pollutant containment, and defending shipping from piracy. If these activities occurred on land, they would be considered matters of law enforcement, not military action, but on the high seas professional navies are often tasked to carry them out; in littoral waters coast guards generally assume these responsibilities.

TABLE 1

Targets of Nonmilitary Operations (in order of importance)

CASE STUDY	DIRECT TARGET	INDIRECT TARGET	COLLATERAL DAMAGE
Slave Trade	slaves (cargo)	abolitionist voters, slave owners, international press	
Venezuela Deterrence	no target—only audiences		
Starvation Blockade	noncombatants in occupied territory	U.S. voters, Entente voters	↓ collateral damage of blockade
Oil Embargo	commerce	Japanese decision makers	↓ U.S. commerce
Vietnamese Refugees	refugees	North Vietnamese government and navy	
Artificial Reefs	ship disposal	sportfishing, tourism, scuba diving	
Sonar and Whales	whales	environmentalists, voters	
Gulf Oil Spill	BP workers, oil cleanup	press, voters, shoreline, fisheries, tourists	
PLAN Antipiracy	pirates	image building at home and abroad, naval training, naval espionage	

Counterintuitively, the indirect, secondary target is often more important than the direct target—for example, domestic voters, who can determine whether politicians remain in office, and the press, which often interprets news items and influences voters. Thus, voters and the press are often the indirect targets of operations to protect the environment and help refugees. After an oil spill, the initial environmental cleanup is the direct target, but press and voter perceptions of the cleanup are often secondary targets. In the case of Britain's "starvation blockade" against Germany in World War I, the strategy might have become unsustainable if it had alienated American and British voters by causing the mass starvation of innocent noncombatants in Belgium and occupied France. Herbert Hoover's humanitarian mission to provide food to those caught in the midst of war avoided this dilemma.

Likewise, if the U.S. Navy can show—by conducting research on sonar and whales—that its activities do not damage marine life, or better yet, if it can improve marine life—by building artificial reefs—voters might view the Navy in an ever more positive light. Although the immediate target of Coast Guard operations following the BP Gulf of Mexico oil spill was the rescue of workers and pressing BP to cap the well, the secondary target of preventing the infiltration of oil into marshlands, which would have outraged conservationists, the fishing industry, and tourists, was even more important for the recovery of the ecosystem. In the case of the Chinese navy's recent antipiracy efforts, the primary target might be the pirates, but the maritime proficiency and intelligence it is gaining, in combination with the pride that Chinese citizens derive from these new power-projection capabilities, are arguably far more important to the Chinese government.

In contrast to these successful operations, it is possible to reach the intended target but in unanticipated and undesired ways. American attempts to pressure Japan to withdraw from China in the 1930s failed; Washington's public ultimatums hardened rather than softened Japanese attitudes. When the United States attempted to deter Japan from further escalation in China, it imposed a succession of sanctions, with great fanfare in the press. Sanctions broadly targeted the Japanese government and people, on the assumption that finance was a central consideration of Tokyo's decision making. Apparently the sanctions did in fact convince Japan's finance minister that war with the United States was untenable; he, at least, received the intended message loud and clear. But Japan's naval and, particularly, army leaders did not wish to accept such a conclusion. They became desperate instead to deter the United States and concluded that attacks across the Pacific constituted their best, albeit remote, hope. So the American strategy backfired with regard to Japan's military leaders and delivered an outcome opposite to what was intended. In this case, the U.S. government correctly gauged Japan's civilian leaders but failed to anticipate the adverse reaction of its military.

Primary targets are often individuals in distress. As various chapters have shown, non-military operations can assist victims of slavery or disaster survivors or help refugees flee a war zone. The number of individuals included can be small or in the tens of thousands, if not more. For example, the Navy's Operation FREQUENT WIND helped thirty thousand refugees flee Vietnam for the Philippines, and melded later into Operation

NEW LIFE, which moved them to Guam for processing before permanent resettlement in the United States and other nations. An important secondary target was the victorious North Vietnamese government, which was denied the ships of the South Vietnamese navy, as well as its officers and their families. Sometimes the secondary targets are audiences—people who witness events and whose subsequent actions may be influenced by the nonmilitary operation.

Audiences of Nonmilitary Operations

In a world connected by instantaneous mass communication, onlookers are far more numerous than participants. Observers can be subdivided into specific audiences with differentiating interests and agendas (see table 2). In the past, the professional press provided the lens through which viewers interpreted events; now, with bloggers and the social media, isolated individuals can unexpectedly attract mass followings. Audiences include voters and political parties at home and in allied and enemy nations, the press at home and abroad, nonstate actors, foreign governments or foreign militaries or foreign intelligence agencies, and also a range of foreign and domestic nongovernmental interest groups, such as environmentalists. In fact, audiences can include any group that has an interest in maritime affairs. The problem for naval strategists becomes reaching the targeted audience without alienating other, unintended audiences.

Publicity is not necessarily an effective method of exerting pressure, particularly in societies concerned with preserving "face," so a navy's ability to stay out of the headlines is valuable. Because naval forces operate far out to sea, their actions generally remain invisible and become public only when a government decides to make them public. The ability to limit the number of audiences is one of the greatest strengths of this "secret service." As Adm. Joseph Prueher, Jr., U.S. ambassador in China during the 2001 EP-3 negotiations, later explained in connection with the success of his efforts to get the aircraft's crew home, negotiating with China often requires building "ladders for the Chinese to climb down" from untenable diplomatic positions.[4] Naval deployments in proximity to the shore but far enough away to be out of the public eye can provide leverage during diplomatic talks without subjecting leaders to public humiliation, let alone to the domestic backlash that such humiliation would entail.

During the Venezuelan crisis, President Theodore Roosevelt's fleet-in-being had no immediate target; rather, its primary audience comprised the highest levels of the German and British governments, whom Roosevelt sought to deter from naval action against Venezuela. A secondary but critical audience was that of South American leaders, whom Roosevelt did not wish to alienate lest they seek outside assistance to counterbalance the United States. In 1906, after forcing Germany to back down, Roosevelt sent Secretary of State Elihu Root on a "goodwill tour" to South America to make it clear that

TABLE 2
Audiences of Nonmilitary Operations and Their Reactions

CASE STUDY	HOME GOVT.	HOME VOTERS	ALLIED GOVTS.	ALLIED VOTERS	ENEMY GOVTS.	ENEMY VOTERS	INTL. PRESS	INTENDED AUDIENCES	UNINTENDED AUDIENCES
Slave Trade	mixed	abolitionists and slave owners	positive	positive	N/A	N/A	positive	abolitionists	slave owners
Venezuela Deterrence	positive	N/A (secret)	N/A (secret)	N/A (secret)	effective	N/A (secret)	N/A (secret)	UK and German governments	South American states
Starvation Blockade	positive	positive	positive	positive	N/A	N/A	positive	home/allied voters, refugee governments	German and UK voters and press
Oil Embargo	mixed	positive	positive	positive	boomerang	boomerang	positive	Japanese government and businessmen	Japanese nationalistic press
Vietnamese Refugees	positive	positive	Philippines unhappy	N/A	angry	N/A	positive	U.S. voters	Filipinos
Artificial Reefs	positive	mixed	N/A	N/A	N/A	N/A	mixed	U.S. voters and press	environ- mentalists
Sonar and Whales	positive	positive	positive	positive	N/A	N/A	positive	U.S. voters and press	environ- mentalists
Gulf Oil Spill	positive	positive	N/A	N/A	N/A	N/A	positive	U.S. voters, U.S. press, Congress	fishermen, sportsmen, tourists
PLAN Antipiracy	positive	N/A	N/A	N/A	N/A	N/A	positive	pirates, foreigners, Chinese people	N/A

the United States desired only to guarantee the independence and sovereignty of the Latin American republics.[5]

But there were other audiences, audiences that Roosevelt wanted to keep in ignorance. He did not wish American voters or the Democratic Party to stir up an anti-British or anti-German crusade that might have strengthened British and German determination to send military forces to the Caribbean. A fourth potential audience was the international press. The mobilization of the entire U.S. fleet was secret to everyone but the American, British, and German governments; it never reached the attention of the press. In the absence of an evident crisis, the American and European press never became an important audience, a fact that avoided unwanted public pressure. Thus, secrecy allowed Roosevelt to reach just the intended audiences without setting off the others.

Even nonhumans can be the targets of naval operations and navy-funded research, with humans the intended audience. In particular, environmentalists are a major, and quickly growing, audience for such issues as marine mammals subjected to intense sound from naval sonar. Navy-sponsored research programs have greatly expanded fundamental knowledge about marine-mammal hearing and have produced innovations in underwater acoustic propagation models, tags for monitoring animals at depth, and increasingly sophisticated operational aids for detecting and predicting movements of individual animals at sea. Such information assists not only the Navy but also a wide range of other audiences in the fields of shipping, fisheries, marine biology, and research to reduce bycatch and ship strikes and to monitor migration patterns, essential behaviors, and population trends.

There is a wide array of audiences associated with environmental disasters. The U.S. Coast Guard, for instance, acted quickly after the *Deepwater Horizon* explosion. The initial target was the rescue of the missing crew members on the oil rig. But the more important audiences of this operation were American voters and Congress, the former wishing to assess the damage and determine which political party to praise or blame, and the latter, in combination with U.S. courts, determining appropriate punishment for BP, with extensive follow-on effects for oil exploration and exploitation in U.S. territorial waters. Restoration of fisheries and coastal economies depended on the efficacy of the environmental cleanup, which affected a number of other audiences, including fishermen, sportsmen, and tourists, to name just a few. Indeed, in the long term, these tertiary audiences may well be the most important politically and restoration of the coastal environment the most important issue economically.

Not all audiences are sympathetic to naval missions conducted during peacetime. For example, most Secretaries of the Navy who served during the antislavery squadron's existence hailed from southern states. Because a primary unintended audience comprised southern plantation owners, who depended on the slave economy, the secretaries were not inclined to suppress the trade. For virtually the entire history of the squadron, the Secretary of the Navy instructed commanders to prioritize the protection of legal American commerce over the suppression of the slave trade. Only when a northerner, Isaac Toucey (1857–61), assumed the post did the primary audience shift to northern abolitionists and the patrols start aggressively targeting the slave trade.

Positive and Negative Objectives and Their Direct and Indirect Effects

The objectives of naval missions can be positive or negative (see table 3). Positive objectives make something happen and so are usually obvious to everyone. These can include facilitating the movement of people or cargo, convoying ships through pirate-infested waters, or promoting research and development to study specific problems. Early in the history of the U.S. Navy, the U.S. Naval Observatory was tasked to become the world's timekeeper and principal authority for navigational astronomical data—a useful, positive objective. A nonmilitary humanitarian-aid mission, such as the Belgian relief effort in aid of noncombatants during World War I, can also contribute to a military operation, in such ways as strengthening the impact of a starvation blockade against the enemy.

TABLE 3

Positive and Negative Objectives

CASE STUDY	POSITIVE OBJECTIVES	NEGATIVE OBJECTIVES
Slave Trade	free slaves (means); catch slave traders (means); halt slave trade (ends)	deter further slave trade (means); prevent movement of banned cargo (ends)
Venezuela Deterrence		deter UK and German intervention in Americas (ends)
Starvation Blockade	feed starving (ends/means); make blockade palatable to voters (ends/means)	prevent collateral damage from blockade (means)
Oil Embargo	force Japan to de-escalate (ends)	prevent cargo movement (means); deter Japan from further escalation (ends)
Vietnamese Refugees	save refugees (means)	prevent NV from taking SV navy (ends)
Artificial Reefs	create new reefs (means); dispose of ships economically (ends)	
Sonar and Whales	research on sonar and whales (means)	avoid hurting whales (ends); avoid alienating environmentalists (ends)
Gulf Oil Spill	rescue BP workers (ends); plug well (ends/means); clean up oil (ends)	prevent spread of oil (means)
PLAN Antipiracy	convoy ships (means); catch pirates (ends)	deter piracy (ends)

NV: North Vietnam
SV: South Vietnamese

While positive objectives are usually easy to document, negative objectives are more difficult to discern, because they seek to prevent undesired actions or situations. Who can prove that anything was prevented or that any attempt was even made? Such "non-events" are virtually impossible to measure and so are often difficult to notice, let alone document. President Roosevelt's "whisper diplomacy," which deterred German and British military intervention in Venezuela, is a rare, well-documented instance of the achievement of a negative objective. His fleet-in-being had a direct effect of deterring European military intervention in the Americas—a very high-value national security objective for the United States.

An equally important indirect effect in that case was the British prime minister's reaction to the crisis (see table 4). Afterward, he chose to cultivate close ties with Washington, an approach that promoted the creation of the Anglo-American "special relationship." While this indirect result was not necessarily sought by Roosevelt at the outset of the crisis, it helped set up the framework of the Anglo-American cooperation that coalesced in World War I, continued through World War II and the Cold War, and arguably remains at the center of American and British foreign policies to this day. Therefore, counterintuitively, indirect effects of negative objectives can be just as

TABLE 4
Direct and Indirect Effects

CASE STUDY	DIRECT	INDIRECT
Slave Trade	slaves; slave owners	press; southern and northern voters
Venezuela Deterrence	British and German governments	British desire to create "special relationship"
Starvation Blockade	hungry noncombatants; UK and German blockade force	U.S., Entente, and Central Powers press and voters; make starvation blockade politically feasible
Oil Embargo	Japanese economy; Japanese people; U.S. businesses	U.S. press and voters; Japanese military
Vietnamese Refugees	refugees; North Vietnam's loss of South Vietnamese navy	morale of U.S. Navy, participants; U.S.-Philippine relations
Artificial Reefs	economical ship disposal; reef creation	environmentalists; recreationists; voters
Sonar and Whales	whales; sonar improvement	environmentalists; voters; pure research
Gulf Oil Spill	rescue BP personnel; oil removal; save fisheries and shoreline	data for lawsuit vs. BP; improvement in U.S. interagency coordination
PLAN Antipiracy	reduce piracy	reduce insurance rates; improve PLAN proficiency; enhance international cooperation

Note: Indirect effects include all audiences influenced.

important as, if not more important in the long run than, the direct effects from the positive objectives that catch people's attention.

Antipiracy missions too concern the negative objective of deterrence. Faced with a growing piracy threat off the coast of Somalia, China's People's Liberation Army Navy (PLAN) began to conduct convoys to achieve the negative objective of deterring Somali pirates from attack. While the primary audience was the commercial shipping, which was directly affected by the success of the convoys, an indirect audience—especially once non-Chinese-flagged ships joined the convoys—was the rest of the world. The international press praised Chinese naval contributions to fighting piracy and China's international image benefited. Increasingly, the PLAN's antipiracy mandate has focused on broad international security objectives to maximize this indirect effect (see table 5).

TABLE 5
Correlation of Positive/Negative Objectives with Direct/Indirect Effects

	DIRECT EFFECTS	INDIRECT EFFECTS
Positive Objective	deliver food to Belgians; rescue refugees (Vietnam); rescue workers, cap well (oil spill); convoy to aid cargo movement (antipiracy); fund R&D (whales)	attract voters (humanitarian or environmental relief); cultivate allies (UK in Belgian relief)
Negative Objective	prevent cargo movement (sanctions); prevent North Vietnam from taking South Vietnamese navy; prevent pollution spread (oil spill)	UK wants "special relationship" with U.S. (Venezuela); prevent environmental damage (oil spill); prevent piracy

R&D: research and development

Deterrence is not always feasible, however. In the early 1940s, an American oil embargo backed up by a fleet-in-being based at Pearl Harbor did not, as had been intended, result in a Japanese withdrawal from China. Rather, it prompted a massive escalation on 7 December 1941—Japan's bombing of Pearl Harbor—along with attacks on British and Dutch interests throughout the Pacific. As one scholar reflects, "It is interesting to speculate whether continuing the oil shipments would have kept Japan out of the war long enough for the deterrent force in the Philippines and in the British Far Eastern Fleet to become completely effective, or whether Japan would have reacted regardless of the oil policy."[6]

Securing the Maritime Commons

One of the Navy's primary missions entails the negative objective of preventing disruption of the global economic order by stopping interference with oceanic transportation. Given that 90 percent of world trade travels by sea, this mission underlies economic prosperity globally. The global commons is often kept open to legal traffic by such non-military missions as elimination of piracy, interdiction of human trafficking, seizure of banned cargoes, prevention of dumping or leaking of pollutants, and research on the maritime environment and other issues.

Focusing on global problems is not new; for the U.S. Navy it dates back to the early nineteenth century. Initiatives by Matthew Fontaine Maury, appointed in 1842 the first superintendent of the Naval Observatory, transformed that institution from a repository for navigational gear and charts to a center for astronomical and oceanographic observation and for data mining of charts and logbooks on currents, winds, and climate. Much of the U.S. Navy's early research, in such areas as hull design, navigational aids, and weaponry, was specific to its missions, but modern-day research and development encompass communications, climate, modeling, deep-sea mapping, visualization of battle spaces, creation of virtual training environments, and physical and cyberspace probes. Many of these research projects provide advantages well beyond war fighting, indeed well beyond the maritime world writ large, to benefit the civilian economy.

Oil spills of the magnitude of *Deepwater Horizon* threaten, if not contained expeditiously, negative environmental effects for decades to come. According to the World Health Organization, dependence on marine resources doubled in a period of about forty years in the twentieth century: "The average apparent per capita fish consumption increased from about 9 kg per year in the early 1960s to 16 kg in 1997."[7] With the oceans already under pressure from overfishing and overuse, the maritime environment may be already damaged beyond repair by permanent ecological changes. Therefore, the protection of the seas from further pollution is not a trivial mission.

The sinking of Navy ships provides for recreational diving an alternative to natural reefs, which diving can damage. Environmental groups such as the Sierra Club and Base Action Network are concerned, however, that the use of the ships for artificial reefs might injure the ecosystem by introducing pollutants and spurring the migration of fish from natural to artificial reefs. But surveys conducted on *Spiegel Grove* off Key Largo, Florida, and anecdotal information from such longer-established artificial reefs as the ex–Coast Guard cutters *Duane* and *Bibb* off Key Largo indicate that the vessels have not diminished marine life on existing reef systems. In fact, artificial reefs can relieve the pressure on the surrounding natural reefs from recreational use and stimulate new populations of reef fish.[8]

In the waters off Somalia, Chinese commanding officers and sailors have worked closely with other navies to secure the maritime commons, through frequent bilateral exchanges as well as multi-stakeholder settings. The PLAN has carefully crafted its antipiracy missions to portray abroad its blue-water operations positively. Initially, China's navy escorted only Chinese-flagged ships through the Gulf of Aden, but recently approximately 70 percent of ships in a given Chinese escort flotilla have been foreign flagged. PLAN antipiracy task forces have called in dozens of foreign ports for a variety of purposes, from core needs, such as replenishment, to diplomatic and friendly initiatives ranging from military parades in Seychelles to the opening of warships for public visits in Malta. Thus, nonmilitary missions can become win-win scenarios for all parties involved.

Win-Win, Lose-Lose, and Mixed-Outcome Operations

Most of the nonmilitary missions discussed in this collection benefited not only the particular nations carrying them out but also many other stakeholders supporting the peaceful use of the global maritime commons. Thus, they were win-win operations for all parties adhering to international law (see table 6). Humanitarian relief, fundamental research, and antipiracy missions all fall into this category.

TABLE 6
Win-Win, Win-Lose, and Mixed-Outcome Operations

CASE STUDY	PROTAGONIST	OPPONENT	GLOBAL AUDIENCE
Slave Trade	win	lose	win
Venezuela Deterrence	win	lose	N/A
Starvation Blockade	win	covert lose	win
Oil Embargo	lose	lose	lose
Vietnamese Refugees	win	lose	win
Artificial Reefs	win	win	win
Sonar and Whales	win	win	win
Gulf Oil Spill	win	win	win
PLAN Antipiracy	win	lose	win

One of the most important humanitarian missions conducted by the U.S. Navy was the post-tsunami Operation UNIFIED ASSISTANCE in Southeast Asia of 2004–2005, in which over thirteen thousand service members on twenty-five U.S. Navy ships delivered essential food, water, and medicine to tens of thousands of desperate survivors.[9] On a much smaller scale, in June 2013 the PLAN deployed hospital ship *Peace Ark* from Zhejiang Province's Zhoushan Port on HARMONIOUS MISSION 2013, in which the vessel visited Brunei, Maldives, Pakistan, India, Bangladesh, Myanmar, Indonesia, and Cambodia over four months. This ship also participated in a combined medical tour with naval ships from Indonesia and Singapore in Labuan Bajo, Indonesia, on 12 September 2013.[10]

Marine research is another win-win. To date, the Navy's Office of Naval Research has supported research for fifty-nine Nobel Prize winners, spanning the fields of chemistry, economics, medicine, and physics (see table 7). Among the first winners were Felix Bloch (physics, 1952), for measurement of magnetic resonance imaging and atomic nuclei, and Georg von Békésy (medicine, 1961), for the biomechanics of hearing, studies seminal to unraveling underwater sound impacts. The Office of Naval Research assisted the *Trieste* deep-sea dives and the development of the deep-diving submersible *Alvin* and experimental underwater habitat Sea Lab, and it funded the remotely operated seafloor vehicle *Jason* and the hunt for *Titanic*. Finally, it has a growing program in unmanned undersea and aerial vehicles deployed for basic research, as well as military uses.

TABLE 7
Office of Naval Research–Supported Nobel Prize Winners, 1952–2010

Felix Bloch	Physics	1952	magnetic measurement in atomic nuclei
Linus Pauling	Chemistry	1954	chemical bond's application to the elucidation of the structure of complex substances
Severo Ochoa	Medicine	1959	synthesis of ribonucleic acid
Donald Glaser	Physics	1960	invention of the bubble chamber
Georg von Békésy	Medicine	1961	explanation of the physical events that take place within the human ear during hearing
Melvin Calvin	Chemistry	1961	explanation of the second stage of photosynthesis
Robert Hofstadter	Physics	1961	electron scattering in atomic nuclei
Charles H. Townes	Physics	1964	invention of the maser and the laser
George Wald	Medicine	1967	identification of visual pigments and their chemical precursors
Haldan Hartline	Medicine	1967	impulse coding in the visual receptors
Hans Bethe	Physics	1967	nuclear reactions, especially energy production in stars
Har Gobind Khorana	Medicine	1968	synthesis of well-defined nucleic acids
Christian Anfinsen	Chemistry	1972	ribonuclease, connection between the amino acid sequence and the biologically active conformation
Robert Schrieffer Leon Cooper	Physics	1972	theory of superconductivity
Gerald Edelman	Medicine	1972	chemical structure of antibodies
Kenneth Arrow	Economics	1972	general economic equilibrium theory and welfare theory
Paul J. Flory	Chemistry	1974	physical chemistry of macromolecules
William Lipscomb	Chemistry	1976	structure of boranes
Herbert Simon	Economics	1978	decision-making process within economic organizations
Peter Mitchell	Chemistry	1978	biological energy transfer through the formulation of the chemiosmotic theory
Herbert C. Brown	Chemistry	1979	use of boron-containing compounds in the organic synthesis
David H. Hubel	Medicine	1981	discoveries concerning the "visual system"
Roald Hoffmann	Chemistry	1981	course of chemical reactions

TABLE 7
Office of Naval Research–Supported Nobel Prize Winners, 1952–2010, continued

Nicolaas Bloembergen Arthur Schawlow	Physics	1981	development of laser spectroscopy
Kenneth Wilson	Physics	1982	critical phenomena in connection with phase transitions
William A. Fowler	Physics	1983	nuclear reactions in the formation of the chemical elements in the universe
Herbert A. Hauptman Jerome Karle	Chemistry	1985	direct methods for the determination of crystal structures
John C. Polanyi Yuan T. Lee Dudley Herschbach	Chemistry	1986	dynamics of chemical elementary processes
Norman F. Ramsey	Physics	1989	atomic precision spectroscopy
Hans Dehmelt	Physics	1989	development of atomic precision spectroscopy
Rudolph A. Marcus	Chemistry	1992	theory of electron transfer reactions in chemical systems
George Olah	Chemistry	1994	carbocation chemistry
Richard E. Smalley	Chemistry	1996	carbon atoms bound in the form of a ball
William D. Phillips	Physics	1997	cooling and trapping of atoms with laser light
Daniel C. Tsui Horst L. Störmer	Physics	1998	quantum fluid with fractionally charged excitations
Walter Kohn	Chemistry	1998	density-functional theory
Ahmed Zewail	Chemistry	1999	transition states of chemical reactions using femtosecond spectroscopy
Eric Kandel	Medicine	2000	signal transduction in the nervous system
Hideki Shirakawa Alan G. MacDiarmid Alan J. Heeger	Chemistry	2000	discovery and development of conductive polymers
Herbert Kroemer	Physics	2000	heterostructures in high-speed electronics and optoelectronics
Wolfgang Ketterle Carl Wieman Eric Cornell	Physics	2001	Bose-Einstein condensation in dilute gases of alkali atoms
John Fenn	Chemistry	2002	identification/structure analyses of biological macromolecules
Paul Lauterbur	Medicine	2003	magnetic resonance imaging
John L. Hall Theodor W. Hänsch	Physics	2005	laser-based precision spectroscopy
Robert H. Grubbs Richard R. Schrock	Chemistry	2005	metathesis method in organic synthesis
Andre Geim Konstantin Novoselov	Physics	2010	two-dimensional material graphene

Source: Darlene R. Ketten, Woods Hole Oceanographic Institution, Woods Hole, Massachusetts.

Antipiracy patrols are a win-win both for those conducting the mission and for shipping companies globally—although they are, of course, a "lose" for the pirates. The *Libera-tion Army Daily,* the PLA's mouthpiece, has described the PLAN as having created by cooperation in the Gulf of Aden an "effective information network with over 50 war-ships from more than 20 countries and organizations through information resource sharing in the Gulf of Aden and the waters off the Somali coast."[11] There are both realist and idealist reasons behind China's antipiracy operations. The former include the "de-sire to protect Chinese shipping, expand China's influence, and to provide opportunities for realistic training that will enhance the PLAN's capabilities in military operations other than war." But the latter involve China's desire to contribute meaningfully to regional security.[12]

Economic win-win scenarios include using naval vessels to create reefs, thereby dispos-ing of old ships cheaply while promoting marine life and recreation. There can be socio-economic benefits from tourism for communities that host artificial reefs. For example, with the *Vandenberg* and the *Spiegel Grove* sinkings, the U.S. Navy, the Maritime Ad-ministration, state and local governments, local business organizations (e.g., chambers of commerce and tourism boards), and advocacy groups were all involved. The *Spiegel Grove* project has recovered most of its costs significantly ahead of schedule, owing in large part to increased tourism from the new diving destination.

Not all win-win scenarios are perceived as such at the time, particularly if there are competing audiences. For example, during the early nineteenth century the U.S. Navy and Royal Navy shared the goal of eliminating the oceanic transport of slaves. The Royal Navy had an active and well-established West Africa Squadron. But the U.S. govern-ment, because of political sensitivities from British searches in the lead-up to the War of 1812, would not allow the British to search American-flagged vessels. Commo. William Edmonstone of the Royal Navy West African Squadron noted, "As vessels engaged in the Slave Trade almost invariably fly the American flag, and our cruisers are prohibited from in any way interfering with them, of course we are to a very serious extent power-less in putting a check on the trade."[13] Thus, American political sensitivity about ship searches undermined what would otherwise have been a clear win for both countries.

Some operations produce public win-win scenarios that are in fact, behind the scenes, win-lose in nature. Herbert Hoover used the fact that his humanitarian relief efforts covertly assisted the blockade of the Central Powers to leverage British support for his efforts, including the free use of British shipping. He also convinced the Germans that if they did not let him feed the noncombatants, Germany would be required by interna-tional law to do so itself. Thus, Hoover presented the humanitarian aid for Belgium and northern France as a win for both parties. However, his private papers show quite clearly that the humanitarian aid allowed Britain to fine-tune its blockade against the Central

Powers so as to affect just their populations, without starving the civilians of occupied countries. The so-called starvation blockade by the Royal Navy proved highly effective: "By the end of World War I there is no question that the German and Austrian populations were suffering as a result of the blockade."[14] In reality, the Belgian relief effort was really a win-lose scenario, in that it assisted the blockaders to defeat the Central Powers.

A win-lose scenario resulted from the rescue of refugees during the final days of the Vietnam War, when thirty-two South Vietnamese naval ships, some in barely seaworthy condition and carrying more than thirty thousand refugees, crossed the South China Sea to the Philippines. The naval escort not only saved the South Vietnamese naval officers and their families from possible persecution but prevented the remaining naval vessels from falling into the hands of the conquering North Vietnamese forces, a clear strategic win for the United States and loss for North Vietnam. For the Philippines it was a win as well: to obtain permission for the ships to land, Ambassador William Sullivan convinced a reluctant President Ferdinand Marcos to give the refugees safe haven in return for the transfer of many of the South Vietnamese naval ships to the Philippine navy.

There is only one lose-lose case study in this collection—the American oil embargo against Japan. Rather than de-escalate the war in China or deter war against the West, the embargo precipitated the escalation of regional wars in Europe and China into a global war. The costs were catastrophic for all sides and produced an outcome antithetical to both American and Japanese interests. By war's end the Japanese had eviscerated the Nationalist forces in China, positioning the communists to win the long Chinese civil war. If there is a lesson to be learned concerning deterrent measures, it would be the requirement for a careful calculation of the value of the undesired behavior to the opponent. Rightly or wrongly, the Japanese government considered prosecution of the war in China to be a matter of regime survival and so felt that it was on "death ground" in late 1941.

Dual-Use Naval Equipment and Cost Efficiency

Given that navies can serve wartime and peacetime missions, the ability to do both promotes cost efficiency (see table 8). The naval capabilities associated with embargo enforcement, reduction of collateral damage from blockades, mitigation of environmental disasters, and fleet-level deterrence enable cost-effective strategies for the United States. Beyond the economies associated with dual use with respect to wartime and peacetime missions, its war-fighting capabilities and nonmilitary missions allow the U.S. Navy to put a combined hard-power and soft-power squeeze on potential enemies, either to predispose to or to deter action.

TABLE 8
Soft- and Hard-Power Capabilities

CASE STUDY	SOFT POWER	HARD POWER
Slave Trade	humanitarian relief	naval task force
Venezuela Deterrence		fleet-in-being
Starvation Blockade	humanitarian relief	focused blockade effects
Oil Embargo	economic sanction	fleet-in-being
Vietnamese Refugees	humanitarian relief	naval escort
Artificial Reefs	environmental protection	
Sonar and Whales	basic research	
Gulf Oil Spill	environmental protection; rescue of workers; disaster relief	use of military planes to fly in extra booms to contain oil spill
PLAN Antipiracy	image building	naval task force

Naval ships are particularly well suited to nonmilitary operations by virtue of these dual-use capabilities. The same naval equipment that can support a war can also support humanitarian missions, patrol operations, or search and rescue. A proficient navy represents a spectrum of capabilities that can be applied in both war and peace. For instance, following the *Deepwater Horizon* disaster the shortage of booms to retain the drifting oil was so severe that military aircraft flew in extra booms from Alaska. In recent years, policy and planning work at the federal level has made an important leap from scenario-based planning for each potential type of event (resulting in reams of planning documents for particular scenarios ranging from pandemics to terrorism) to capabilities-based planning, wherein capabilities are examined and refined to deliver what is needed as circumstances arise. Capabilities-based planning has resulted in the more economical integration of much-needed Department of Defense capabilities into the existing domestic response structure, all the while observing the legal limitations on domestic use of the military.

Many nonmilitary missions involve saving lives and so are extremely time sensitive. Either people are reached in time and saved, or they perish. Such missions involve refugees at sea, people blown overboard from oil rigs, hungry noncombatants, and innocents threatened by pirates. Such problems are solved either quickly or not at all, so speed can be essential. The early-nineteenth-century antislavery patrols were such a mission; they constituted law enforcement, not war fighting, but warships conducted them quite effectively, especially as steam-driven units became available. Similarly, off the coast of Somalia today, *Qingdao,* a Type 052 Luhu-class destroyer commissioned in 1996, served as the PLAN's eleventh successive escort task force's command ship.

High-tech vessels can be assigned relatively easily to nonmilitary missions, thus allowing governments to get the most effective and efficient use out of modern navies. If wartime is supposed to be the exception and peacetime the rule, nonmilitary uses of navies might actually be the most frequently called-for missions and therefore deserving of budgeting attention. Even more importantly, having overpowering naval force on call in times of state-to-state tension can provide sea powers enormous diplomatic leverage to de-escalate crises, even while remaining largely outside public view. Both of these points argue for retaining a large navy composed of many capable ships rather than downsizing or building ships with lesser capabilities. Given the cost of warfare, the ability to avoid war is worth an expensive military force structure. World War II made clear the false economy of failing to maintain military forces in Europe and Asia sufficient to deter expansionist ambitions.

The military use of navies remains their primary purpose, because of the horrendous stakes involved in wars, which one enters with the navy one has, not with the navy one wishes one had. As a former Chief of Naval Operations, Adm. Gary Roughead, has made clear, "I am also a firm believer that the hard power can soften up, but the soft power normally cannot harden up."[15] In wartime, naval coalitions will fail if they lack the naval capabilities to get soldiers and supplies into the theater, to protect overseas trade, or to shut down the commons for enemy use. In peacetime, these naval assets can inspect ships for contraband, act as fleets-in-being to dissuade attack, and conduct a wide range of humanitarian missions.

Many nonmilitary operations involving naval task forces or fleets-in-being can help keep ships in readiness for war. Even while performing useful missions of a nonmilitary nature, crews continue to train for duties essential to warfare. If these humanitarian missions can supplement training exercises, and in particular if some activities turn out to be even more useful than training exercises, they will be viewed in a different financial light—that is, as maximizing tax dollars by incorporating dual-use missions and training.

While the term "MOOTW" dates only to the 1990s, the U.S. Navy has a nearly two-hundred-year history of sponsoring nonmilitary missions that affect many aspects of our lives. After the Cold War ended, the U.S. military developed the "3/1" strategy, in which a big circle called "major combat operations" encompassed several smaller inner circles—stability operations, the global war on terrorism, and homeland defense. This framework was an important first step in the creation of a new maritime strategy. These smaller circles also included counterterrorism, peacekeeping, antipiracy operations, and even humanitarian assistance and disaster relief.[16]

The Navy's March 2015 maritime strategy, *A Cooperative Strategy for 21st Century Seapower,* provides for humanitarian missions: "Naval power projection capabilities also facilitate other elements of 'smart power' missions in the form of humanitarian assistance and disaster response. . . . Positioned to respond rapidly to disasters in key regions, forward naval forces working with allies and partners are ready to save lives, provide immediate relief, and set the conditions for effective civilian response without relying on damaged or inaccessible ports or airfields ashore. This function supports the naval missions of defending the homeland, responding to crises, deterring conflict, defeating aggression, and providing humanitarian assistance and disaster response."[17] Working with allies and coalition partners is key for success. As Ray Mabus, Secretary of the Navy, points out in his preface to the maritime strategy, one of the primary missions of America's sea services is "supporting an ally with humanitarian assistance or disaster relief."[18]

Modern navies should be envisioned not as comprising either military or nonmilitary capabilities but rather as being extraordinarily flexible "hard power" platforms with an infinite array of "hard" and "soft" extension packages at their disposal. While in the past the U.S. Navy has taken the lead in many soft-power missions, in recent years other global navies, such as China's, have performed a wide range of nonmilitary operations as well, such as patrolling sea-lanes against pirates, searching for missing airliners, or conducting a noncombatant evacuation operation in Yemen. These activities break the traditional mold of what most people think of as primary missions. In fact, navies can be important providers of soft-power solutions across a spectrum of natural and man-made threat scenarios ranging from environmental disasters to the outbreak of war.

Notes

The thoughts and opinions expressed in this essay are those of the authors and are not necessarily those of the U.S. government, the U.S. Navy Department, or the Naval War College.

1. Geoffrey Till, *Seapower: A Guide for the Twenty-First Century*, 3rd ed. (London: Routledge, 2013), chap. 12.

2. John T. Fishel and Edwin G. Corr, "Thinking and Writing about COIN," *Small Wars Journal*, 17 July 2013, smallwarsjournal.com/.

3. Alan Vick et al., "USAF MOOTW Operations, 1916–1996," appendix A in *Preparing the U.S. Air Force for Operations Other than War* (Santa Monica, Calif.: RAND, 1997), pp. 79–162, available at www.rand.org/.

4. See John B. Hattendorf and Bruce A. Elleman, eds., *Nineteen-Gun Salute: Case Studies of Operational, Strategic, and Diplomatic Naval*

Leadership during the 20th and Early 21st Centuries (Newport, R.I.: Naval War College Press / U.S. Government Printing Office, 2010).

5. James R. Holmes, *Theodore Roosevelt and the World Order* (Washington, D.C.: Potomac Books, 2007), pp. 190–91.

6. James H. Herzog, *Closing the Open Door: American-Japanese Diplomatic Negotiations, 1936–1941* (Annapolis, Md.: Naval Institute Press, 1973), p. 238.

7. "Global and Regional Food Consumption Patterns and Trends: Availability and Consumption of Fish," *World Health Organization*, www.who.int/.

8. V. R. Leeworthy, T. Maher, and E. A. Stone, "Can Artificial Reefs Reduce or Alter User

Pressure on Adjacent Natural Reefs?," *Bulletin of Marine Science* 78, no. 1 (2006), pp. 29–37.

9. See Bruce A. Elleman, *Waves of Hope: The U.S. Navy's Response to the Tsunami in Northern Indonesia,* Newport Paper 28 (Newport, R.I.: Naval War College Press, 2007).

10. "'Peace Ark' Hospital Ship Participates in Joint Medical Tour in Indonesia," *China Military Online,* 12 September 2013, eng.mod.gov.cn/.

11. Cao Jinping and Wu Dengfeng, "PLA Navy Deepens Cooperation with Naval Escort Forces of Various Countries," *Liberation Army Daily,* 26 December 2012, www.chnarmy.com/.

12. Erik Lin-Greenberg, "Dragon Boats: Assessing China's Anti-piracy Operations in the Gulf of Aden," *Defense and Security Analysis* 6, no. 26 (2010), pp. 213–30.

13. Quoted in Christopher Lloyd, *The Navy and the Slave Trade: The Suppression of the African Slave Trade in the Nineteenth Century* (London: Frank Cass, 1968), p. 179.

14. Paul Halpern, "World War I: The Blockade," in *Naval Blockades and Seapower: Strategies and Counter-strategies, 1805–2005,* ed. Bruce A. Elleman and S. C. M. Paine (London: Routledge, 2006), p. 103.

15. Gary Roughead, telephone interview, 14 December 2012.

16. John Morgan, telephone interview, 28 November 2012.

17. Joseph F. Dunford, Jr., Jonathan W. Greenert, and Paul F. Zukunft, "A Cooperative Strategy for 21st Century Seapower," March 2015, pp. 24–26, available at www.navy.mil/.

18. Ibid., p. i.

Selected Bibliography

安部彦太 [Abe Hikota]. "大東亜戦争の計数的分析" [A Statistical Analysis of the Great East Asian War]. In 近代日本戦争史 [Modern Japanese Military History]. Vol. 4, 大東亜戦争 [The Great East Asian War], edited by 奥村房夫 [Okumura Fusao] and 近藤新治 [Kondō Shinji], pp. 823–59. Tokyo: 同台経済懇話会, 1995.

American Colonization Society. *African Repository*. Vol. 37. Washington, D.C.: C. Alexander, 1861.

Aristotle. *The History of Animals*. Translated by D'Arcy Wentworth Thompson. Oxford, U.K.: Clarendon, 1910.

Asada, Sadao. *From Mahan to Pearl Harbor: The Imperial Japanese Navy and the United States*. Annapolis, Md.: Naval Institute Press, 2006.

Au, W. *The Sonar of Dolphins*. New York: Springer, 1993.

Barnhart, Michael A. *Japan Prepares for Total War*. Ithaca, N.Y.: Cornell Univ. Press, 1987.

Barrett, David P., and Larry N. Shyu, eds. *Chinese Collaboration with Japan, 1932–1945*. Stanford, Calif.: Stanford Univ. Press, 2001.

Bartlett, Ruhl J., ed. *The Record of American Diplomacy*. New York: Knopf, 1964.

Beale, Howard K. *Theodore Roosevelt and the Rise of America to World Power*. Baltimore, Md.: Johns Hopkins Univ. Press, 1956.

Benzon, Anne Cipriano, ed. *The United States in the First World War: An Encyclopedia*. New York: Garland, 1995.

Best, Antony, ed. *Imperial Japan and the World, 1931–1945: Critical Concepts in Asian Studies*. London: Routledge, 2011.

Bix, Herbert P. *Hirohito and the Making of Modern Japan*. New York: HarperCollins, 2000.

Bove, A. A., ed. *Bove and Davis' Diving Medicine*. Philadelphia: W. B. Saunders, 2004.

Bowen, Herbert W. *Recollections Diplomatic and Undiplomatic*. New York: Grafton, 1926.

Brooks, George E., Jr. *The Kru Mariner in the Nineteenth Century: An Historical Compendium*. Newark, Del.: Liberian Studies Association in America, 1972.

Brubakk, A., and T. Neuman. *Bennett and Elliotts' Physiology and Medicine of Diving*. 5th ed. New York: Elsevier, 2002.

Burkman, Thomas W. *Japan and the League of Nations: Empire and World Order, 1914–1938*. Honolulu: Univ. of Hawai'i Press, 2008.

Canney, Donald L. *Africa Squadron: The U.S. Navy and the Slave Trade, 1842–1861*. Washington, D.C.: Potomac Books, 2006.

Collin, Richard H. *Theodore Roosevelt, Culture, Diplomacy, and Expansion: A New View of American Imperialism*. Baton Rouge: Louisiana State Univ. Press, 1985.

———. *Theodore Roosevelt's Caribbean*. Baton Rouge: Louisiana State Univ. Press, 1990.

Collinge, Robert A., and Ronald M. Ayers. *Economics by Design: Principles and Issues*. Upper Saddle River, N.J.: Prentice Hall, 2000.

Conroy, Hilary, and Harry Wray, eds. *Pearl Harbor Reexamined: Prologue to the Pacific War*. Honolulu: Univ. of Hawai'i Press, 1990.

Cotran, R. S., V. Kumar, and T. Collins. *Robbins Pathologic Basis of Disease*. 6th ed. Philadelphia: W. B. Saunders, 1999.

Cowman, Ian. *Dominion or Decline: Anglo-American Relations in the Pacific, 1937–1941*. Oxford, U.K.: Berg, 1996.

Croston, Glenn. *The Real Story of Risk: Adventures in a Hazardous World*. Amherst, N.Y.: Prometheus Books, 2012.

Crow, Hugh. *The Memoirs of Captain Hugh Crow: The Life and Times of a Slave Trade Captain*. Oxford, U.K.: Bodleian Library, 2007.

Dennis, Alfred P. *Adventures in American Diplomacy, 1896–1906*. New York: E. P. Dutton, 1928.

Dewey, George. *Autobiography of George Dewey*. New York: Charles Scribner's Sons, 1913; repr. Annapolis, Md.: Naval Institute Press, 1987.

Diène, Doudou, ed. *From Chains to Bonds: The Slave Trade Revisited.* New York: Berghahn Books, 2001.

Do, Kiem, and Julie Kane. *Counterpart: A South Vietnamese Naval Officer's War.* Annapolis, Md.: Naval Institute Press, 1998.

Dow, George Francis. *Slave Ships and Slaving.* Salem, Mass.: Marine Research Society, 1927.

Drake, Richard. *Revelations of a Slave Smuggler: Being the Autobiography of Capt. Rich'd Drake, an African Trader for Fifty Years—from 1807 to 1857; During Which Period He Was Concerned in the Transportation of Half a Million Blacks from African Coasts to America.* New York: Robert M. DeWitt, 1860; repr. Northbrook, Ill.: Metro Books, 1972.

Eargle, Lisa A., and Ashraf Esmail, eds. *Black Beaches and Bayous: The BP Deepwater Horizon Oil Spill Disaster.* New York: Univ. Press of America, 2012.

Edmonds, C., C. Lowry, J. Pennefather, and R. Walker. *Diving and Subaquatic Medicine.* 4th ed. London: Arnold, 2002.

江口圭一 [Eguchi Kei-ichi]. 十五年戦争小史 [A Short History of the Fifteen-Year War]. Tokyo: 青木書店, 1996.

Elleman, Bruce A. *Waves of Hope: The U.S. Navy's Response to the Tsunami in Northern Indonesia.* Newport Paper 28. Newport, R.I.: Naval War College Press, 2007.

Evans, David C., and Mark R. Peattie. *Kaigun: Strategy, Tactics, and Technology in the Imperial Japanese Navy 1887–1941.* Annapolis, Md.: Naval Institute Press, 1997.

Ewell, Judith. *Venezuela: A Century of Change.* Stanford, Calif.: Stanford Univ. Press, 1984.

Fromm, D. M., and J. F. McEachern. *Acoustic Modelling of the New Providence Channel.* Washington, D.C.: U.S. Office of Naval Research, 2000.

Gay, George I. *Statistical Review of Relief Operations.* Stanford, Calif.: Stanford Univ. Press, 1925.

Gilliland, C. Herbert. *USS* Constellation *on the Dismal Coast: Willie Leonard's Journal, 1859–1861.* Columbia: Univ. of South Carolina Press, 2013.

———. *Voyage to the Thousand Cares: Master's Mate Lawrence with the African Squadron,* 1844–1846. Annapolis, Md.: Naval Institute Press, 2004.

Gleaves, Albert. *The Admiral.* Pasadena, Calif.: Hope, 1985.

Goldberg, David Isaakovich. *Внешняя политика Японии (сентябрь 1939 г.–декабрь 1941 г.)* [The Foreign Policy of Japan (September 1939–December 1941)]. Moscow: Издательство восточной литературы [Eastern Literature Publishing], 1959.

Gottschall, Terrell D. *By Order of the Kaiser.* Annapolis, Md.: Naval Institute Press, 2003.

Hall, John W., Marius B. Jansen, Madoka Kanai, and Denis Twitchett, eds. *The Cambridge History of Japan.* Vol. 6, *The Twentieth Century.* Cambridge, U.K.: Cambridge Univ. Press, 1988.

Halusky, J. G., ed. *Artificial Reef Research Diver's Handbook.* Gainesville: Univ. of Florida, Florida Sea Grant College Program, 1991.

Hamilton, Keith, and Patrick Salmon, eds. *Slavery, Diplomacy and Empire: Britain and the Suppression of the Slave Trade, 1807–1975.* Portland, Ore.: Sussex Academic, 2009.

Harries, Meirion, and Susie Harries. *Soldiers of the Sun: The Rise and the Fall of the Imperial Japanese Army.* New York: Random House, 1991.

Hendrix, Henry J. *Theodore Roosevelt's Naval Diplomacy: The U.S. Navy and the Birth of the American Century.* Annapolis, Md.: Naval Institute Press, 2009.

Herman, Donald L. "Democratic and Authoritarian Traditions." In *Democracy in Latin America: Colombia and Venezuela.* New York: Praeger, 1988.

Herman, Jan K. *The Lucky Few: The Fall of Saigon and the Rescue Mission of the USS* Kirk. Annapolis, Md.: Naval Institute Press, 2013.

———. *Navy Medicine in Vietnam: Oral Histories from Dien Bien Phu to the Fall of Saigon.* Jefferson, N.C.: McFarland, 2009.

———. *Navy Medicine in Vietnam: Passage to Freedom to the Fall of Saigon.* Washington, D.C.: Naval History and Heritage Command, 2010.

Herwig, Holger H. *Germany's Vision of Empire in Venezuela.* Princeton, N.J.: Princeton Univ. Press, 1986.

————. *Politics of Frustration: The United States in German Naval Planning, 1889–1941*. Boston: Little, Brown, 1976.

Herzog, James H. *Closing the Open Door: American-Japanese Diplomatic Negotiations, 1936–1941*. Annapolis, Md.: Naval Institute Press, 1973.

Hill, Howard C. *Roosevelt and the Caribbean*. Chicago: Univ. of Chicago Press, 1927.

Holmes, James R. *Theodore Roosevelt and the World Order*. Washington, D.C.: Potomac Books, 2007.

Hoogenboom, Ari. *Gustavus Vasa Fox of the Union Navy: A Biography*. Baltimore, Md.: Johns Hopkins Univ. Press, 2008.

Howard, Warren. *American Slavers and the Federal Law, 1837–1862*. Berkeley: Univ. of California Press, 1963.

Ike, Nobutaka, trans. and ed. *Japan's Decision for War: Records of the 1941 Policy Conferences*. Stanford, Calif.: Stanford Univ. Press, 1967.

International Military Tribunal for the Far East. *The Tokyo War Crimes Trial*. Compiled by R. John Prichard and Sonia Magbanua Zaide. 17 vols. New York: Garland, 1981.

Iriye, Akira. *The Cambridge History of American Foreign Relations*. Vol. 3, *The Globalizing of America, 1913–1945*. Cambridge, U.K.: Cambridge Univ. Press, 1993.

Jones, F. C. *Japan's New Order in East Asia: Its Rise and Fall 1937–1945*. London: Oxford Univ. Press, 1954.

Kamphausen, Roy, David Lai, and Travis Tanner, eds. *Learning by Doing: The PLA Trains at Home and Abroad*. Carlisle, Pa.: Army War College Press, 2012.

Karnow, Stanley. *Vietnam: A History*. New York: Viking, 1983.

Kneer, Warren G. *Great Britain and the Caribbean*. East Lansing: Michigan State Univ. Press, 1975.

Knox, Dudley W. *A History of the United States Navy*. New York: G. P. Putnam's Sons, 1936.

Kryter, K. D. *Handbook of Hearing and the Effects of Noise*. New York: Academic, 1996.

LaFeber, Walter. *The Cambridge History of American Foreign Relations*. Cambridge, U.K.: Cambridge Univ. Press, 1993.

Lee, Bradford A. *Britain and the Sino-Japanese War 1937–1939*. Stanford, Calif.: Stanford Univ. Press, 1973.

Liss, Sheldon B. *Diplomacy and Dependency: Venezuela, the United States, and the Americas*. Salisbury, N.C.: Documentary, 1978.

Lloyd, Christopher. *The Navy and the Slave Trade: The Suppression of the African Slave Trade in the Nineteenth Century*. London: Frank Cass, 1968.

Lu, David J. *Japan: A Documentary History*. Vol. 2, *The Late Tokugawa Period to the Present*. Armonk, N.Y.: M. E. Sharpe, 1997.

Lundgren, C., and J. Miller, eds. *The Lung at Depth*. New York: Marcel Dekker, 1999.

Lustgarten, Abrahm. *Run to Failure: BP and the Making of the* Deepwater Horizon *Disaster*. New York: W. W. Norton, 2012.

Magner, Mike. *Poisoned Legacy: The Human Cost of BP's Rise to Power*. New York: St. Martin's, 2011.

幕内光雄 [Maku'uchi Mitsuo]. 満州国警察外史 [An Unofficial History of the Manchukuo Police]. Tokyo: 三一書房, 1996.

Marks, Frederick W. *Velvet on Iron*. Lincoln: Univ. of Nebraska Press, 1979.

Marolda, Edward J. *By Sea, Air, and Land: An Illustrated History of the U.S. Navy and the War in Southeast Asia*. Washington, D.C.: Naval Historical Center, 1992.

Massie, Robert K. *Castles of Steel: Britain, Germany, and the Winning of the Great War at Sea*. New York: Ballantine Books, 2004.

McBeth, Brian S. *Gunboats, Corruption, and Claims: Foreign Investment in Venezuela, 1899–1908*. Westport, Conn.: Greenwood, 2001.

Morison, Elting E. *Admiral Sims and the Modern American Navy*. Boston: Houghton Mifflin, 1942.

Nash, George H. *The Life of Herbert Hoover: Master of Emergencies, 1917–1918*. New York: W. W. Norton, 1996.

————. *The Life of Herbert Hoover: The Humanitarian, 1914–1917*. New York: W. W. Norton, 1988.

National Research Council. *Low-Frequency Sound and Marine Mammals: Current Knowledge and Research Needs*. Washington, D.C.: National Academies, 1994.

————. *Marine Mammal Populations and Ocean Noise: Determining When Noise Causes Biologically Significant Effects.* Washington, D.C.: National Academies, 2005.

————. *Marine Mammals and Low-Frequency Sound: Progress since 1994.* Washington, D.C.: National Academies, 2000.

————. *Ocean Noise and Marine Mammals.* Washington, D.C.: National Academies, 2003.

Nevins, Allan. *Henry White: Thirty Years of American Diplomacy.* New York: Harper and Brothers, 1930.

Paine, S. C. M. *The Wars for Asia 1911–1949.* New York: Cambridge Univ. Press, 2012.

Payne, Roger. *Among Whales.* New York: Scribner's, 1995.

Pinfold, John. "Introduction: Captain Hugh Crow and the Slave Trade." In *The Memoirs of Captain Hugh Crow: The Life and Times of a Slave Trade Captain.* Oxford, U.K.: Bodleian Library, 2007.

Resnick, D., ed. *Diagnosis of Bone and Joint Disorders.* Philadelphia: W. B. Saunders, 2002.

Reter, Ronald. "The Real versus Rhetorical Theodore Roosevelt in Foreign Policy Making." PhD diss., University of Georgia, 1973.

Reynolds, J. E., and S. A. Rommel, eds. *Biology of Marine Mammals.* Washington, D.C.: Smithsonian Institution, 1999.

Richardson, James D., ed. *Compilation of the Messages and Papers of the Presidents.* New York: Bureau of National Literature and the Arts, 1920.

Robinson, Margaret. *Arbitration and the Hague Peace Conferences.* Philadelphia: Univ. of Pennsylvania, 1936.

Roosevelt, Theodore. *The Letters of Theodore Roosevelt.* Edited by Elting Elmore Morison. Cambridge, Mass.: Harvard Univ. Press, 1951.

Ross, Steven T. *American War Plans 1890–1939.* London: Frank Cass, 2002.

Snepp, Frank. *Decent Interval.* New York: Vintage Books, 1977.

Society of Friends. Philadelphia Yearly Meeting. *An Exposition of the African Slave Trade, from the Year 1840, to 1850, Inclusive, Prepared from Official Documents, and Published by Direction of the Representatives of the Religious Society of Friends, in Pennsylvania, New Jersey, and Delaware.* Philadelphia: J. Rakestraw, 1851; repr. Detroit, Mich.: Negro History, 1969.

Spector, Ronald. *Admiral of the New Empire.* Baton Rouge: Louisiana State Univ. Press, 1974.

Spitz, W. U., ed. *Spitz and Fisher's Medicolegal Investigation of Death: Guidelines for the Application of Pathology to Crime Investigation.* 3rd ed. Springfield, Ill.: Charles C. Thomas, 1993.

Swanson, Bruce. *Eighth Voyage of the Dragon: A History of China's Quest for Seapower.* Annapolis, Md.: Naval Institute Press, 1982.

Thayer, William R. *Life and Letters of John Hay.* Boston: Houghton Mifflin, 1915.

Tilchin, William N. *Theodore Roosevelt and the British Empire: A Study in Presidential Statecraft.* New York: St. Martin's, 1997.

U.S. State Dept. *Foreign Relations of the United States Diplomatic Papers 1939: The Far East, the Near East, and Africa.* Vol. 4. Washington, D.C.: U.S. Government Printing Office, 1955.

————. *Foreign Relations of the United States Diplomatic Papers 1940: The Far East.* Vol. 4. Washington, D.C.: U.S. Government Printing Office, 1955.

————. *Foreign Relations of the United States Diplomatic Papers 1941: The Far East.* Vol. 4. Washington, D.C.: U.S. Government Printing Office, 1956.

————. *Papers Relating to the Foreign Relations of the United States, 1903.* Washington, D.C.: U.S. Government Printing Office, 1904.

————. *Papers Relating to the Foreign Relations of the United States: Japan: 1931–1941.* Vol. 2. Washington, D.C.: U.S. Government Printing Office, 1943.

Wagenknecht, Edward. *The Seven Worlds of Theodore Roosevelt.* New York: Longman, Green, 1958.

Wang Yizhou. *Creative Involvement: The Evolution of China's Global Role.* Beijing: Peking Univ. Press, 2013.

Williams, Glenn F. *U.S.S. Constellation: A Short History of the Last All-Sail Warship Built by the U.S. Navy.* Virginia Beach, Va.: Donning, 2000.

吴景平 [Wu Jingping]. "抗战时期中美租借关系述评" [Sino-American Lend-Lease Relations during the War against Japan]. 历史研究 [Historical Research], no. 4 (1995), pp. 48–64.

Young, Arthur N. *China and the Helping Hand 1937–1945*. Cambridge, Mass.: Harvard Univ. Press, 1963.

———. *China's Wartime Finance and Inflation,`1937–1945*. Cambridge, Mass.: Harvard Univ. Press, 1965.

About the Contributors

Bruce A. Elleman: William V. Pratt Professor of International History and Research Professor, Maritime History Department, U.S. Naval War College, with a BA (1982) from the University of California Berkeley; an MA (1984) and PhD (1993) from the History Department, Columbia University; an MS (1985) in international history, London School of Economics; and an MA in national security and strategic studies, with distinction (2004), Naval War College. His twenty-two books include *Modern Chinese Warfare, 1795–1989* (Routledge, 2001); *Naval Mutinies of the Twentieth Century: An International Perspective,* edited, with Christopher Bell (Frank Cass, 2003); *Naval Blockades and Seapower: Strategies and Counter-strategies, 1805–2005,* edited, with S. C. M. Paine (Routledge, 2006); *Waves of Hope: The U.S. Navy's Response to the Tsunami in Northern Indonesia,* Newport Paper 28 (Naval War College Press, 2007); and *Naval Coalition Warfare: From the Napoleonic War to Operation Iraqi Freedom,* edited, with S. C. M. Paine (Routledge, 2008).

Andrew S. Erickson: Associate professor in the China Maritime Studies Institute (CMSI), Strategic Research Department, U.S. Naval War College; associate in research at the John King Fairbank Center for Chinese Studies, Harvard University; and a term member of the Council on Foreign Relations. He is author of the Jamestown Foundation monograph *Chinese Anti-ship Ballistic Missile Development* (2013), coauthor of the CMSI monographs *No Substitute for Experience: Chinese Antipiracy Operations in the Gulf of Aden* (2013) and *Chinese Mine Warfare* (2009), and coeditor of *A Low-Visibility Force Multiplier: Assessing China's Cruise Missile Ambitions* (National Defense University Press, 2014) and of *Rebalancing U.S. Forces: Basing and Forward Presence in the Asia-Pacific* (Naval Institute Press, 2014). He also serves as an expert contributor to the *Wall Street Journal*'s "China Real Time Report." In 2012 the National Bureau of Asian Research awarded him the inaugural Ellis Joffe Prize for PLA Studies.

Henry J. Hendrix: Captain, U.S. Navy; doctor of philosophy in war studies, King's College London; MA in extension studies in diplomatic history, Harvard University; MA in national security affairs, Naval Postgraduate School, Monterey, California; and BA, political science, Purdue University, West Lafayette, Indiana. His publications include *Theodore Roosevelt's Naval Diplomacy: The United States Navy and the Birth of the American Century* (Naval Institute Press, 2009), and book chapters in *Leadership Embodied,* edited by Joseph J. Thomas (Naval Institute Press, 2005), and

Theodore Roosevelt, the U.S. Navy, and the Spanish-American War, edited by Edward Marolda (Palgrave Press, 2001).

Jan Kenneth Herman: Chief Historian of the Navy Medical Department from 1979 to 2012 and also curator of the Old Naval Observatory, in the Foggy Bottom district of Washington, D.C. He was the editor in chief of *Navy Medicine,* the journal of the Navy Medical Department, for thirty years. Since 2000 he has written and produced documentaries for the U.S. Navy, highlighting its medical service during World War II, the Korean War, and the Vietnam War. *The Lucky Few: The Story of USS* Kirk, a documentary about the closing days of the Vietnam War, provided the stimulus for a companion book of the same name (Naval Institute Press, 2013). He has authored more than fifty articles and monographs and has presented lectures to audiences across the United States on military medicine, nineteenth-century astronomy and oceanography, and the medical history of World War II in the Pacific.

Darlene R. Ketten: Chief Scientist, WHOI CT Facility, Biology Department, Woods Hole Oceanographic Institution, Woods Hole, Massachusetts; and Assistant Clinical Professor, Department of Otology & Laryngology, Harvard Medical School. She received her PhD from the Johns Hopkins University, MS from the Massachusetts Institute of Technology, and BA from Washington University, Saint Louis, Missouri. She is the author of over a hundred publications on hearing abilities and hearing loss in marine mammals, including possible impacts from human activities in the ocean, such as sonar, explosives, construction, shipping, and ship shock trials. Recent publications include a feature article in *Acoustics Today* on sonar and beaked-whale strandings and three coauthored articles in a special edition on sonar stranding correlations for *Aquatic Mammals:* "Correlating Whale Strandings with Navy Exercises off Southern California," "Correlating Military Sonar Use with Beaked Whale Mass Strandings: What Do These Historical Data Show?," and "Beaked Whale Strandings and Naval Activities."

Mary E. Landry: Rear admiral, retired, in the U.S. Coast Guard and former commander of the Eighth Coast Guard District and of Task Force 189.8, headquartered in New Orleans, Louisiana. She has held various assignments on the East Coast, West Coast, Gulf Coast, and Hawaii. Most notably Rear Admiral Landry served as the federal on-scene coordinator for the *Deepwater Horizon* incident in the Gulf of Mexico. Ms. Mary Landry is the current Director of Incident Management and Preparedness at Coast Guard Headquarters. She has a master's in management from Webster University and a master's in marine affairs from the University of Rhode Island; also, she is a National Security Fellow at Harvard University.

S. C. M. Paine: William S. Sims Professor in the Strategy and Policy Department, U.S. Naval War College, with a PhD (1993) in Russian and Chinese history, Columbia

University, and MIA (1984) from the School for International and Public Affairs, Columbia University. She is the author of *The Wars for Asia, 1911–1949* (Cambridge University Press, 2012), winner of the Leopold Prize and a PROSE award; *The Sino-Japanese War of 1894–1895: Perceptions, Power, and Primacy* (Cambridge University Press, 2003); and *Imperial Rivals: China, Russia, and Their Disputed Frontier, 1858–1924* (M. E. Sharpe, 1996), winner of the Jelavich Prize; editor of *Nation Building, State Building, and Economic Development: Case Studies and Comparisons* (M. E. Sharpe, 2010); and coauthor with Bruce A. Elleman of *Modern China: Continuity and Change 1644 to the Present* (Prentice Hall, 2010).

John Pentangelo: Managing director of the Naval War College Museum and previously chief curator at Historic Ships in Baltimore, Maryland (formerly the USS *Constellation* Museum). During his tenure in Baltimore he spearheaded several initiatives to commemorate the 2008 bicentennial of the abolition of the transatlantic slave trade in the United States. The capstone of these efforts was the passage of two congressional resolutions honoring *Constellation* for its role in fighting the slave trade. He holds an MA in history museum studies from the Cooperstown Graduate Program and a BA in American history from Manhattanville College.

Austin M. Strange: Research associate at the Institute for the Theory and Practice of International Relations at the College of William and Mary. He was a research associate from 2011 to 2014 in the China Maritime Studies Institute, Strategic Research Department, U.S. Naval War College. He received a BA in economics and Chinese language and literature from the College of William and Mary. Currently, he is a PhD student in Harvard University's Department of Government studying international relations and comparative politics, with a focus on Chinese politics and foreign relations.

Thomas Williams: PhD in public policy and administration, urban studies, and planning, with a concentration in environmental policy, Virginia Commonwealth University; master's in public administration, with a concentration in human resource management, Virginia Commonwealth University; and BA from Indiana University. The title of his 2006 PhD dissertation was "Sinking Poor Decision Making with Best Practices: A Case Study of Artificial Reef Decision-Making in the Florida Keys." Currently, he is Director of Planning and Community Development for the Ketchikan Gateway Borough, Ketchikan, Alaska.

Index

Vitter, David 153

volcano 130

von Holleben, Theodor 23, 27, 33, 36, 40, 41

von Marbod, Erich 106

von Metternich, Paul 31, 40

von Reuter, Ludwig 110

von Sternburg, Speck 31

Vung Tau 99

W

Wakasugi Kaname 80

Walker, John 26

Walsh, Mike 152

Wang Jingwei 82

Wang Yizhou 172

Wang Yongxiang 166

War Department 70

War of 1812 7, 194

War Office 42

War Plans Division 83

War Risk Insurance Scheme 56, 57

warship 7, 8, 12, 22, 101, 105, 110, 115, 121, 122, 124, 166, 167, 168, 169, 170, 173, 174, 191, 194, 196

Washington (state) 121

Washington, D.C. 28, 31, 33, 36, 112, 127, 154

Washington Evening Star 36

Washington Navy Yard 32

water column 113

Watson, Jim 159

Webster-Ashburton Treaty (1842) 2, 7, 8

Weise, Adam 147

Welles, Gideon 17

Welles, Sumner 81

wellhead 145, 147, 148, 156, 157, 158, 160

Wenz curve 130

Wenzhou 168, 169

West African Squadron 2, 7, 8, 9, 10, 11, 12, 13, 16, 17, 194

Western Hemisphere 21, 23, 31, 78, 81

West Flanders 49

West Morning News 60

whales 4, 127–41, 182, 183, 185, 187, 188, 189, 191, 196

wheat 48, 50

WHEC cutter 100

White, Henry 39

White, John 55, 56–57

"White Christmas" 95

Whitehall 51, 56

White House 24, 27, 31, 32, 33, 153, 154, 160

Whitlock, Brand 56, 57, 60

Whitmire, Donald 93, 98, 99

Wickes, Francis Cogswell 64

Wilhelm II 23, 27, 28, 30, 40, 41

Willamette 115

Wilson, John 15, 16

Wilson, Stephen B. 12

Wilson, Woodrow 61, 62

Wood, E. F. L. 80

Wood, Leonard 31

World Health Organization 190

X

X-ray 130

Y

yachting 2

Yangzi River 71, 111

Yankee 16, 27

yeast 50

Yemen 166, 198

Yiyang 167, 169

Yorktown 8

Yukon 116, 119–20, 121

The Newport Papers

Writing to Think: The Intellectual Journey of a Naval Career, by Robert C. Rubel (no. 41, February 2014).

Commerce Raiding: Historical Case Studies, 1755–2009, edited by Bruce A. Elleman and S. C. M. Paine (no. 40, October 2013).

Influence without Boots on the Ground: Seaborne Crisis Response, by Larissa Forster (no. 39, January 2013).

High Seas Buffer: The Taiwan Patrol Force, 1950–1979, by Bruce A. Elleman (no. 38, April 2012).

Innovation in Carrier Aviation, by Thomas C. Hone, Norman Friedman, and Mark D. Mandeles (no. 37, August 2011).

Defeating the U-boat: Inventing Antisubmarine Warfare, by Jan S. Breemer (no. 36, August 2010).

Piracy and Maritime Crime: Historical and Modern Case Studies, edited by Bruce A. Elleman, Andrew Forbes, and David Rosenberg (no. 35, January 2010).

Somalia . . . From the Sea, by Gary Ohls (no. 34, July 2009).

U.S. Naval Strategy in the 1980s: Selected Documents, edited by John B. Hattendorf and Peter M. Swartz (no. 33, December 2008).

Major Naval Operations, by Milan Vego (no. 32, September 2008).

Perspectives on Maritime Strategy: Essays from the Americas, edited by Paul D. Taylor (no. 31, August 2008).

U.S. Naval Strategy in the 1970s: Selected Documents, edited by John B. Hattendorf (no. 30, September 2007).

Shaping the Security Environment, edited by Derek S. Reveron (no. 29, September 2007).

Waves of Hope: The U.S. Navy's Response to the Tsunami in Northern Indonesia, by Bruce A. Elleman (no. 28, February 2007).

U.S. Naval Strategy in the 1990s: Selected Documents, edited by John B. Hattendorf (no. 27, September 2006).

Reposturing the Force: U.S. Overseas Presence in the Twenty-first Century, edited by
Carnes Lord (no. 26, February 2006).

The Regulation of International Coercion: Legal Authorities and Political Constraints, by
James P. Terry (no. 25, October 2005).

Naval Power in the Twenty-first Century: A Naval War College Review *Reader,* edited by
Peter Dombrowski (no. 24, July 2005).

The Atlantic Crises: Britain, Europe, and Parting from the United States, by William
Hopkinson (no. 23, May 2005).

China's Nuclear Force Modernization, edited by Lyle J. Goldstein with Andrew S.
Erickson (no. 22, April 2005).

Latin American Security Challenges: A Collaborative Inquiry from North and South,
edited by Paul D. Taylor (no. 21, 2004).

Global War Game: Second Series, 1984–1988, by Robert Gile (no. 20, 2004).

The Evolution of the U.S. Navy's Maritime Strategy, 1977–1986, by John Hattendorf (no.
19, 2004).

*Military Transformation and the Defense Industry after Next: The Defense Industrial
Implications of Network-Centric Warfare,* by Peter J. Dombrowski, Eugene Gholz, and
Andrew L. Ross (no. 18, 2003).

The Limits of Transformation: Officer Attitudes toward the Revolution in Military Affairs,
by Thomas G. Mahnken and James R. FitzSimonds (no. 17, 2003).

*The Third Battle: Innovation in the U.S. Navy's Silent Cold War Struggle with Soviet
Submarines,* by Owen R. Cote, Jr. (no. 16, 2003).

*International Law and Naval War: The Effect of Marine Safety and Pollution Conven-
tions during International Armed Conflict,* by Dr. Sonja Ann Jozef Boelaert-Suominen
(no. 15, December 2000).

*Theater Ballistic Missile Defense from the Sea: Issues for the Maritime Component
Commander,* by Commander Charles C. Swicker, U.S. Navy (no. 14, August 1998).

Sailing New Seas, by Admiral J. Paul Reason, U.S. Navy, with David G. Freymann
(no. 13, March 1998).

What Color Helmet? Reforming Security Council Peacekeeping Mandates, by Myron H.
Nordquist (no. 12, August 1997).

*The International Legal Ramifications of United States Counter-Proliferation Strategy:
Problems and Prospects,* by Frank Gibson Goldman (no. 11, April 1997).

Chaos Theory: The Essentials for Military Applications, by Major Glenn E. James, U.S. Air Force (no. 10, October 1996).

A Doctrine Reader: The Navies of the United States, Great Britain, France, Italy, and Spain, by James J. Tritten and Vice Admiral Luigi Donolo, Italian Navy (Retired) (no. 9, December 1995).

Physics and Metaphysics of Deterrence: The British Approach, by Myron A. Greenberg (no. 8, December 1994).

Mission in the East: The Building of an Army in a Democracy in the New German States, by Colonel Mark E. Victorson, U.S. Army (no. 7, June 1994).

The Burden of Trafalgar: Decisive Battle and Naval Strategic Expectations on the Eve of the First World War, by Jan S. Breemer (no. 6, October 1993).

Beyond Mahan: A Proposal for a U.S. Naval Strategy in the Twenty-First Century, by Colonel Gary W. Anderson, U.S. Marine Corps (no. 5, August 1993).

Global War Game: The First Five Years, by Bud Hay and Bob Gile (no. 4, June 1993).

The "New" Law of the Sea and the Law of Armed Conflict at Sea, by Horace B. Robertson, Jr. (no. 3, October 1992).

Toward a Pax Universalis: A Historical Critique of the National Military Strategy for the 1990s, by Lieutenant Colonel Gary W. Anderson, U.S. Marine Corps (no. 2, April 1992).

"Are We Beasts?" Churchill and the Moral Question of World War II "Area Bombing," by Christopher C. Harmon (no. 1, December 1991).

Newport Papers are available online (Acrobat required) at www.usnwc.edu/press/.